THE TRAIL LESS TRAVELED

*The Yukon's Dawson City-to-Ottawa
Stanley Cup Reenactment*

**by
DON REDDICK**

Published by Nauset Sound Publishing Company.
P.O. Box 101
Stockbridge, VT 05772
nausetsound@myfairpoint.net

Reddick, Don, 1954-
The Trail Less Traveled

ISBN 978-0-9842380-0-2

Visit the author's website www.donreddick.com

Printed and bound in the Untied States
10 9 8 7 6 5 4 3 2 1

Cover photograph of Steve Craig on the ferry Malaspina, by Don Reddick.
Back cover photograph by Terry Reddick.
Edited by Sarah Reddick.
Book design by Cynthia Ryan.

To their grandchildren's grandchildren,
who will do it again in one hundred years

"His is one of those cases which are more numerous than those suppose, who have never lived anywhere but in their own homes, and never walked but in one line from their cradles to their graves. We must come down from our heights, and leave our straight paths, for the byways and low places of life, if we would learn truths by strong contrasts; and in hovels and forecastles, and among our own, outcasts in foreign lands..."

— R. H. Dana,
Two Years Before The Mast, 1840

"He who sits still in a house all the time may be the greatest vagrant of all."

— Henry David Thoreau, *Walking,* 1851

"The Northwest Passage, in the imagination of all free people, is a short cut to fame, fortune and romance—a hidden route to Golconda and the mystic east. On every side of us are men who hunt perpetually for their personal Northwest Passage, too often sacrificing health, strength and life itself to the search; and who shall say they are not happier in their vane but hopeful quest than wiser, duller folk who sit at home, venturing nothing and, with sour laugh, deriding the seekers for that fabled thoroughfare—that panacea for all the afflictions of a hum drum world."

— Kenneth Roberts,
foreward to *Northwest Passage,* 1935

"The trails of the world be countless,
and most of the trails be tried;
You tread on the heels of many,
till you come where the ways divide;
And one lies safe in the sunlight,
and the other is dreary and wan,
You look aslant at the Lone Trail
and the Lone Trail lures you on."

— ROBERT SERVICE, *THE LONE TRAIL,* 1911

"It's not that we love to be alone, but that we love to soar,
and, when we do soar, the company grows thinner, till
there is none at all."

— HENRY DAVID THOREAU,
WALDEN, OR LIFE IN THE WOODS, 1854

"Hospitality consists of a little fire, a little food, and an
immense quiet."

— RALPH WALDO EMERSON,
JOURNAL, 1841

Acknowledgements

When Troy Suzuki released his documentary *From Moccasin Square Gardens,* he told audiences that he had traveled the whole way with the team, was frustrated that he could not play in the Ottawa game, and that the film was his contribution, completing the journey for him. His words mirror precisely my sentiments regarding this book.

The Trail Less Traveled is actually the culmination of three books, and twenty years of research. As such, the depth of my gratitude reaches far and wide.

I'd like to thank first my brother Ken, for making me want to step onto the ice, and my father John, who bought the skates. I recognize in my brother Gordon an invaluable historical reference, and thank sisters Connie and Pat, and my mother Ruth for their past, and ongoing support.

As a product of my environs, I'd like to reach back and thank those of the generation past who gave themselves to Norwood youth hockey, Ernie Higgins, Tom Clifford, and Tom Brown, as well as their progeny, Mike Martin, Bill Clifford, Peter Brown, Bill Pieri, and Ed King, who made my boyhood dreams come true on Boston Garden ice.

I'd like to thank the muscle behind the hockey history, Bill Fitsell, Ernie Fitzsimmons, Lloyd Penwarden, and Paul Kitchen, without whom the context of these stories would be bare. Descendents of original players provided invaluable insight, and deserve my deepest thanks, including Lydia Watt, Ken Forrest, Dave Hannay, Art Moore's grandson Ted Evans, and the late Honorable Frank McGee.

Ed Bennett, president of the Joe Boyle Repatriation Committee, and Nancy Newham, descendant of Frank Slavin, deserve mention, as do filmmakers Keith MacNeill, Vaughan Killin, and Kevin Kelly, for their patience with a sometimes inarticulate, stumbling subject.

My appreciation extends to those who sat for interviews during and after the trip, including Patricia Dahlquist, Margo Anderson, Rick Smith, Roy Johnson, Steve Craig, Harvey Downes, Troy Suzuki, Larry Smith, and Willie Gordon. Bruce Duffee and Earl McRae deserve special thanks, not only for their interviews, but ongoing friendship, support, and advice regarding the manuscript. I'd like to specifically thank those three eloquent ambassadors of Dawson City, Kevin Anderson, John Flynn, and Pat Hogan, for inviting me on their journey, and helping me through.

For this book my gratitude extends to Nauset Sound Publishing, managing editor Alby Mason and editor Sarah Reddick, as well as book layout and designer Cynthia Ryan.

And finally, we all come home from work; thank you Rebecca, thank you Sarah, and thank you Allison and Paul; more than thanks I convey to my wife Terry, who has, more than anyone, shared the trials and tribulations of one wanting to write.

Don Reddick
Stockbridge, Vermont
October, 2009

BEFORE

*"No labor of historian, no eloquence of orator, will stir
the heart of youth to the love of country, and a desire to
emulate the great deeds of the past, like a visit to the spot
which has been familiar with the presence of great men,
or the scene where great deeds have been enacted."*

— GEORGE FRISBIE HOAR, MASSACHUSETTS SENATOR, 1866

Henry James he wasn't. From a Dickensian childhood on the docks of Oakland emerged an uneducated, racist, alcoholic, opinionated, and arrogant individual. He declared to his first wife on their wedding day that he did not love her, enjoyed the company of prostitutes and derelicts, never paid a bill on time, abandoned his young family for another woman, and ran from every problem he ever faced. I would have loved to have known him.

Jack London was woefully unprepared for the overnight fame he achieved at the tender age of twenty-one. He probably would have remained obscure and undistinguished had he not joined the Klondike gold rush. After traveling up the coast and traversing the Chilkoot Pass, London and his companions were caught by a sudden winter onset on an island at the confluence of the Yukon and Stewart Rivers. Huddled inside a cabin for the winter of 1897–98, he read, depending on which source you quote, Charles Darwin, Herbert Spencer, or Frederick Nietzsche. Known for certain is what blossomed in the writer's imagination during the hollow silence of that Yukon winter. In unintended parody of the common writer's expression, "write what you know,"

London developed his most brilliant, intriguing character: a dog.

He began the novel December 1st, 1902, and finished three and a half months later. *The Call of the Wild* was published the following July, and has since been translated into more than eighty languages. It is considered the most widely read American classic, and exists in several film adaptations. No one was more astounded by the sudden success of the novel than the young author himself. The weighty allegory of the primal human condition ascribed to the novel's unusual protagonist was born of the darkest recesses of his subconscious mind. "I was unconscious of it at the time," he would later recall. "I did not mean to do it." More telling was his attitude on writing: "I have no unfinished stories. Invariably I complete every one I start. If it's good, I sign it and send it out. If it isn't good, I sign it and send it out."

Such was the genesis of the Yukon's myth-making lore. Even before the gold rush, the public was drawn by articles of the far north in *Frank Leslie's Illustrated Newspaper, Scribner's Magazine,* and *Harper's Weekly.* News of the Yukon gold strike reached the west coast in the spring of 1897, accentuating an already established interest in the mysterious, remote region. Before drinking himself to death at age forty, London continued to mine the great vein he'd struck with numerous Yukon stories and novels, anxiously received by a public hungry for tales of their generation's great adventure. Movies followed as well as the more obscure novels of Rex Beach, assuring the Yukon Territory's stubbornly growing legend accompanied its inevitable decline. So much did the world venerate this last image of the final frontier, this pot of gold at the furthest end of the rainbow, perpetuated by steady sales of London's prose and Robert Service's poetry, that it manifested itself in a famous promotion a half century later.

As this legend of advertising goes, Bruce Baker, ad man for Quaker Cereal, was sitting on the toilet, sweating out a deadline, when the idea struck: Quaker Cereal would offer one square inch of Yukon land with each box of cereal sold. When presenting the idea, lawyers rejected the scheme as too costly. "Don't register the deeds," replied Baker, and Quaker's council proceeded to find a Yukon lawyer "who thought it was legal." Up to the Yukon these lawyers ventured, purchasing Lot 2,

Group 243 located three miles upstream from Dawson City for $1,000. Thus was created the infamous Great Klondike Big Inch Land Caper.

Twenty-one million certificates were printed and inserted into Quaker Cereal boxes. On January 27, 1955 a promotion began on the *Sergeant Preston* TV show. The response was phenomenal. Some of the proud new owners complained when they didn't receive tax statements. One kid sent four toothpicks to fence in his inch. Another wrote to the prime minister of Canada, formally declaring the independence of his four square inches. A lad from Michigan offered to donate his three square inches to become the world's smallest national park. But the fate of the Great Klondike Big Inch Land Caper was really set from the start. The eleven acres purchased by Quaker Cereal was repossessed for nonpayment of $37.20 in back taxes in 1965.

The myth of the Yukon continues to this day, albeit more subtly and perhaps subconsciously. Associating wilderness imagery with truck and SUV sales, Detroit offered Explorers, Expeditions, and Escapes; once the American west was conquered with Siverados, Tahoes, Sequoias and Wranglers, they pushed on to the ends of the North American continent to offer Tundras, Denalis, and finally, Yukons. When writing the screenplay for 1997's Academy Award-winning movie *Titanic*, writer-director James Cameron needed a name for his young, worldly-wise, turn-of-the-century protagonist he hired Leonardo DiCaprio to play. He named the character *Jack Dawson.*

I shared this love from afar, and understood it implicitly. As a youngster I read London's stories, *To Build a Fire* my favorite. A friend's father could recite from memory, verbatim, line after line of Service's poems. In 1972 came the call for tradesmen to build the Alaskan pipeline, and my subsequent disappointment when I found I had no viable skill to offer. I remember former high school teammate Bobby Rosata landing a welding job. How I stared when Rosy returned, pockets full of cash and reveling in his stories of the wilderness by Delta Junction. Industrial league teammate Danny McCarthy and I applied for jobs in the nickel mines of Thompson, Manitoba, only to be rejected. It wasn't until years later that I finally came to my decision.

Thirty-years-old, a wife, three kids, and a new mortgage, I realized if I didn't do it now, I never would. Pacing the floor, I confessed my problem to my wife Terry. And one of those beautiful things that happens in a marriage—"Go to Alaska," she said. No malice, no strings, an honest response to an honest, life-long desire, a wife to a husband, go and see what you have to see, we'll get by. Just come back.

In August of 1985 friend Mike Lydon and I traveled more than two thousand miles of Alaskan and Yukon roads. We were introduced to the weather-beaten characteristics of the far North, culminating in a bizarre invitation to a ninety-year-old woman's birthday party held in Millie's Moose River Lodge on Alaska's Kenai peninsula. The old woman never showed up, nor did anyone else. Mike and I found ourselves pulling up chairs in front of the stage to be serenaded by a local country band who, despite the otherwise empty room, obliged our every request.

The highlight of the trip was far to the northeast in the Yukon Territory. I had insisted that we visit Dawson City, that famous old gold rush town. We stumbled into Dawson after driving fifteen hours across the Top of the World Highway only to lose our money inside and our car outside of Diamond Tooth Gerties, the northernmost casino in the world. Finally locating the vehicle, we discovered that there were no rooms available in the entire town, so made our way to its edge where we slept on the gravel bed of a large sand pit.

Once home, I bought one of those little hockey books that list all the players, a short synopsis of each, award winners, and Stanley Cup champions. This book was different, however, listing not only Stanley Cup winners, but also losers. It was then that I saw that Dawson City had once played for the Stanley Cup. This seemed remarkable. Dawson is so remote, so distant, the reality of a challenge from literally the end of the earth intrigued me. I learned that in the winter of 1904–05 a rag-tag hockey team traveled three hundred and fifty miles by dog-sled and bicycle from Dawson to Whitehorse in the dead of winter. From Whitehorse they rode the narrow gauge train to Skagway, where they boarded a steamer for its run down the inside passage to Seattle. Backtracking to Vancouver, they then caught the Canadian Pacific

Railway for its cross-country run to Ottawa to play the greatest hockey team of its time, the Ottawa Silver Seven. The first thing I did was try to find a book about it. Finding none, I decided to take matters—literally—into my own hands.

Seven years later, on a book tour promoting my novel *Dawson City Seven*, I stood once again in Dawson City, in the home of John and Jennifer Flynn. I had given a talk on my book and John had invited various Dawson hockey intelligencia back for an after party. A guy named Anderson was there, as well as a guy with the strange name Poncho Rudniski. A wild-looking Indian named Farr and a quiet man named Duffee were there. A young woman named Marjorie Logue told me she wanted to be the first woman to travel from Dawson to Ottawa to play goal. I had no idea what she was talking about. One individual hovered in the background, his hand clutching a beer, and finally came forward and shook my hand. I recognized him as the individual who had stood up during my talk and blurted, "Hey, I've read half this book and they haven't even left Dawson yet. *What's the story?*" We spoke of the Boston Bruins and my book until he hesitated. He took his Dawson City Generals hat off his head and placed it on mine.

"We're thinking," he said softly, "of recreating that trip, eh?"

"You're kidding."

"The whole trip. The dog sleds through the wilderness, the inside passage, across the whole country on a train, to play Ottawa again."

I stuck out my hand.

"If you do that, you've got to invite me." The man grabbed my hand and looked me square in the eye.

"We will," Budd Docken replied.

CHAPTER ONE

"Be a good man to camp out with."

— TEDDY ROOSEVELT, 1910

Gravel ice streets, an occasional car, boardwalks fronting the Jack London Grill, Bank British North America and the Downtown Hotel. It is cold and dusky at 8:00 A.M. Hills rise abruptly at the rear of town. Across the Yukon River cliffs are topped with black spruce, some sinking down ravines, toward the ice.

Quiet. The hum of a distant truck. Stones thrown by wheels of a passing automobile. Kitty-corner from the Klondike Nugget and Ivory Shop sits the decaying, boarded-up former Bank of Commerce, Robert Service's work place. Beside it the refurbished sternwheeler Keno, white and regal beside fading yellow, frozen in both time and place.

A cold wind lifts up across the 400-yard-wide Yukon River. The isolated slam of a car door, the tell-tale ice-gravel crunch of a human being. A Canadian flag half-mast. The river iced and ominous, coursing endlessly northward, bending under the sharp cliffs.

The long levy on Front Street protects a line of frontier facades and boardwalks from the river. Queen Street slightly undulates upward to its end against the forested white hill, seven streets up. Streetlights line the way. The facade: Dawson City General Store, River West Food & Health, Maximillion's Emporium, River West Cappuccino Bistro. Houses uneven, bent, rusted, pilfered, new, a blue flag hanging from a second story window, a Union Jack with a series of stars. Snow encrusted, tarpaulin draped piles of wood. Signs. Red buildings,

1

grey buildings, blue buildings; back alleys cluttered with snow-topped wheels, ladders, wooden steps, and fuel tanks. Nothing even, nor level. Jacked-up permafrost dizzy. Yellow CIBC Banking Center, banking hours 10:00–5:00. "SATURDAY CLOSED."

At 8:30 A.M. high clouds over the back of town are tinted pink by a hidden sun. Over buildings falling up, building down. The line of flags draped in a row on the Downtown Hotel gently sway in the cold breeze. Boardwalks and gravel. A log cabin, "Beauty Salon 933–5222." One block past the Midnight Sun Hotel a vacant parking lot with logs lining the perimeter. A store: "K.T.M. Co." with subtitle: "Store That Sells Most Everything." Diamond Tooth Gerties slant roof next, white with green trim.

The sound of one truck loud, intrusive. Looking down the streets each way you see the past and imagine the present. Down Third Street toward the signature gash in the rear hillside is a boarded-up log cabin. Ramshackle tin buildings waving along the ground, new next to old, the new boarded up, the old open. An old dog slowly waddling down the middle of the street, so little noise the low wing "whoop-whoop-whoop" of a raven seems loud and magnified. Satellite dishes black and shiny. Empty flag poles. Toward the rear of town vacant lots more numerous. For Sale signs plenty: "Century 21 667-7000, ask for Marg."

At Third and King the Post Office sits regal and Victorian new, kitty-corner Klondike Kates, yellow. The building across from the Post Office (For Sale) has written on its side "The Spell of the Yukon" with the first eight lines of the famous poem, beside a mural of Robert Service, reading at a table.

A banged-up red van with a two-foot by two-foot blue metal sign bolted to the front grill, a big, white question mark on it. A barbershop poll red and swirling white, a cuff and hand, pointing, at the top. The Downtown Hotel dining room. Old beaten caps and chamois shirts. Lots of coffee. Old Indian couple slowly walk in. Country music. Wounded First Nation persons straggling in, long black hair, pony tails. Missing teeth. Small. Picking teeth with fingers. Off season, no rush for the tables of men. Time as they know it. Anger while discussing the parking situation on Front Street. Everything old, worn, used, weathered; the shirts, the coats, the faces. Especially the hats.

It is the rough in the diamonds; it is Dawson City.

DAWSON CITY TO MONTANA CREEK

Saturday, March 1

We assemble on dry, crunching snow in the town maintenance yard, a flurry of pickup trucks, snowmobiles, dogs, and men. Everyone busy packing sleds we will pull behind our snowmobiles. Twenty below zero Fahrenheit. I left John Flynn's house ahead of Pat Hogan and Earl McRae and immediately discovered that my machine can turn neither left nor right on the ice-laden Dawson streets. Waves of panic. How will I manage 400 miles on wilderness trails if I can't turn on a damn city street? And then—where is everyone? I realize not only do I have to dismount and yank my machine ninety degrees to make each turn, but I can't find the maintenance yard either.

Finally in the yard, everyone is excited. Local newsmen are interviewing various characters that make up this expedition; leaders Pat Hogan, John Flynn, and Kevin Anderson, local color in the intimidating form of one Larry "Cowboy" Smith, and the two writers from outside, *Ottawa Sun* correspondent Earl McRae and the lone American and novelist from Massachusetts. Gasoline fumes mix with the wafting aroma of dog feces. I am concerned when Hogan decides that the hundred pounds of extra dog food must be stored in my sled. There is laughter here and there, nervous proclamations, white wisps of frost forming on the faces of those with beards. Margot Anderson, wife of Kevin, approaches me.

"Do you realize how lucky you are?" she asks. "Do you realize you're going to see the Yukon in a way that most Yukoners never will?" Brendan McEwen, CBC cameraman filming a documentary on our trip, pipes up in his British accent.

"McRae's a nervous wreck, and look at you Don, like you have all the confidence in the world!"

Sure enough McRae is warily gazing about, struggling to move in his fifty pounds of clothing. He is muttering to himself. When I walk over he says to me, "I'm gonna die. I know I'm gonna die. What the Christ was I *thinking?*" As for myself, I'm glad my facade is holding up. When approached by newspaper reporter Michael Onesi of the *Whitehorse Daily Star*, McRae tells him, "I have a sense of fear and foreboding as I stand here now. It's like the calm before the storm."

"To have written a book about this," I say into the reporter's microphone, "and then do it—I'm the luckiest guy in the world right now. I truly believe that."

Tires crunch fast-frozen snow, dogs wail. Bundled wives hugging bundled husbands, bundled girlfriends hugging bundled boyfriends. Eccentrics standing alone. Everyone's breath a blown cloud in the air. Jokes. Hockey sticks. But where are all the towns-people? I thought we'd have a better turnout, though it is awfully cold. Surely more people are interested in our trip than this, but where are they?

Bicycles appear, and snowshoes. With two nights in Dawson I've met so many people, and I try to place names with faces. Wes Peterson, the guy I can't understand for the life of me, is filling his gas tank. Earl MacKenzie, the sixty-year-old Dawson hockey benefactor is here, bulky in his red parka, icicles forming from the end of his nose. Kevin Anderson never stops chattering, insulting all around him, swearing, declaring he won five hundred bucks last night in Diamond Tooth Gerties. Gerard "Doc" Parsons is here, Errol Flynn with a pony tail and Dawson City's lone doctor, always smiling, tying up his sled next to the quiet, earnest preparation of Bruce Duffee. The Indians stick together, wild-looking Freddy Farr in his tattered clothing, and others who will not take part in this first leg of the trip but join us later in Vancouver, or Toronto.

Two pickup trucks pull into the yard with wood-panel caps housing two layers of dogs. These are Frank Turner's dogs, but I overhear indignant dismay that local legend Turner, the only man to run every Yukon Quest dog sled race and two weeks previous this year's runner up, has decided not to accompany us. He has sent two interns in his place, Patrick Riopel from the Laurentians north of Montreal, a quiet individual who speaks little English, and Steve Christianson, a cheerful New Zealand adventurer immediately nicknamed "Kiwi." They struggle mightily, unloading dogs, strapping them into harnesses, pulling the lunging creatures from one another, all in a cacophony of animal yelps and human cursing. Next to them the Rangers stand, Trevor Williams, Bruce Taylor, and the lone woman on the trail Agata Franczak, drinking coffee. The Rangers are to accompany us for the first two days, guiding us along the trail and assisting with the camps.

Hogan, his red beard gathering a porthole of ice, surveys the scene and is satisfied the sleds are ready. Since I was the last to arrive at the maintenance yard, I am first in line when we turn around.

"Where am I going?" I ask, and Hogan answers, "Front Street." I pull out of the yard, my iron sled loaded with gear and dog food. Sensing my uncertainty, Adam Killick, reporter with the *Yukon News*, jumps on the back and pats my arm left and I turn toward Front Street and finally see the crowd.

Hundreds of souls stand in the bitter cold, stomping feet and shaking hands to summon any last vestige of warmth. When they see my snow machine they begin cheering and a phalanx of cameras emerge from warm hiding places and flash in unison as the Rangers, who have moved ahead of us to organize the exit strategy, direct me to my place at the intersection of 3rd and King. I switch off my machine, turn and watch as the line of snowmobiles noisily settles in behind me. A mechanical whining and coughing crescendo. I meet the gaze of Deb Belinsky, owner and operator of DCB Productions, who, along with assistant Jim Nicol, is in charge of publicizing this event, and wave. I strain to listen as someone raises a microphone and issues a brief speech I know has ended only because of scattered applause. There are moments in life that sear themselves into the fabric of memory, and here on the streets of Dawson City, immersed in this marvelous scene, I realize I'm experiencing one of them.

John Flynn and Kevin Anderson appear on snowshoes, stepping side-to-side, awaiting Hogan's word. Anderson brandishes his hockey stick above his head, a Yukon flag tied to it, yelling, "Bring on Brad Marsh!" Assistant coach Dave Millar, Bob Sutherland, and Doc Parsons appear on bicycles, recreating a mode of transportation used ninety years before by original team members. Box lunches consisting of a sandwich, two juice boxes, and an apple, compliments of the Downtown Hotel, are distributed; I stick mine in my sled. And to the rousing cheer that a couple of hundred souls can muster, Flynn and Anderson clomp off in their snowshoes down the road, toward the Yukon River. Hogan announces, "I'm ready to go!" and jerks his snowmobile forward and I pull out behind him, chugging through cheers, thumbs-up waves, and winks. My machine lurches up the levy and down the steep slope onto the river, the horizon a bleak black and white. As the procession whines down the road and onto the river, well-wisher Marco Jiocamoli turns to reporter Onesi and says, "They might not win, but who cares?"

Out on the Yukon River the machines stop to regroup. The dog teams fall down the banks and onto the ice, mushers Riopel, Christianson, Craig, and Gudmundson waving as they pass, Cowboy Smith following grim-faced, without a hint of acknowledgement. Up on the bank the crowd strings out along the levy, waving goodbye as we head south. Immediately we turn east onto the Klondike River. Up the Klondike we run, turning south onto Bonanza Creek, passing original gold claims, the wooden Discovery Claim historical marker, and reconditioned Dredge #4. Here the first of the day's problems occur when two dog teams miss the turn and continue on the Klondike. We stop for a long while as someone chases them down, and suffer our first accident. Steve Craig is working on a sled runner when another dog team races by dragging its anchor claw. The bouncing steel claw catches the outside runner of Craig's sled and jerks it against him, bruising his thigh and cutting his hand.

The line of snow machines jolts ahead, passing the CBC crew which has driven ahead to film our departure. We leave Bonanza where it bends to the east, running along the banks of Eldorado Creek. Shortly we turn up into the hills, the thin forest closing in around us. My inexperience on a snowmobile surfaces quickly when I cannot manage a turn on an icy incline. Hogan takes my machine, guns it and makes the corner. Continuing on we encounter a harrowing diagonal stretch across an open, steep slope, where I must rise and lean far to my left to keep the machine from toppling.

Crossing a low ridge and advancing toward the Indian River valley, we enter the heart of the Yukon wilderness. The temperature, once out of the Yukon River valley, rises noticeably. With the Rangers breaking trail and Cowboy and his dogs ahead, we begin our journey in earnest. We pass through forests sparse and in places burned-out, affording views of neighboring snowy peaks and a winding, ice-encrusted river below. When we stop for coffee I discover what frozen food truly is. I take my box lunch from my sled only to find the sandwich frozen. To eat it requires a difficult bite, a pause of about thirty seconds as the warmth of my mouth reduces it to a chewable consistency, and then a crunching attempt.

The beauty of this land unfolds with every turn of the trail. Overwhelming is the landscape and its cold blanketed, haunting stillness. When I pause and turn off my machine, I sense silence's staggering presence, a natural resource invaluable and unexportable, yet available here in the Yukon to anyone willing to step outside. I hear the faint slide of a dog sled runner through the vacant, deadened air. But on this first day of our journey, there is little inclination to pause, and admire. Hour after hour we grind our way over open slopes and through forests of willow and white spruce, until Hogan and Flynn finally pull over on a long, straight stretch of trail, with level ground for the tents.

Sounds and sights of camp: chainsaws buzzing in the woods, voices and laughter up and down the trail, guys splitting firewood, tying up tents, balancing cooking pots on rocks encircling roaring fires. Snow machines and dog teams line the trail for seventy, eighty yards. Echoing voices ringing through the woods. White tents held up by cut pines, seven trees four to five inches thick necessary for each. Parsons carries ten-foot-long logs out of the woods on his shoulder, and flips them to the snow. With a jerk of his arm his chainsaw whines, and he slices them up. Log after log the Doctor retrieves, the amount of wood needed for the campfires and tent stoves formidable, the amount of energy he burns remarkable. Others gather spruce boughs and dump them into the tents, matting the snow for bedding. I pitch in as best I can, grabbing a shovel and digging out a place for the tent, and then the campfire.

The expedition is divided into three groups, each with its own tent. The sites are separated by forty or fifty yards, delineated by slowly rising wood smoke through the pines. Each Dawson member is responsible for two meals on the trail. Hogan serves us peppercorn rib steaks along with some John Flynn bannock, an excellent meal devoured by men who have spent twelve hours in the Yukon cold. After dinner I almost make a terrible rookie mistake. I have eaten inside our group's tent, which has become quite warm by the roaring camp stove. Going outside to clean my plate and spoon, however, I am sidetracked by a short conversation with McRae before turning to the snow. The only way to clean up in the bush is to rub snow on everything, until a semblance of cleanliness is achieved. Standing in the snow, needing both hands to accomplish this, I take the spoon and begin to place it in my mouth. I feel the metal, which has had time to acclimate to minus thirty degrees, begin to bite my tongue and stick, and I quickly jerk it out before suffering any damage.

The other camps quickly quiet, the days excitement and toil taking its toll. But our campfire is animated, Anderson and Hogan in particular happy to finally be in the wilderness, and relieved of their more pedestrian duties and obligations as leaders of this adventure. Hogan is interesting, a burly man with an imposing red beard and no-nonsense demeanor. He is as eloquent as he is intelligent, and settles himself fireside, telling stories the others have no doubt heard before, but which are new to me. He talks of growing up in Port Hope, Ontario before wandering north to Dawson City, and spending winters in Latin American. He mentions a friend recently spotting a Sasquash in the Yukon woods.

"You speak as though you believe your friend," I say to him.

"Well, he was out of jail and sober when he told me."

"Tell him about Bob," Parsons suggests.

"They're splitting up the Northwest Territories," Hogan says, "and they held a referendum for what to call the new Territory. 'Bob' won."

Doc Parsons sits on a log smiling and nodding to the conversation, breaking out a bottle of whiskey he passes to Anderson. Hogan hesitates, then grabs the bottle and takes a swig. McRae staggers up to the fire, hollering and pointing up into the Yukon night. We look up to see, in the clear night sky, the long, thin tail of a comet.

"It's Elvis!" he declares, pointing to the line of light streaking the sky. "It's Elvis come back to earth!"

"It's Hale-Bopp," Parsons replies, and pulls out a magazine that describes the latest meteorological incursion into our atmosphere, the Hale-Bopp Comet, and passes it around.

"Have you heard of Tagish Elvis?" Anderson asks. "There's this guy Gilbert Nelles from Carcross, he claims aliens visited him and revealed to him that he's actually Elvis Presley. Drives around in this big, pink Cadillac, dresses up and sings as Elvis Presley. Fucken scream."

"Has an album with a picture of his transformation under a hovering spaceship on the cover," Parsons adds.

I sit with them listening, watching. I stare at the fire. It is so cold that logs burning furiously harbor ice and snow on their back sides, barely inches from the flames. To step away a foot removes all benefit of the heat. The northern lights emerge and begin their rose swirl beside the tail of the comet. A circle of hollow voices surrounded by a million square miles of wilderness. Soon I retreat from the fire and enter the tent to settle in for the evening. It is hot inside and I remove my layers of clothing. I awake the next morning to find my feet sticking out of my sleeping bag, and the stove out. Next to me I hear McRae stirring.

"Oh Gawd," I hear him mutter. "Here we go again."

CHAPTER TWO

*"I have, for some time, been thinking it would be a good
thing if there were a challenge cup, which should be
held, from year to year, by the champion hockey club
of the Dominion. There does not appear to be any such
outward and visible sign of a championship at present,
and considering the interest the hockey matches now elicit
and the importance of having the games fairly played...I
am willing to give a cup that shall be annually held by
the winning club."*

— LORD STANLEY OF PRESTON, 1892

Six thousand people inhabited Dawson City in 1903, another
15,000 working the outlying gold fields. Athletics were a
popular distraction from the harsh conditions, with organized
leagues playing indoor and outdoor baseball, curling, lacrosse, and ice
hockey. As early as 1901 four rinks were set up on the Yukon river
ice. The Dawson Amateur Athletic Association, known as the DAAA,
built the first enclosed hockey rink west of Winnipeg during the fall of
1902. That winter a four-team hockey league was formed consisting of
the Eagles, the Mounties, Joe Boyle's DAAA, and the powerhouse Civil
Service team, under the watchful eye of Jack Eilbeck. Of those involved
in the evolution of the original Dawson City Klondikers, it was Eilbeck
who played the most prominent role.

The Kingston, Ontario native was described in the *Dawson Daily
News* as, "not only president, but also financial backer, chief rooter and

mascot," of the Civil Service club. He was an aging athlete, "famed in
the Yukon as a star baseball player," who boasted of playing against
Albert Spaulding, the early American baseball star and sporting goods
tycoon, in the 1870's. He spared no effort in building up Civil Service
teams, and rumors of bribes, payoffs, and awarding government jobs
to good athletes simmered and occasionally boiled over, garnering
outraged headlines in local newspapers. One of the more controversial incidents was Eilbeck's attempt to lure Sureshot Kennedy from the
Idyll Hour's baseball team to the Civil Service in June 1903, promising
a $7.50-a-day government job and a spot on the Civil Service's hockey
tour the following winter.

This is one of the first indications that a hockey tour was being
discussed. Athletic touring, at the turn of the century referred to as
"barnstorming," was common in the days before far-flung, organized
leagues. It was a way for athletes to gain some money, as well as a little
adventure, in the days of amateur sport. An all-Indian hockey team
from Calgary was preparing to tour, and Joe Boyle had toured with
Australian boxer Frank Slavin, "the Sydney Slasher." Two of the Civil
Service hockey players had touring experience; Randy McLennan's
Queen's University hockey team had toured the United States in
1894, and goalie E. C. Senkler had toured England with the Canadian
Association football team.

Eilbeck went outside in the spring of '03, "promoting the hockey
idea." During this trip the inclusion of a Stanley Cup challenge
evolved—and was initially frowned upon. Cup trustees John Sweetland
and Philip Ross, empowered by Lord Stanley to implement a method
of awarding Cup challenges, did not recognize Dawson's league as a
legitimate senior league, disqualifying the Civil Service team for con-
sideration. Eilbeck countered that an all-star team, drawn from all four
Dawson clubs, could represent the Klondike. Though the participation
of an all-star team in Stanley Cup play had never before been considered, this engendered a more favorable response, and Eilbeck returned
to Dawson City encouraged.

Though the Ottawa games would be the focus of the trip, a series
of games was sought for afterward. Letters were written to prospective

opponents, eliciting interest from teams across the Dominion as well as in the United States. Eilbeck wrote to the CPR for particulars on securing a train car, determining the cost of transporting and feeding the team on their four-month-long journey. The *Dawson Daily News* reported that, "the replies are satisfactory. They show that the trip will not cost the barrel of money many people expected." It is unknown who wrote the official challenge, directed at the powerhouse defending champion Ottawa Silver Seven and delivered to the Cup trustees, but it almost certainly was Eilbeck. And so it must have been heartbreaking for the Kingston man when on September 3rd, 1904—just six days before Philip Ross officially acknowledged receipt of the Dawson challenge—Sheriff Jack Eilbeck was dismissed from his presidency of the Civil Service athletic club due to one final, inexcusable attempt to fix the championship of the Dawson baseball league. Eilbeck would soon leave the Klondike, and instead of standing on the bench behind his team in Ottawa, would lie in a San Francisco hospital during the games, recovering from a broken leg amidst the tremors of a soon to be ruined city.

Joe Boyle, who had played on Eilbeck's curling team, became prominent in the Cup challenge, probably because he was outside tending business in Detroit and Ottawa, and therefore in a position to petition the Cup trustees in person. A businessman known as a very tough, charming individual, Boyle was persuasive, and although the games would not be officially sanctioned until December 10th, Ross and Sweetland conveyed to Boyle that the Dawson City challenge would be accepted.

On October 27th the *Dawson Daily News* reported that the hockey players were petitioning Ottawa for a postponement of the games so that they could participate in elections scheduled for December 16th. Meanwhile, a committee was established to select the team's players. The day after the DAAA rink opened the Klondikers held their first practice, announcing that the team would practice every night until their departure for Ottawa. With more than twenty players trying out, it was decided to hold a series of scrimmages to determine the final roster. One of the men entrusted with the decisions and expected to play himself was former Ottawa star Weldy Young.

Young had played seven tumultuous seasons on defense for Ottawa, six of them alongside future Hockey Hall of Fame inductee Harvey Pulford. For four years in the mid-nineties he was elected vice-president of the Amateur Hockey Association of Canada. In 1894 he played in a losing cause against Montreal in the second "league" Stanley Cup play-off game ever played.[1] Having been charged with brutality in Quebec in '95, and later charging into the stands in Ottawa to assault a fan in '98, Young left a checkered, notorious past when he decided that gold was more valuable than silver after the 1899 season. His decision to leave for the Klondike was catastrophic as far as his hockey-playing legacy is concerned; the Ottawas were on the verge of dominating senior hockey and the Stanley Cup. Had he remained he almost surely would be in the Hockey Hall of Fame today, as are six other members of what became known as the Ottawa Silver Seven: Harvey Pulford, Alf Smith, Bouse Hutton, Harry Westwick, Billy Gilmour, and the legendary Frank McGee.

Challenging his former teammates for the Stanley Cup must have been an exciting possibility, but Young faced a dilemma. When the Cup trustees agreed to delay the start of the Stanley Cup series so that the Yukoners could vote in their elections, the first game was pushed back to Friday, January 13, 1905. For Young, this delay was accompanied by disconcerting news. His new Civil Service job required him to assist in tabulating the election returns, which would prevent his departing immediately after the elections with the team. Torn by his dilemma, Young continued supervising practice sessions and scrimmages, and was elected captain of the team by a vote of the players.

The all-Klondike team was selected in early December. Chosen to play alongside Young were Captain Lionel Bennett, "formerly of Nova Scotia and a star," Norman Watt of Aylmer, Quebec, "left wing, a fast, scientific player, quick on his feet and a good combination player,"

---

1 In its early history, there were two ways in which to win the Stanley Cup. First was by winning the league in which the Cup resided, second by challenging and defeating the league champion. In 1894 four Amateur Hockey Association teams improbably tied for best record in league play. One team dropped out, and the other three had a playoff for the league championship, and the Stanley Cup.

Dr. Randy McLennan, "with all the craftiness of the veteran and a hard player," and George Kennedy, "or 'Old Sureshot' as he is called, who received his first lessons in hockey at Winnipeg and played on a number of teams in that city and also for Rat Portage, Selkirk and similar places." Also selected were Jimmy Johnstone of Ottawa, and, despite never having played goal before, Albert Forrest, formerly of Three Rivers, Quebec and later Grass Valley, California.

The *Dawson Daily News* proclaimed, "The boys are in much need of financing and are working like beavers to get it." Practice games with teams drawn from rejected players, with the gate added to the tour kitty, were played, and not without rancor. But as time grew short, two calamities befell the team. Weldy Young, after agonizing for weeks, decided he could not leave his Civil Service job. Suddenly the team was without its star player-coach. The blow was compounded when Captain Bennett also declined the tour. His wife had been severely injured the previous winter when she was dragged sixty feet by a runaway sleigh in front of the Northern Hotel, and Bennett decided he could not leave her. To fill their places Hector Smith, from Kennedy's hometown of West Selkirk, Manitoba, and Archie Martin, formerly of Aylmer, Quebec and an employee of Boyle's, were selected. It was also determined to arrange for the addition of Lorne Hannay, "formerly of the Yukon," and now living in Brandon, Manitoba.

Hannay was from the Maritimes and had played in Brandon's Stanley Cup challenge to the Silver Seven the previous March. He had scored twice, but more importantly had seen first-hand Ottawa's fearsome stars Frank McGee and Alf Smith, who between them had scored thirteen of Ottawa's fifteen goals in the two-game Brandon series. It's possible that the Klondikers felt Hannay was eligible simply because he had once been in the Yukon. And so the team was set: Smith, Kennedy, Watt, and McLennan the forwards, Hannay and Johnstone on defense, Albert Forrest in goal, with Archie Martin as spare.

On December 14, 1904 Frank Slavin, Boyle's old pugilist partner, arrived off the trail from Whitehorse suffering from appendicitis and with bad news: there was little snow. Martin, Kennedy, and Smith, hoping for snow, would leave with dog teams. The rest of the players would depart on bicycles the following day. The newspaper of the day reported, "If the snow is well packed the time will be much better than otherwise. If much light snow is encountered the lads will have the experience of pushing their wheels through the accumulation until good stretches can be found..."

On Sunday morning, December 18th, 1904 it was ten degrees below zero Fahrenheit as Martin, Kennedy, and Smith assembled their dog teams on the streets of Dawson City. And with the release of their claw-brakes and first running steps toward the wilderness, amidst cheers and well-wishes of teammates, friends, and families, the legend began.

MONTANA CREEK TO STEWART RIVER

Sunday, March 2

I sit on a log by the fire, it is twenty-two below zero. Bacon is frying and coffee pots boiling from precarious perches upon rocks ringing the flame. Men are cooking breakfasts in bent and blackened cast-iron pots and pans that appear as old as the gold rush. Everyone in good moods, cheerful and joking, a half-moon hanging in the dull sky at the north end of the trail, back toward Dawson.

I walk down the trail to get a better look at the dogs. They respond eagerly, perhaps looking for food. They seem to have a sophisticated language. Despite what I have read, they can bark as well as howl, but mostly just hack. They emit endless, quick hacks, and the wars they wage are frightful. While the world below is watching the re-release of *Star Wars*, we're watching Dog Wars. Individual teams appear to hate all others, and must be kept separate. A warning is called up and down the trail as the dog teams surge through camp, trampling anything in their path.

I sit on my snowmobile and try to write in my journal, but find the ink in my pen has frozen. I stick the pen in my glove to warm it up. McRae has experienced the same problem, tells me felt-tipped pens work better and retrieves a spare from his pack. Ice has already formed on my beard. The ice builds down from my mustache, and I find I must continually clean it off with my teeth, reaching up with my lower jaw to scrape it away, melting it in my mouth for a bit of fluid.

Once the dog teams have left, we pull out of camp in our designated groups. Ours, with John Flynn the primary navigator, always leads. We immediately experience rough going, facing a two-thousand-foot climb with difficult switch backs. These are at terrible angles, essentially u-turns, and must be hit hard enough not to stall, yet slow enough to manage the turn. Chugging, skidding, gunning our machines we charge up the mountain trail, hanging on for dear life as we traverse glaciers and slide into switch backs. Up we climb, emerging onto a wondrous trail, the jagged teeth of the Ogilvie Mountains snarling down on us from the north, and unending rows of smaller, rounded mountains stretching as far as the eye can see in all other direction.

We stop to marvel at the scene. The trail here is spectacular, running along a mountain crest through old mining camps. We continue on and pass ancient, fallen-in roadhouses of the old Dawson road, and are climbing again when problems arise. The trail snow becomes packed where we run, remaining a couple feet deep on each side. I come up behind Steve Craig's dog team and the musher waves me around and I try, but my machine and steel toboggan sink like stone and I'm stuck. Hogan and Flynn stop, Hogan pulling a wrench from his sled with which to disengage my sled from my snowmobile. A few others stop to assist in stomping out a path, and we pull my machine and toboggan back onto the trail.

Yesterday I usually had someone right on my tail, as I am inexperienced and go slowly. Today I suddenly find myself alone. This is a wonderful turn of events; I drive along for a long time until I come up behind Cowboy Smith and his dog team. He looks back and waves me around, but after sinking earlier there's no way I'm going to attempt this again. I motion to Smith 'No,' and soon he finds a place to pull off the trail, allowing me to pass.

I run on, and Hogan catches up telling me that McRae ran twenty yards off the trail down a steep embankment and they had to haul everything back up. Told me that everyone who came upon the accident stopped to help except Wes Peterson, who just laughed and kept going. Now we enter a hard section, lurching and jerking continuously over six-inch-high bumps that last for miles. We travel through woods and brush, terrible going, but I'm doing it without tipping or running off the trail. It takes effort to maintain control of the machine. Just as I begin feeling good about my snowmobiling ability, I enter a long, closed-in path through dense woods where I see a log half buried in snow. The path bends to the right and I hit the log with all my weight to the right and I am thrown headlong into the snow, my machine coming to a stop ten yards further. I lay still and play dead, thinking Hogan isn't far behind. But as minutes creep by and no Hogan appears I get too cold, and finally get up and sit on my snowmobile, awaiting the leader. When he pulls up he hollers over the roar of his machine, "Did you see the martin in the trap back there?"

We continue along this difficult stretch and finally break onto the banks of the Stewart River. I had heard that there was a cabin at this campsite, and now that I see it on the opposite bank my heart becomes set on the luxuries I imagine this Shangri-La possesses. But before I can reach Shangri-La I see the steep embankment that descends onto Stewart River ice, and worse, the precipitous rise on the opposite shore. I wait as Hogan and Flynn drop down onto the river, and watch with mounting concern as they accelerate up the opposite bank, their machines flying through the air when they gain the top, falling onto unseen turf. I advance, easily fall down onto the ice and then gun across the river gaining the necessary speed, then run up the bank. I'm ecstatic when my machine makes the grade, flies through the air and lands, my life still intact, upon level ground. I pull up to the cabin, considering myself fortunate that I am first in line to claim it.

Here the Stewart River is 400 yards wide with hills rising from the opposite bank, from which we've emerged. It is roughly fifteen miles upstream from its confluence—and Jack London's 1897–98 wintering site—with the Yukon River. We find two standing tents, remnants of previous Ranger maneuvers. MacKenzie and I start the campfire as others slowly filter in. I return to the cabin to stake my claim only to find McRae has claimed the top bunk and Ranger Bruce Taylor the bottom, so I push my gear under his, on the ground. The potbellied stove has been stoked, and the cabin begins to warm. MacKenzie dumps his gear inside, and Cowboy Smith arrives and ties a rope across the room, hanging dog booties along it to dry.

It is MacKenzie's night to feed our group, and he heats up a pot of chili with little hot dogs mixed in. After dinner with the camp settling down, I dig out a bottle of Jack Daniels I had been given in Dawson the night before our departure. Realizing that many were bringing along bottles, I had gone out only to find that all the Dawson liquor stores had closed. Later, during the going-away party held in Dick Van Nostrand's Downtown Hotel, I bemoaned this fact to Van Nostrand, who promptly went to his barroom and returned with the bottle of whiskey. And then I searched for the toy I've had since I was a kid.

Sometime back in the early 1960's, my parents gave me and my brothers one of those flapping, hand-operated hockey games for Christmas. It came with a little plastic replica of the Stanley Cup. Before departing for the Yukon, my wife Terry had handed the Cup to me, suggesting that I take it on the trip. Here on the banks of the Stewart River with the already-dangerous temperature plummeting, I determine what to do with it. Grabbing the Cup and the bottle of Jack Daniels, I make the rounds, offering everyone a shot from the Cup, "to remind us of our goal." All accept a shot and some have two, a lone exception Freddie Farr, who gazes longingly but declines. The Rangers, coaches, and players all participate, many posing to have their picture taken with it. When I hand it to McRae he accepts, raises it and pays homage to my roots: "From Milt Schmidt down to Ray Borque," and throws back the shot.

Back in the little cabin, I find myself next to Agata Franczak. She is a blonde, eastern-European woman with a heavy accent. She endures a remarkable consequence of frozen breath on hair similar to the ice that forms on men's beards, except that her breath condenses and freezes on the fringe of her hair falling on each side of her face.

"What position do you play?" she asks me.

"I'm not on the team, I'm an author. I wrote the book about the original team."

"Oh! I've wanted to talk to you!" she exclaims, and I explain to her the path which led to this moment on the banks of the Stewart River. Agata, in turn, tells me she is concerned with her ability to keep up with the other Rangers on the trip; she wants very much to hold her own. She does not want them to know her real age.

"They will say I am too old to be a Ranger," she says, a rueful smile on her face. "So don't tell them! Don't tell anyone!"

The temperature continues to fall, and I abandon any campfire-side society for what comfort the little cabin provides. Inside is crowded, many coming and going, some cooking on top of the woodstove, mushers drying dog booties on lines strung rafter to rafter. Several of us lay about still bundled in our bunny boots, bibs, and great overcoats. I watch as Cowboy Smith picks among the booties, examining each and tossing rejects into the stove. McRae, who sits on the floor beside me, puts the back of his hand to his mouth.

"Strangler," he whispers. I turn my head toward him.

"There's a rumor."

"What's the rumor?"

"They say we're slowing them down, we're an accident waiting to happen to screw up the timetable. The bastids are thinkin' of pulling us out."

CHAPTER THREE

*"Anyone who'd willingly take twenty-one days to go
to Ottawa from the godforsaken frozen steppes of the
North when a plane could accomplish it in a few hours
of warmth and comfort has to be the most extreme of
lunatics."*

— EARL McRAE, *OTTAWA SUN,* JANUARY 31, 1997

The effect of the far North on mental health has long been recognized as a distinct malady. Polar Eskimos, long adapted to protracted, dark winters, recognized the extreme depression that could result and called it "perlerorneg," translated, "to feel the weight of life." Pioneers who followed called it, "bushed." Author and Queen's Attorney Vernon Frolick brilliantly documents Michael "Shesley Free Mike" Oros' slow disintegration in the darkness and isolation of the British Columbia–Yukon borderland from idealistic hippie, to paranoidal murderer in his book, *Descent into Madness.*

He relates that Gunter Hans Lishy was born in a decidedly bad time and place. At age sixteen he was sent to the Russian front where he was captured by partisans. He spent two hellish years of torture and deprivation at the hands of female guards before being liberated by western funds from the coffers of his wealthy, aristocratic family. But years languished under eyes that despised all Germans left an indelible scar on the man's soul. In 1957, paranoid of all things official and fearing most the horde of Soviet soldiers massed in Eastern Europe, Lishy disappeared, forsaking a personal fortune. An intense search ensued, but no trace was ever found of the troubled young man, and German courts declared him legally dead. But Gunter Lishy was very much alive and well just south of the Yukon border in 1981, where Michael Oros fired a bullet through his back.

I was fortunate to spend an evening with Vernon Frolick. A guest of Carol Pettigrew, wife of then Yukon Premier John Ostashek, during my book tour, Frolick was on his own tour, and Carol had arranged a writer's evening in her home. *Descent into Madness* was also Frolick's first published book, and the evening started slowly, until Frolick got going. Feeling more comfortable he began speaking, and I soon found myself mesmerized by this storyteller, an intelligent, educated, wonderful speaker who held the room spellbound. Traveling with his buddies Rick Lawton and Art Mitchell, Frolick made the night a success, putting me in possession of another remarkable Yukon story.

When I was younger I devoured the books of Danish explorer Peter Freuchen, who related one of the more harrowing examples of northern insanity in his book, *Adventures in the Arctic*. A Greenland trapper named Olav had quarreled with his long-time partner, and had formed a new partnership with a man named Gustav Krakau. Krakau was new to the Arctic, and Olav found that he enjoyed teaching his new friend the things trappers needed to know in the deep cold. He appreciated Krakau's endless wonder at all that Olav and his old partner had come to take for granted. The men divided the territory, Olav heading north and Krakau south, working their traplines a week at a time before meeting back at their base cabin. Olav found himself looking forward to seeing his new companion, for they always seemed to have something to talk about.

One day Olav returned from his traplines and entered the cabin to find Krakau hunched up in his bed, facing the wall. The cabin was cold, the dogs howling with hunger, and Olav immediately sensed that Krakau was dead. When he looked more closely, he noticed a wry smile frozen on his friend's death face. But Olav scolded him for letting the cabin grow so cold, and for not heating up the water. He fell into bed exhausted, and when he arose the next morning asked Krakau if he wanted breakfast. He pulled the frozen body from the bed, and with its legs pulled up toward its chest, was able to set the corpse on a chair at the wooden table. Olav spoke to his friend, prepared his meals and chastised him when he would not eat. Finally coming to his senses, he placed his friend on a sled, pulled him to the edge of a cliff and carefully buried him, so that his remains would not be eaten by wolves.

But Olav could not bear to think of his friend out in the terrible cold. He dug Krakau out and brought him back inside the cabin, placing him again at the table. In the middle of the night Olav awoke and swore the body was moving! In his fright he realized his mistake, but still could not accept that his friend was gone. He reburied the remains, but each weekend when he returned from his traplines he disinterred Krakau's corpse, and placed it at the wooden table. With the advent of spring and the imminent return of the ship scheduled to take them home with their winter's catch, Olav knew he must reconcile the situation.

He returned from his last trapline run very much afraid. He was frightened of ghosts and goblins, frightened of Krakau and himself, and deathly frightened of what others would think of him if they were to discover what he had done. His behavior embarrassed him, and suddenly Olav realized what he must do. Talking to Krakau as he sat at the table, Olav acted as though nothing were amiss. But when he saw his chance he snuck outside, leaving the door ajar, and returned with his rifle. And from the doorway of the cabin, furious with the man for scaring him so, Olav shot the corpse in the back of the head. Convinced that his friend was now truly dead, Olav made a proper coffin from some wooden boxes and reburied Krakau. Calm for the first time in months, Olav awaited the spring ship.

On the journey home, his companion's body stored in the hold, Olav confessed all. He could not bear the truth of what he had done, and the only reason he did not throw himself overboard was that he did not want his reputation sullied further. Once back in Denmark, the police came to Olav's house and arrested him for the murder of Gustav Krakau. Despite protesting that he had only killed a dead man, he was imprisoned, where he was taunted mercilessly by guards who called him a murderer. This broke the man once and for all, for he could not bear the thought that anyone could believe that he would take the life of his great new friend.

When the coroner performed an autopsy on Krakau's corpse, he determined that the man had indeed been dead, his head frozen solid, when the bullet had struck. But it was too late for Olav, for he had lost his mind completely, and shortly after was deemed incurably insane.

One of the first murders of a white man in the Yukon was more a cultural misunderstanding than the result of mental illness. In the mid 1880's, a period in the secluded North when the white man's initial influence was having a dramatic effect on the native population, a Han Indian was transported to Sitka to testify in a murder trial. Upon his return to the primitive shores of the Yukon River, he described to a rapt audience of fellow tribesmen how the murderer had been convicted and now lived a life of ease, fed and clothed by the United States government, housed in a "skookum," or strong house that was constantly heated. Such, the Indian concluded, was the reward for murdering a white man.

A young Han Indian took the story to heart, and shortly thereafter encountered a man known to history only as Frenchy. The young Indian promptly dispatched poor Frenchy, and when his body was discovered by fellow gold seekers on their way to Fortymile, they immediately approached the nearby village to investigate. To their surprise the young Indian eagerly presented himself and confessed all, and elders corroborated his bizarre confession, explaining that the boy had vowed to kill the first white man he encountered, so that he too could enjoy a life of ease in the white man's skookum.

The miners, furious with the murder of their companion but dumbfounded by this surprising twist, quickly agreed that it was merely a sad misunderstanding. To ensure no further misunderstandings, they promptly hung the enterprising young Indian from a nearby tree and repeatedly shot through his body with their rifles.

STEWART RIVER TO PELLY FARM

Monday, March 3

We wake in our camp on the banks of the Stewart River to an ominous dawn—it is forty degrees below zero. The stove is dead cold, no one willing to rise during the night to replenish it. I realize that my haste to claim a bunk in this cabin was ill-advised; without the stove heat, the holes in the walls next to my sleeping bag remove all protection from the cold. When I turn to check my Wal-Mart thermometer I find that the mercury has frozen. The air is something beyond imagination. I shift in my sleeping bag and discover that two days of rocking and rolling on a snowmobile has taxed every muscle in my body. I am so sore I can barely move. I am the only person on this expedition without face protection, and sense that my face is frost bitten. My right hand, from constantly depressing the accelerator lever, has frozen in place, and is essentially paralyzed. It is so weak I could not cut pasta with a hand-held fork. Someone mentions the cold and Duffee mutters what will become an oft-repeated joke: "But it's a *dry* cold."

We want to get out before the dog teams so that we won't be held up by them on the narrow trails we expect to run this day, but fail to do so. Packing up camp is a painstakingly slow process, further complicated by the severe cold that blankets the central Yukon this morning. Everything we pack must be wrapped in plastic, to guard against "the dreaded overflow," as Hogan calls it. Despite extreme cold, rivers and streams do not freeze entirely, and will often form a thin layer of ice which cracks, allowing water to overflow. This overflow can be obscured by yet another thin topping of ice and snow, creating a dangerous trap for the unwary wilderness traveler. We prepare for a long day on the trail, some sixty-five miles to our next camp at Pelly Farm. The Rangers are enjoying their time in the woods. Caught up in the excitement of this reenactment, they quietly confer, and decide to accompany us one more day.

The trail continues much as it had late yesterday, if not worse. We travel along Scroggy Creek, the path perilously close to its steep, twenty foot banks. We run through forests and emerge into an open valley, substantial mountains surrounding us. At first we're bunched together, but again I break free after a particularly bad accident behind me where several machines went off the trail and into the trees and deep snow, everyone desperately trying to avoid crashing into the man in front of him. It would take a long time to haul the machines back out and onto the trail, allowing me this break, traveling ten or fifteen miles completely alone.

This is a marvelous development. I run through miles of burned-out forest. Absent pressure to move more quickly than I am comfortably capable of, I take my time, pulling over and taking pictures. The land is mesmerizing when you turn the machine off and the silence descends. Crystallized clarity. Silence doesn't just envelop the land, it enshrouds it, penetrates it, consumes it. It is more than the mere absence of a sense, it is a timeless presence, a consuming identification, an imprint. There is simply no sound. The reach of low mountains and sparkling slopes speaks fluently, more eloquently than any man-made sound that perchance breaks its long-cast spell. Sitting in a mountainside snow bank, I catch a glimpse of an absolutely wonderful sight, Cowboy Smith and his dog team gliding slowly, steadily along the trail far below.

Onward into the forest I ride, entering a clearing where a small pond, or maybe a meandering stream lies hidden beneath the snow. I don't know how far anyone is in front of me, or behind. I run onto unpacked snow and begin to bog down, and desperately gun the machine, leaning far forward, willing it out of the trap. I break free onto the trail and jerk forward, barely escaping another embarrassing accident where I'd have to wait God knows how long to be helped out. This pleases me immensely, confidence in my snowmobiling abilities once again mounting.

The trail improves with long stretches of straight running. Along one portion the path straddles the very top of a mile-long ridge, and I notice McRae gaining from behind. I find myself pausing after particularly bad places and turning to see that McRae makes it over them. He does so every time. I pull over and wait. When he arrives we shut down and relax, taking in the views and rehashing the events of the day. Earlier, while still running with Hogan, we had stopped on a high, burned-out ridge and built fires for the dog teams still behind, which must pause to rest once or twice a day. After loitering for an hour, enjoying a leisurely cup of coffee, I had left as others began to arrive, hoping for more miles alone. McRae tells me now of the ruckus that followed.

"Cowboy pulls in, digs out a side-path for his team to lay down and rest, then goes up to the fires and starts heating up some of that shit they feed the dogs," he tells me. "Then what's-his-name the French kid pulls up, but he pulls up and stops right where Cowboy has beaten down a path for his team to come back onto the trail. Anderson warned him, but for some reason—what's his name?—he shrugged it off. You know how wary and aware all those guys are of Cowboy, Riopel—that's it! Patrick Riopel!—probably felt he had enough time. So the Cowboy comes back and gets his team up and ready, and what does he do but just runs over Patrick's team! Just yells 'Go!' and his dogs run right over Patrick's, everything getting entangled and the dogs eating each other alive, a mess! Didn't even ask Patrick to get out of the way, just bowled over them!"

We reluctantly remount our hogs, as McRae now calls our snowmobiles, and continue onward. Miles mount, weariness develops, and I stop observing the woods and snow, and start to think of nothing but completing this day's journey. Sixty-five miles over mountain trails becomes arduous. I recall with a smirk my brother-in-law asking before the trip what I had done to get into shape.

"Get in shape?" I had replied. "What for? We're riding snowmobiles." I recall some sense of fearing the cold more than anything, and rationalizing that if it got too bad I would simply run full-speed ahead and settle into the cozy camps I was told the Rangers would have waiting. I laugh out loud at that now—not only is there no cozy camp ahead, if I was truly traveling alone I would become so lost in this maze of mountains I'd never find it anyway.

Onward we run, McRae and I sticking together for the rest of the afternoon, pausing at one point to allow others to move ahead of us. At dusk, despairing of ever reaching camp, we come to a fork in the trail with tracks leading in each direction. Through a thin bank of willows we see the deep, broad Pelly River valley, the red outbuildings of Pelly Farm far off to our left, settled in the middle of the forested valley floor, like toys. I run down the left branch a bit but see no sign of camp, and return to the fork and shut down my machine. Agata Franczak buzzes up and joins us. She says there have been several accidents, that she herself had bogged down in the snow and had to be pulled out by the other Rangers. McRae and I are relieved to hear that it isn't just the cheechakos who are having problems, but even a Ranger! We rest, but soon hear the tell-tale buzz of Doc Parson's chainsaw ringing dully in the distance, down the right hand path. Agata mounts her machine and pulls out and down the trail, McRae and I remain.

"Hey Earl, whaddaya say we're still, like, far behind."

"Let *them* set up the gawdamn camp," he agrees, and we laugh like two fools with our hands in the cookie jar. We lean shamelessly on our machines, laughing at the foibles and idiosyncrasies of the Yukoners. But it's beyond mere laziness; we are spent. Three long, frozen, machine-shaking days have taken their toll. And five more days to go! McRae's right hand is also paralyzed. He has developed a frostbite scab on the bridge of his nose. My soreness has taken on a life of its own. We sit giddily in our exhausted sloth for ten or fifteen minutes, until finally suffering vague pangs of guilt. We drag ourselves back on our machines and travel the last mile into camp.

The site chosen is dramatic, the dull, grey remains of the day allowing views from a ridge through a grove of willows over a wide, expansive valley. A thin wisp of smoke rises from a building far below, in Pelly Farm. Here great campfires are built but I am so tired that I consider going to bed without eating. This is not an idle comment; to have struggled through sixty-five mountain miles in cold that began at a bit lower than forty below and climbed no higher than thirty below, to imagine the calories burnt, to be so tired as to not even care if one eats is a statement. Kevin Anderson pulls into camp on someone else's dog team, and I ask him how the mushing was. He swears a reply, hustling on. As the gang falls in and the various camps are setting up, it becomes apparent that Steve Craig and his dog team are still out there, and what begins as a simple observation develops, with the passing of an hour, into concern.

Unlike Gudmundson and the professionals, Craig is a novice musher, having borrowed dogs to put a team together. Another hour passes as we mill about our smoky campfires, and our concern becomes alarm. There is talk of a search party going out after him. There were several trails crossed today that he may have mistakenly followed, but the danger of traveling back down darkened trails prevents an immediate rescue attempt. But in true Yukon manner, the alarm is shrugged off and everyone goes about their camp duties amidst the sound of spoons scraping tins, the hiss of spilled water on flame, and its ensuing, billowing steam cloud.

Dinner is served on plates containing the frozen remains of every preceding meal. No one cares. Campfires are surrounded by a twelve-foot radius of yellow holes in the snow. White tents forty yards off through the willow trees, each accompanied by their own slow swirl of smoke. A miscellaneous howl from otherwise silent dogs curled in the snow, snouts buried beneath their tales. I'm sitting at one of the fires when Craig's headlamp finally shimmers, then gleams on the trail leading into camp. The musher halts his team, jams the claw brake in the snow. He stumbles rigidly up, eyes vacant, and sinks onto a log and just stares into the fire. Anderson hands him a dinner plate that has been kept waiting for him. Craig doesn't even look at it, but stares at the flames.

Inside our tent I pull out my journal. I use my headlamp in an attempt to jot down the events of the day. McRae is propped up against a duffel bag, his own headlamp shining down on the newspaper column he is writing. Brian Gudmundson enters the tent and starts rummaging through a pack.

Gudmundson is a former Royal Canadian Mounted Policeman running his own dog team on the trail. He looks fifty-ish, a big, balding individual with a blunt, sober expression. He emits an aura of total, utter competence.

"No one gets to know him," Duffee had told me earlier. "He was a RCMP in the Arctic, quite a smart man, police mind, phenomenal memory. Everything is cut and dried to Brian. He did the Lost Patrol reenactment a few years back. I've been in a car with him and his wife, and they'd play games. We'd be driving along and he'd say to May, 'What was the third car we passed?' And she'd say, 'Toyota.' 'How many people in the front seat?' 'Two, and a dog,' she said. He'd go up the Dempster Highway and memorize every license plate he passed. He solved the last murder in Dawson. Arrived in Dawson two weeks before the murder, and he figured it out. Said, 'This is our man.' Put the guy away. He was unshakeable on the stand.

"Brian's one of the men that fears no other man on earth. How do you get to that state? He must realize that there are people bigger, stronger, can shoot harder—I hit him pretty good one time in front of the net, and he just looked at me and I never hit him again. I saw him go look at one of Cowboy's dogs one time. Cowboy had this vicious dog and Brian just stared at him and that dog just went to the other side of the pen..."

I observe the man. There is something arresting in his combination of competence and calm. I attempt to make small talk, but it's apparent he is not receptive to such a task. I mention that there appear to be some characters among us on the trip, and that there seem to be many such characters in the Yukon. This strikes a wooden chord, and Gudmundson pauses.

"The North seems to attract those out of the mainstream," he replies. I ask Gudmundson to tell me of Dawson's last murder. He finishes whatever he's doing in the pack, and shifts his blunt, emotionless eyes to me.

"I would but I don't have time. I must take care of my dogs."

As Gudmundson leaves the tent, Hogan enters. He shares his version of the day's big story.

"We were by Jane Creek and Cowboy pulled off to snack his dogs," Hogan tells us. "What he does is run the dogs off the trail, up and around and then pulls them back on the trail he just made. He lays them down there, so when they get up they have an easier time getting out. Well, he had them all bedded down on his little part of the trail, and the Frenchman, Patrice with Turner's team, strings them out right in front and leaves his sled and his team strung out right in front of Larry's trail. And Larry says to me, 'That fucken French cocksucker, I'm gonna run this team right over his wheelers when I come outta here.' And that's exactly what he did. The sled was there, and he ran his whole team right between the wheel dogs and the sled!"

McRae and I shake our heads, and go back to our notes. I write about the best bannock John Flynn has made yet, with raisins in it. When I complimented Flynn on it, he mentioned that in Dawson there is a TV show called *Bannock of the Week*. As usual I find that so much is occurring, yet I manage to record so little of it. I'm just too tired. I finish up by writing, "Not much more tonight to write—just a long, hard day through beautiful, wild country." I look up at McRae, earnestly scribbling away.

"What's this column about, Earl?"

"Ronnie McPhee."

"Who's Ronnie McPhee?"

"Anderson's dead buddy. Great story, Strangler, great story!"

I'd seen the large picture that Anderson had taped to the windshield of his snowmobile, and had heard the short version earlier.

"What's the whole story?" I ask McRae now.

"It's the picture Kevin has taped on his hog. I look at him, and he's talking to it! I asked him who it was, and he says, 'It's Ronnie McPhee. Great guy, great friend of mine. He would have been here, but he's dead. So I'm bringing him with us anyway. Ronnie's coming with us the whole way.'

"This guy McPhee was some kind of wild man, great friend of Kevin's, and he picked some foreign girl up in a downtown Dawson bar, and drove her up to Hunker Creek.[2] On their way back he pulled over to take a leak, stepped outside the truck, and the truck rolled on him and killed him. Great story! At his funeral they threw a bunch of empty rum bottles into his grave. And Kevin's bringing him with us the whole way. Great, great story!"

Investigating further, I find another member of our troop not as enamored of our honorary teammate. "I don't like McPhee," I am told. "He was revered in his certain circle, he had a tremendous mind, but he wasted it. When I heard he used to be a teacher, I almost fell off my chair. I thought, how did this reprobate do this... He was totally irresponsible. I mean totally. I know people like that—in a small town

---

2 In 1998, the year after his death, an article about McPhee appeared in *The Colorful Five Percent*, a magazine dedicated to the larger-than-life characters of the Yukon. The opening paragraph read, "When asked how Yukoners pass the time, Ronnie McPhee once said with a gleam in his eye, "In the summer, we fish and we f***, and in the winter, we don't fish." It's impossible to sum up the guy, but that succinct phrase gives a fair indication of his two primary passions in life."

there are people for reasons I'll never understand that are revered. Hockey players get a kick out of that. Yeah, Ronnie was…I formed my opinion of him the first time I met him. I had a loader and he had a boat, and he came up to me and he wanted his boat moved and said the city foreman said I was to move that boat. The city foreman was my boss. So I moved the boat. It was strictly a con, but that was it. I never respected him from that point on. My first two years in the Yukon I found these kinds of people really interesting, but I slowly came to realize that the better you get to know them, the better off you are not knowing them."

Even before hearing these words, I disliked the story. I told McRae as much. I am from an Irish neighborhood outside of Boston, and though I am by no means opposed to drinking, the tragedy of alcohol holds no romance for me. I dismissed it as just another pathetic waste of life due to alcohol. I felt Anderson's involvement of this guy was sophomoric, ill-advised sentiment. It would take another two weeks and four thousand miles before I learned how wrong I was.

CHAPTER FOUR

"The thousand and one gentlemen whom I meet, I meet despairingly and but to part from them, for I am not cheered by the hope of any rudeness from them. A cross man, a coarse man, an eccentric man, a silent, a man who does not drill well—of him there is some hope."

— HENRY DAVID THOREAU,
WALDEN, OR LIFE IN THE WOODS, 1854

When I climbed upon my grandfather's knee, I was regaled with tales of riding with the United States cavalry as a sixteen-year-old flag carrier, chasing Pancho Villa across the Mexican border. What effect this had on a wide-eyed seven-year-old can only be imagined, but it was the beginning of my obsession with people who did things out of the ordinary.

The Northeast, perhaps more so than other American regions, shares a common bond with Canada in that we are closely tied to the mores and manners of England. Among these mores and manners is a well established tolerance of eccentricity. The Society of Folly Fanciers, founded in London in 1871, boasted of Lord Nubble's 1872 attempt to cross the English Channel in an armchair pulled by "water dogs." This episode prompted not only the premature demise of Lord Nubble, but a local newspaper to claim that the Fanciers "have proven beyond all question that there is no relationship between wealth and brains." A more recent example of English eccentricity appeared in a Reuters press release entitled, *His Parting Shot*, "London—The ashes of the 7th

Lord Newborough, an eccentric British peer, were fired from an 18th century cannon to their final resting place—a wooded copse on his country estate."

Legendary New York promoter Jim Moran once planned to fly midgets on kites over Central Park as an advertisement for a client. Hiring several and fitting them with matching uniforms and caps, Moran assembled his group in Central Park and was prepared to launch them when police interfered, citing the lack of a permit. Moran later held a press conference during which he stated, "It's a sad day for American capitalism when a man can't fly a midget on a kite over Central Park."

This legacy of eccentricity includes as a historical tenet the desire to remove oneself from the mainstream. Two of the more famous contemporary American outposts are Provincetown, Massachusetts, and Key West, Florida, the latter referred to by locals as, "the Last Resort." But before these remote, sleepy fishing villages became Meccas for artists, writers, and eccentrics during the early part of the 20th century, it was the far western reaches of the continent that attracted these outcasts. Toward the end of the century there was a sense that the vast North American wilderness was finally closing, the restless, romantic possibilities finally ending. "The Wild West is tamed, and its savage charms have withered," wrote Francis Parkman in his book, *Oregon Trail,* in 1892. Six years later the Yukon gold rush challenged such assessments, and those who had historically gone west, "Psychological types who found forest solitudes more acceptable than the company of their fellow men," as Billington characterized these individuals in *Westward Expansion,* found a new opportunity for their precious isolation. And so Dawson City, a new end of the rainbow in the eyes of the disaffected, became a magnet for "those out of the mainstream."

The far North historically has had its share of eccentrics, more than a few who have met cruel fates, usually at the hands of the uncompromising climate. Editor Michael Korda relates that he was once persuaded by a student of animal psychology to publish a book the young man proposed to write about an attempt to have Alaskan wolves raise his infant son as one of their pack. Armed with a $2,500 advance from

Simon and Schuster, the student promptly "disappeared into the tundra with the boy, never to be heard from again, leaving me to many years of difficult correspondence with the boy's mother…"

Jon Krakauer documented in his book *Into the Wild* the foolish demise of one Chris McCandless. Krakauer dismissed McCandless' penchant for self-destruction, focusing instead on the young man's alleged Thoreauvian qualities. McCandless, forsaking his education, family, and a substantial amount of money, began drifting about the western United States in 1991. Like many out of the mainstream he eventually reached Alaska, with the intention of entering the wilderness north of Mount McKinley and living off the land. Unprepared, ill-informed, and full of hubris, McCandless trekked into the wilderness and was dead of starvation within three months.[3]

In his book Krakauer recalls Victor Rosellini, the Mayor of Hippie Cove. Krakauer met the Seattle native in 1981 while awaiting a job on a seiner outside of Cordova, Alaska. The Mayor was locally infamous for having forsaken a normal life to conduct what he had planned to be a life-long anthropological study of whether a modern man could live as a stone age man. He felt that modern man had diminished as a species and he wished to know, as he explained to the *Anchorage Daily News*, "if it was possible to be independent of modern technology." The Mayor conducted his experiment, living off the land without benefit of any modern conveniences, surviving on roots, berries, seaweed, and animals he killed with hand-fashioned spears and knives. But in 1991, years after Krakauer had met him, the Mayor faltered. After fourteen years of proving that modern man could indeed live under stone age conditions, Rosellini came to a more cerebral conclusion that he had failed. "I learned that it is not possible," he wrote to a friend, "for human beings as we know them to live off the land." The man then declared his intention of walking around the world, but that plan was

---

3 Krakauer was impressed that McCandless lasted three months on his own in the wild. Michael Oros lasted *ten years* before his descent into madness. The subject of McCandless came up in the wilderness. The consensus of the Yukoners was best summarized by Kevin Anderson's fireside assessment: "Fuck him, he got what he deserved."

never realized. Victor Rosellini was found face down in his hovel, a knife thrust through his heart. Although no note was discovered, it was determined that the Mayor of Hippie Cove had committed suicide.

A stunning example of incompetence occurred in 1981 when Carl McCunn was dropped off by a bush pilot on a remote lake near Coleen River, Alaska. Deposited in the wilderness in March, the wildlife photographer had intended on being retrieved the following September. When the plane failed to return, McCunn realized he had not confirmed the pickup. His emaciated body was discovered the following February, a self-inflicted gunshot wound to the head. His diary included the entry, "I think I should have used more foresight about arranging my departure."

PELLY FARM TO PELLY CROSSING

Tuesday, March 4

I watch dog teams surge through camp and down the trail, disappearing around a bend. Morning campfires crackle under frying pans loaded with moose sausage, kielbasa, and bacon. I stand with Earl MacKenzie, who I have come to know as "The King of Coffee" for our morning ritual. Hovering close to the flames, it is sobering to see what goes into his blackened, dented coffee pot. MacKenzie scoops snow with the cap of his thermos, carefully avoiding yellow holes. His recipe is precise: ten cups of snow to three fistfuls of coffee grounds. Into this soup also goes any number of foreign objects mixed in the snow, dirt, leaves, pine needles, twigs. As he carefully tends the brew, the burley red bear notices my dubious gaze.

"Fifty-seven secret herbs and spices," MacKenzie says, winking.

He is a monster of a man with a broad white beard, instantly recognized by his bulky, bright red parka. Sixty-years-old. He has long been a benefactor to Dawson hockey, outfitting at his own expense numerous teams. I am told he was thrilled and honored when Hogan asked him to accompany the Nuggets to Ottawa as our modern-day Joe Boyle. MacKenzie manages to cultivate remarkable nose icicles in the frigid air, the longest over an inch long, extending out over his white mustache.

McRae calls them snotcicles. I am told he is a millionaire. He seems a gentle soul, but carries a reputation as one who does not hold his liquor well. He tells me not to tell his wife he's drinking on this trip. McRae joins us and I point to MacKenzie and say, "Earl MacKenzie—a man so big they named a river after him—the *Earl* River." Neither gets it.

McRae watches MacKenzie wander off, making eyes as if to say, "this one's *another* crazy bastid." He wants to talk about Cowboy Smith. I first laid eyes on Smith at the going-away party in Dick Van Nostrand's Downtown Hotel the night before we left Dawson. Told he was a Vietnam veteran, I assumed him to be American. I walked over, extended my hand and said, "I can't wait to talk to you." Smith looked at my hand and replied, "Yes you can," and walked away.

"He's not American, he's from B.C.," a local explained to me. "Came back from Vietnam and spent ten years in the bush by Coffee Creek, then he came to Dawson. He's run six or seven Iditarods. He's known for his balls-to-the-walls effort, doesn't know what it means to pace himself. Breaks the trail every race, full speed, knowing his dogs will get tired toward the end. Everyone else knows it too, they let him break trail and follow him, knowing they'll overtake him in the end. He knows it and they know it, but he can't do it any other way. Only knows how to do anything one way—all out. Hates the media. Won't allow his picture to be taken. Doesn't like anyone who hasn't proven himself in the bush. I'd stay out of his way, most people do."

I watch this legendary musher amongst us on the trail and in camp, and see he possesses a certain charisma. He appears deeply respected by all the Yukoners, though some with a degree of reluctance. One described him as "a legend in his own mind." Another suggested his legend is carefully self-promoted. He carries a confidence about him that challenges with a stare, withers with a look. Just under six feet tall with milky, lost eyes that seem hardened beyond ordinary trials. He is running his dog team with us as far as Whitehorse, representing the dog teams of the original argonauts. Out on the trail, Smith keeps to himself. He builds his own camp and tends his dogs away from everyone else. He seems to have suffered an injury; it is painful watching him stiffly move about. As the most colorful character in our entourage, he has captured McRae's attention. The *Ottawa Sun* columnist has dubbed Smith the "Deranged Whacko."

"He hates everyone," McRae tells me. "He has the million-mile stare, won't look you in the eye but stares over your shoulder when he speaks to you. And the cadence is wrong, there's no rhythm to his conversation. He's a certifiable Deranged-fucken-Whacko. I went up to him this morning:

'Hello, Cowboy. How's it goin'?'

'Hmmm.'

'Well, Larry, are there any animals around here?' Now I know that's a stupid question, but that's what I asked him, 'Larry, are there any animals around here?'

'Fucking animals.'

'I say, Larry, any animals here?'

'Fucking animals.'

'Larry, I noticed you never wear any sunglasses. Doesn't the sun on the snow bother your eyes?'

'Guess the fuck not.'

'Larry, do you ever get lonely up here?'

'Why the fuck would you get lonely up here? There's people in cities more lonely.'

'Nice talking to you, Larry,'" and McRae roars.

"You know what he says when you ask him anything personal? I asked him about Vietnam. 'That's classified information,' he says. Anything personal is 'classified information.'

'Larry, did you see any action in Vietnam?'

'Guess the fuck I did.'

'What did you see?'

'That's classified information.'"

Now obsessed, McRae tries to engage Smith in conversation whenever possible. In camp he approached the musher as he tended one of his dogs.

"'Larry, I notice you put a blanket on one of your dogs. Why did you do that? Is something wrong with the dog?'

'Obviously there's something fucking wrong with the dog.'

'Well, what's wrong with the dog?'

'What's it matter?'"

This has become a private joke between McRae and I—What's it matter?

"Hey Earl, how many miles do they say to the next campsite today?"

"What's it matter?"

We pack up camp and begin down the trail, the whole gang excited because we have a short day's run into the Indian village of Pelly Crossing. We are scheduled to play the local teenagers in a road hockey match, and will have a chance to shower and sleep under a real roof in the village Community Center.

Though warmer, I have a difficult time this morning with the cold air on my face. I wear a neck warmer that I can pull up over my nose, and a red fleece skull cap that covers my ears. But my right ear, despite all effort to protect, has become permanently numb. I've lost my sunglasses. John Flynn notices my face, and points out that my wire-rim glasses are a problem, and I start wearing a patch of white hockey tape over the bridge of my nose.

We descend into the Pelly River basin, turning onto a lumber road which is easy traveling compared to what we have been through. I realize Flynn is trying desperately to flag me down. I pull to a stop and he yells, "You're on the left side of the road! This is a used road!" and roars off. I realize the danger, that turning any corner on the wrong side will put me head-on into oncoming traffic. I move to the right, but drift back a while later, and Flynn again pulls up beside me, waving frantically.

We come upon a car-load of young people out on a cross-country skiing excursion. First human beings we've encountered since leaving Dawson. They are surprised to see a line of machines filing out of the wilderness, and astonished to hear we've been in the bush for four days. Continuing on, we climb out of the valley and gain the bluffs overlooking the broad Pelly River. We gather on a prominent overlook, witnessing yet another wonderful sight far below. The dog teams, taking a gentler route for the dog's sake, have emerged from the wilderness and are running the river. One after another they glide by, the faint yipping of the dogs reaching us, the guys around me hollering and waving their arms to attract the mushers' attention. Anderson pulls out his bottle of whiskey, and the players gather to take their swig from the jug.

"Pelly's a dry town," he explains earnestly, in his dead-pan expression. "We have to drink it all before we go in."

Pelly Crossing is home to three hundred Selkirk First Nation people, who settled here in the 1950's after the overland road between Whitehorse and Dawson City was completed. Loose-running dogs, pickup trucks with snow plows, and single dogs tied to red plastic sleds, pulling toddlers across the parking lot, dodge our entry. The Community Center is a long, wooden structure; other outbuildings, garages, and storage sheds edge the parking lot. We line our snowmobiles outside the Center, unpack fresh clothes and carry them inside, dumping our bundles along the walls of the large, open main room. Some fall into folding chairs arrayed about tables in the middle of the room, while others peruse messages pinned to the Community bulletin board.

McRae is anxious to find a fax machine to send his latest article to Ottawa. We walk to the grocery store to inquire within. Players chat with local acquaintances. I pick up a handful of Cup-O-Soups, which have proven easy to prepare on the trail. I buy two sausages, then sit on the bench outside the door with Duffee. Players come and go, everyone picking up supplies, gassing up, sharing newspapers. We watch the silent, gloomy inhabitants.

"Look at their faces," Duffee whispers. "They're all cut, all of them have been cut."

Our story is prominently covered in the Yukon newspapers. I read the taunts of my fellow travelers toward the Ottawa Alumni.

Earl MacKenzie: "Tell Mr. Boschman when we get through with him, he'll be ready for the old folk's home."

Wes Peterson: "Let's see them challenge us in a return match by traveling to Dawson City by the way we're going there. I doubt they will. You have to be a man to do it."

Kevin Anderson: "Boschman better have his suspenders up and good and tight. And if Brad Marsh thought he was standing in cement when he played he'll think he's been mummified when I blow past him."

Pat Hogan: "We're in serious liver training as we speak..."

We play a road hockey game against local teenagers in front of the Community Center. Women and children crowd the front porch of the center, old men stand here and there, staring in muted silence. Our opponents are interesting. I can see in their eyes that they are excited, that the game means a great deal to them. They're playing the Dawson City Nuggets on their way to Ottawa! These youngsters, Kenny Harper, Kenny and George McGinty, Allen Joe, calling themselves the Pelly Crossing North Centrals, warm to the task. The young First Nation legs out-race us, running up an 11–6 victory over their middle-aged adversaries. Kenny Harper leads their team with four goals, Freddy Farr, one of our own Indians, the star on our side with three. Idiosyncrasy: they show no emotion. When they score, I see excitement in their eyes, but they remain silent in some age-old cultural restraint. Solemn, barely noticeable congratulatory acknowledgements. When the game ends, I approach the youngsters and ask all to sign my personal copy of *Dawson City Seven* and they eagerly do so, thrilled to sign their autographs.

I have carried this copy of my book since publication, gathering autographs from anyone touching the story. Every talk I've given, every participant I've met, the families, the researchers, the fans, all are asked to sign my personal copy. And tonight inside the Community Center, showered, warmed, lining up for moose stew and bannock the natives have prepared for us, I go about adding signatures. Aedes Scheer, one of the Nuggets' most avid supporters, is following the team through the Yukon, and planning to fly to Ottawa for the big game. She signs my book. Wendy Burns of Yukon Anniversaries signs it, as do Rangers Williams, Taylor, and Franczak. Frenchman musher Patrick Riopel signs, but when I approach Kiwi Christianson he declines, raising his hands to show the dreadful sight: his hands are frozen and lacerated, covered with gaping, bloodless cuts. He promises to sign later, when he can hold a pen. I sit at one of the long tables in the center of the room with several of the players, Kevin Anderson, Doc Parsons, and Bruce Duffee all signing my book. I see Cowboy Smith in line to get his bowl of moose stew.

"Hey, do you think Cowboy will sign my book?" I ask the players.

"Oh, he'll sign it," Anderson replies, but I see him grin at the others.

"I don't think he knows how to read or write," Parsons says. When someone expresses disbelief, the Doctor adds, "Honestly, he comes in once a year for a physical and he refuses to sign anything, and *tells* me he can't read or write." Nevertheless, I decide that Cowboy Smith must be able to produce some sort of signature or sign, and as the others watch I saunter up to the musher. I wait for him to break away from a couple of First Nation men before speaking.

"Hey Cowboy, you got a minute?"

"No," he says, and blows by me, bowl of moose stew and spoon in hand. The others are watching, so I follow him.

"Hey Larry, all the guys on the trail are signing this book I wrote, would you?"

"No."

He's trying to make me look foolish in front of the others; I shrug and give up. I walk back to a table full of winking, knowing smiles.

"You call this guy a legend?" I ask the table. "Know what we'd call a guy like this back home?" The players look at me expectantly.

"An *asshole...*"

With a chance to wind down, McRae and I talk with Pat Hogan about the more organizational aspects of the trip. We ask how the team was chosen.

"We formed a committee of five," Hogan tells us. "There was John Flynn, Bob Sutherland, Kevin Anderson, Rod Dewell, and myself. So there was five of us, mostly like a steering committee for the whole thing. And what we said was, if you'd ever played for the Dawson City oldtimers hockey club, whether you played just a weekend in a tournament or whatever, you were eligible to play. And to get in you had to submit your name and a five hundred dollar check to apply. So put your name in the hat, and put a five hundred dollar check in the hat. Your name is no good without the five hundred dollar check.

"And we'd take as of a certain date, we'd take all the names that had a check attached, and five guys would each pick separately five different teams. Those five guys each picked the team they wanted to go, and that was based on who, you know...there were a lot of factors, how long had you played with the club, could you make a contribution, were you reliable, could we count on you to make the whole thing, or were you a guy who never paid his dues for hockey, that kind of thing. So at the end of the day we had five separate teams picked by five different guys, we compared notes, and there was only about four guys difference between them all, and we resolved we would take 'X' number of people, which amounted to eighteen or twenty-one. And the gig was that you had to pay your own way. We estimated it would cost up to two thousand bucks, and then whatever else you spend. Right now it looks like it's about sixteen hundred bucks per person.

"The five of the steering committee sat down and said this is what we got, unanimous, unanimous, unanimous, no I don't have him I got this guy, these are the maybes, OK, we have three maybes here for this name, and the other two had different guys, what do you think, OK he's in, no he's out, OK end of story. There weren't a lot we said no to, I think there were twenty-five or thirty guys applied, and ah, we picked about twenty because we figured a couple would drop out. We put them on a waiting list. Wes Peterson said he'd be the coach, so that Steve Craig could play. Rod Dewell, at no time did he want to play, said no, he wasn't going to play, he didn't feel he could make a contribution, but he'd help in any way. And he had been in on it from the beginning.

"Troy Suzuki had only been here for a couple years, he was under-age, he was under thirty-five. We would have loved to have Troy play. He fit into the community, he fit into the league, he's a great guy, he has a lot of talent, he's a hell of a hockey player. But there were a lot of other people with more time, and really had paid a few more dues, and were better justified to take that place on the ice irregardless of their skills. We wanted a team that was representative of our community. We didn't want to go and solicit a whole bunch of ringers from around the territory in the hopes of stacking the team. They picked up one guy in 1905, but they went with the talent pool that they had in Dawson City that had played with them, irregardless of where they came from. So that was sort of the idea, to stay true to that spirit as much as possible.

"Who's our best players? Johnny Flynn's a hell of a hockey player, has the ability to score goals, good wheels, good leader, lots of determination. Mike Fraser's a real fine hockey player. Steve Craig's a good hockey player, Kulych, Dale Kulych has great hands. Who else. Those are the guys that spring to mind. In my mind, I think John Flynn is probably the best. Kulych scored more often, but he was up and down. And he was younger. You know, some days he was hot, some days he was cold, but when he was hot, he could put it in. Steve Craig is probably one of the steadiest, and the highest skilled player. Mike Fraser is the same, when he gets pissed off he can make things happen."

Bruce Duffee offered his opinion: "I think the best players in Dawson are Kevin Anderson, Mike Fraser, and Dwayne Taylor. Taylor isn't with us, he waited to be asked to go. A prima donna, Dwayne Taylor. He had fantastic balance and speed, I thought he was the best, he was the toughest for me. But he wanted to be asked to come along..."

The evening ends with the first, albeit minor, ugliness. Earl McRae and I sit at a table swapping stories. We have much in common, we are the two outsiders invited to participate in this odyssey, we are both writers. I have agreed to supply a running account of the trip to a couple of Yukon newspapers, and have tentative alliances with some larger ones back east. I am trying to write an article on the beginning of our trip for the *Ottawa Citizen* and McRae knows it. As a writer for the *Citizen's* competition, I sense McRae wants to know what I'm writing, and maybe even slow me down.

"Anderson talks to the picture of his dead buddy," McRae tells me. "*Talks* to him! Told me he was a great guy. Said he got more women than you could shake a stick at, he was a bachelor. A loner, a fisherman, originally from Nova Scotia." McRae's eyes go distant and his hands move as he speaks, shaping his image of the man.

"A loner...a fisherman..."

Our conversation descends into what has become a daily comparison of notes about the trip, the players, the adventures. We begin laughing, and are approached by Troy Suzuki. Suzuki has accompanied the team to document the trip on film. He asks us to do the dishes.

"Well, I'm trying to write an article right now," I say.

"Hey," McRae adds, "I didn't come along to do dishes, my contribution is national exposure."

Suzuki stands stunned.

"I can't believe you two..." he says, disgusted.

"We—" McRae began, but it's clear Suzuki isn't kidding, and that McRae and I are in the wrong.

"I'm an invited guest," I interrupt. "I'm willing to do my part." McRae relents, apologizes and says of course he'll do dishes, too. But it is too little, too late for Suzuki.

"I can't believe you two..." he repeats and storms away, shaking his head. We quickly find ourselves in the kitchen, McRae scrubbing dishes and handing them to me to dry.

"Doin' the gawdamn dishes..." the columnist mutters.

Later, with most asleep and no audience to entertain, Cowboy Smith sidles up to me.

"So, where's this book?"

CHAPTER FIVE

"The first milk cow ever in Dawson arrived on Wednesday. She is not very well pleased with her surroundings and did not give much milk. H. I. Miller is the man who brought her in along with nineteen male companions. The gentleman is more favorably known as 'Cow' Miller, and as Cow Miller let him be known from this on."

— The *Dawson Nugget*, July 8, 1898

One of the more interesting place names in the United States is Intercourse, Pennsylvania, but perhaps more curious is the unincorporated township of Sugar Tit, South Carolina. At the University of Massachusetts many of the dormitories are named after famous Massachusans. Thus there is Emerson House, Thoreau House, etcetera. The lone exception a woman's dormitory named after Edmund Hoar, which has been judiciously named, Edmund House. Canada has its share of unique place names. There is a Bastard, Ontario named after John Pollexfen Bastard, an eighteenth century English M.P. There is a Punkeydoodles Corner, Ontario. North of Toronto are the villages of Mono Centre, Mono Mills, and Mono Road, all, no doubt, sleepy little towns. But Newfoundland by far leads in the unusual, containing the towns of Leading Tickles, Happy Adventure, Jack of Clubs Cove, Little Hearts Ease, and of course, Dildo.

Indian names, their literal translations eluding European cartographers, often contain surprises. There is the town of Quanqtaq, Quebec, which in Inukitut means, "intestinal worms." Metchosin, B.C. may mean, "the oil of a beached dead whale." Coquitlam, B.C. was named by a Salish tribe and is believed to mean, "stinking with fish slime." Skagway, the jump-off town to the Klondike, is thought by some local historians to mean in Tlingit, "lady relieving herself on a rock."

Nicknames can be fascinating. The best Canadian town nickname belongs to Owen Sound, whose inhabitants have informed me enjoys the sobriquet, "The Elephant's Asshole." Take a map of Ontario and locate Owen Sound, turn it ninety degrees clockwise, and you'll see why. The history of the American west is rife with individuals referred to exclusively by their nicknames, such as Wild Bill Hickock, Calamity Jane, and Billy the Kid. The far North has its own legendary nicknames in Swiftwater Bill Gates, Soapy Smith, and more recently, Shesley Free Mike Oros. Obscure men carried great nicknames. James Gray, a steamboat Captain for the Northern Navigation Company, was known as, "The Master of Impressive Profanity." The town of Likely, B.C. was named after Plato John Likely, a miner who enjoyed lecturing on Greek philosophers. Phantom Archibald dreamed continually of being chased by a long, black python.

Tappan Adney mentioned the predilection of frontier men to rename themselves in his book, *The Klondike Stampede*: "A man's real name is not of much consequence in this country. Not half a dozen men in camp know that Old Man Harper's front name is Arthur. Like as not some peculiarity of manner or appearance has instantaneously fixed a nickname upon a man, and the name has clung. Swiftwater Bill was plain William Gates. Nigger Jim in civilization was James Dougherty. And there is Happy Jack, Circle City Mickey, Long Shorty, Kink Miller, French Curley, Skiff Mitchell, Siwash George, Hootchinoo Albert, Tom the Horse, Dog-Salmon Bob, etc."

In its hey-day Dawson City had its share of colorful monikers; besides Swiftwater Bill there was The Lucky Swede, Klondike Kate, and Diamond Tooth Gertie. Prostitutes enjoyed great nicknames. In the crib-lined alleys of Lousetown, Dawson's red-light district across the Klondike River, worked such characters as The Oregon Mare, Nellie the Pig, and Dog-faced Kitty. Circle City had a famous whore called

The Virgin, thus named, a contemporary once mused, because "possibly they thought she had seen one." Robert Service is responsible for some of the most famous fictional Yukon nicknames, including Dangerous Dan McGrew, Athabasca Dick, and Blasphemous Bill.

Here in Pelly Crossing Cowboy Smith is with us, as well as Kiwi Christianson and Doc Parsons. McRae develops a lexicon of his own: because it is difficult to understand every word he utters, McRae has dubbed coach Wes Peterson, "Mumbles." Smith, of course, is the "Deranged Whacko." Associating me with my hometown of Boston, McRae calls me "Strangler." Kevin Anderson stomps up to me through the snow and declares, "They're calling you 'Dangerous Dempster Don' in Dawson."

PELLY CROSSING TO YUKON CROSSING
Wednesday, March 5

We awake in the large, warm Community Center hall to dual dilemmas: outside the ravenous village dogs have torn into our sleds, and it is thirty-eight degrees below zero. The Rangers have finally decided, after sticking with us two days extra, to abandon the trip. Our First Nation hosts, unhappy with the havoc the roving dogs have wreaked, apologize profusely and help clean up the mess as we tie up our sleds. Wishing us luck in Ottawa and waving gently, they see us off and out of town, and back into the wilderness.

We immediately confront a steep, rugged hill, but I make it up after grinding away over the bumps, bowls, and twists of the broken trail. We enjoy a nice run over several lakes, a traveling luxury after what we have experienced. We run easily over the snow-covered ice for several hours, this area for the next twenty-five miles all burned-out. An aged black and white photo.

Following the Yukon Quest trail, Flynn and Hogan are constantly on alert for the colored markers at the end of each lake delineating the trail connecting us to the next. Over six thousand of these markers are produced each year in the Whitehorse Correctional Center and placed along the trail in the weeks leading up to the race. But now, three weeks post race, some are missing and others obscured by drifted snow, so that care must be taken to follow the right path. There are times when we halt and wait as Hogan holds up his hand while Flynn reconnoiters the surrounding shoreline, before waving us on. A wrong turn is made at one point this morning, but we quickly right ourselves and reenter the woods, and for the first time encounter "the dreaded overflow."

Cowboy Smith and his dog team wait trailside, Cowboy pointing, explaining that his team has broken through thin ice. We are confronted by an overflowed creek forty yards wide, and we search up and down the edges of the bad ice until Duffee locates a viable path through the dangerous mess. As more dog teams approach we dismount and grab their harnesses, three or four men to each team, and lead them the hundred yards safely across the ice. The dogs have no traction on the ice in their colorful booties and must be pulled across. As McRae, MacKenzie, and I struggle Craig's team through, Flynn notches trees with his axe to guide the following teams, Hogan tying red ribbons on branches to attract attention.

The trail takes us to the Klondike Highway. We run a portion of the road toward McCabe Creek, where we will reenter the wilderness. This is not an easy task, as we cannot run on the snow-less road, but must stay up on the snow banks lining the sides of the highway. This proves treacherous; MacKenzie's machine side-swipes a stump and flies through the air into the branches of a pine. "Joe Boyle" is lucky to escape injury. I climb onto the side snow and ride along, struggling to maintain my balance. We continue on until we pull up to the ruins of Midway, a desolate spot along the highway where a broken-down, wood frame of a former store reaches up through the crusted snow.

I watch as MacKenzie dismounts and stomps through the snow to one of the posts, a pink ribbon rising lightly in the breeze as he approaches. He bends down and picks up a "Forty Pounder" of Ballantine Scotch Whiskey, much to the delight of the rest. It seems MacKenzie's friend George Abernmath, who had ridden out to our first camp on Montana Creek to deliver a bottle of whiskey only to find it had shattered in his pack, had arranged with McKenzie then to leave another bottle here. As the Wild Bunch rides up, Anderson's group with Peterson and Parsons, the bottle is opened and we stand in a circle, passing it around. It is soon half gone. With the exception of MacKenzie, my group takes one sip only and after a short rest we pull out, leaving the sight of Kevin Anderson, bottle tilted upward, guzzling whiskey on the side of the Klondike Highway amidst the ruins of Midway. This is when Earl McRae earns his Yukon nickname.

For some reason he has pulled out ahead, all business, running south along the highway toward Carmacks. He would tell me later that he was just hell-bent on reaching the next camp, to get warm. As we regroup at McCabe Creek, Flynn notices McCrae's absence, and we determine he was last seen heading south. Duffee, not one to tarry with a whiskey bottle in the wilderness, comes up, and volunteers to chase McRae down. He takes off full throttle down the road, while Hogan, Flynn, MacKenzie, and I shut down our machines, and wait. A short while later we see the two men returning. As they pull up, Duffee shakes his head.

"I couldn't yell loud enough for McRae to hear me, so I had to bump into him from behind! Screaming at the top of my lungs, I had to hit him twice before he'd stop!" And it's then that someone first utters the words that will grace the *Ottawa Sun* columnist for the remainder of our journey.

"He's Wrong Way. Wrong Way Earl."

We wait for the Wild Bunch to catch up, enjoying this newest nickname, Wrong Way Earl, until someone, with even more laughter, realizes the absurdity of Wrong Way *Earl* compared to the more alliterative, Wrong Way Mc-*Rae*. And thus is born Earl McRae's Yukon moniker: Wrong Way McRae.

We descend the bank onto McCabe Creek and follow it to a house on the edge of the Yukon River. Here Flynn and Hogan dismount and knock on the door, seeking directions. We follow the leaders behind outbuildings onto the jagged, heaved jumble of ice that covers the wide river. Carefully navigated is a smaller tributary with frightening, gaping round holes in the ice twenty feet wide and four feet deep, the result of some bizarre dynamic of the river current. We clatter across the ice and locate the Quest trail, weaving through huge shelves of ice heaved up upon themselves, blocks fifteen inches thick creating a lurching, bone-jarring ride.

The river ice conditions worsen, and we find ourselves at a snail's pace bumping hither and yon. Finally leaving the river and enjoying a benign run through woodland, we come upon two trees fallen across the path. Hogan and Flynn pull their axes and chop out a section wide enough for our machines to pass. We continue on, entering a difficult area where Hogan is thrown from his machine, striking his neck on the plexiglass shield. Where the trail begins to descend back onto the Yukon River, Anderson suffers a bad accident when his machine rolls onto him. Destroyed in this accident is one of the camp stoves. Back on the river ice we pause, Anderson and Peterson get into a wrestling match, Anderson tipping the coach backward and hard onto the jagged ice. Peterson is hurt but says nothing while Anderson howls, threatens, laughs, a bundle of energy, a never-ending line of chatter.

We run the ice and with a collective sigh of relief reenter the woods on the far side of the river. Soon we pull over under the shadow of a one hundred fifty foot bluff, a small stream and island separating us from the main course of the river. Here the leaders decide to pitch camp, and once again we dismount to begin the arduous process of cutting timbers, gathering spruce boughs, and shoveling aside snow for the tents and fires.

I am very, very tired. As no one ever gives any direction, any overt orders, I simply seek out a shovel and begin clearing a twelve-by-twelve foot area for our tent. McRae staggers up to me, a shovel in hand, gasping for breath. His face is ghastly, he is done in. He begins mumbling almost incoherently.

"He owns a golf course!" he blurts out, throwing an arm out toward the river. "The image is destroyed!"

"What are you talking about?"

"The Deranged fucken Whacko is part owner of a golf course! They just told me! Ruins my image of the man..." But it is apparent McRae is suffering from exhaustion. I grab his arm.

"You'll have a heart attack," I warn him. "Take a break, Earl, the hell with them. Take a break and catch your breath."

"Jesus Christ," he responds, leaning on his shovel, glancing about at the primitive, stark site. He seems to calm, to catch his breath, and I frown at him.

"He owns a golf course?"

"He owns a golf course!"

The sky is overcast for the first time during our trip, a slow drift of snowflakes dusting our shoulders. I am completely done in, but there is no rest. We shovel out the square for the tent, then an area for the campfire. Chainsaws ring in nearby woods, and I attempt to help with the raising of the tent until I see my hands are not needed, and gladly retreat to sit on my snow machine. Freddy Farr, arms full of spruce boughs, spies me.

"Come on, Don," he says, dumping his boughs inside the tent, then handing me an axe. "Help me gather the boughs." We tromp off through the snow into the woods. I cut down a small tree, and begin to strip the boughs.

"No, no," Freddy instructs me. "Drag the whole tree back, and strip it at the tent. It's easier."

He leaves me alone in the gathering darkness. I take his axe and barely manage to cut down another small tree, then jerk the entangled mess free of the bushes. I stop, drop the axe and bend over, my hands on my knees. *It's easier*, I remind myself. My breath billowing, my face hot with sweat. I stare at the rising fires, hear the laughter and profanity. I grab the trees under my arms and drag them through the knee-deep snow, struggling against the brush, breaking out onto the trail and passing the Deranged Whacko's dog team curled alongside the trail, in the snow.

I am so tired I don't even care if I drag my trees over them, desiring with all my soul just to drop in the snow and rest. But I stagger into camp, strip my trees of their boughs and place them carefully inside the tent. I stay up for the campfire, and listen as the stories flow in from the day.

"I had that high windshield on, eh?" Hogan tells the campfire. "We come down across McCabe Creek and across the Yukon and we're going down the trail, and there's fresh wolverine signs, right? And I'm watching the wolverine signs, I wonder where that fucker went? And it went off, the trail went off like this, and the wolverine went off like that, and I'm kinda still steering around still watching and there's a log lying across the trail and I pranged the log, went forward ass-over-tea kettle right over the machine, and got the windshield *right here*. And I'm lying on the ground laughing like hell at being so dumb, eh?"

The cloud cover dissipates and again we sight Hale-Bopp, as the northern lights appear. To the north they form one sky-long band of grayish white, to the south rise beams of light straight up into the heavens. I sink down in the snow, watching the campfire hiss and pop, listening to Anderson's never-ending chatter. Taps of spoons on kettles, the crunch of boots as the mushers deliver pots of food to their hacking dogs. Men rising from the campfire, walking ten feet back and urinating in the snow. A wonderful scene here, our quieting camp in the snow and cold, on the banks of the Yukon River.

I soon relent, and make my way back through the snow toward the tent. Crawling inside, I find Kevin Anderson packing away the satellite phone.

"Did you hear about the Indians back at Pelly Crossing?" he asks me.

"What about them?"

"They were embarrassed that the stray dogs broke into our sleds, and rounded them all up." I look at him, barely making out his face in the glimmering light of the distant fire.

"They shot them all."

CHAPTER SIX

"I saw a sign that said, 'Drink Canada Dry,' and I've just started."

— Brendan Behan, Irish author, when asked
by a reporter why he was in Canada

"CARMACKS ROADHOUSE"
*"Located on the NORDENSKIOLD River, it operated
from 1903 to 1943. Of the 16 original roadhouses along
the overland trail from WHITEHORSE to DAWSON
CITY, this is the last intact structure. Travelers could
rest in the bar or one of the twelve bedrooms upstairs.
There was also a stable man's room and a linen room.
The building was converted to a single story structure in
the 1940's and the dirt roof was replaced with tin. It was
then used as a private residence until the 1960's."*

— Inscription on Souvenir Coffee Mug,
purchased at Carmacks

American bashing is a common, worldwide practice with, unfortunately, some reason for it. Larry Pynn writes in his book on the Stikine route to the Klondike *The Forgotten Trail*, "...it is at this point that I begin to perceive another aspect of Albrecht's personality: his disdain for Germans. The Swiss view of

Germans is not unexpected and not very different from that of any people forced to endure a louder, larger neighbor—the relationship, say, between Canadians and Americans..." This is a common notion, one not much different from the feelings the Midwestern United States has for, say, New York City. In South America a recurrent theme is that Americans are a fat, overweight people. Of course there is some truth to this, but not because Americans are a less thoughtful people, it's a matter of circumstance. Given the same resources, South Americans would evolve a similar culture. In India, it's our vast moral vacuum that they point out, which of course strengthens their self-image.

A man in Mumbai, India once told me that all western music was of the devil, and proceeded to explain, line by line, the chilling horror of *Hotel California*. When the man went to the men's room I escaped his table, moving to another to speak with a friend. When my Indian acquaintance returned he was enraged at this perceived offense, and revealed the true nature of his vast inferiority complex by screaming at me in the middle of the restaurant how arrogant, thoughtless, and Godless *all* Americans were.

I have had some success in disseminating a more favorable American impression. A co-worker in Brazil, a former officer in the French army, once told me I was the only American he liked because I was the only American he ever met that didn't talk solely of money and cars. After drinks in The Pit the night before we left Dawson, Wes Peterson turned and mumbled the ultimate Canadian compliment: "You're not very *American*." Ken Forrest, grandson of original Dawson goalie Albert Forrest, rendered a similar verdict after meeting for the first time in his home in Marysville, Washington. Forrest is a character, a guy with whom you can hunker down next to and share stories. He hits the ball back over the net. We had enjoyed a wide-ranging, engaging conversation and as I left, Ken paused in his doorway and said to me, "You know, you're not anything like I imagined. You're a *regular guy*."

The ugly American is not a new phenomenon. Robert McCormack, former owner of the *Chicago Tribune*, used to travel the world aboard his reconditioned B-17 bomber. McCormack reported back to his readers his various impressions of the rest of the world, often declaring people lazy, dirty, and lacking Midwestern virtue. He once reported from Libya, "No water in river, and country full of Wops." One can only imagine his personal contact with these people.

I have seen the ugly American in action, the most astounding display occurring in one of Buenos Aires' finest restaurants. A fellow American and I had been taken to dinner by an entourage of Argentine co-workers. In the middle of one of the most elegant steak houses in a country known for its beef, I sat next to my compatriot who inadvertently knocked over his Cuba Libre. Somehow triggering a heretofore hidden primordial beast, my erstwhile companion suddenly staggered to his feet, pointed across the crowded tables and shouted, "*You people are the dumbest goddamn stupid motherfuckers I've ever seen in my entire life, the most backward, ignorant, dumbest motherfuckers imaginable…in fact, this WHOLE COUNTRY is the most…*" As the man energetically and profanely disparaged all things Argentine, I observed the laughter of those who did not speak English, as well as the silence of those who did. Concluding his tirade, he slapped my arm and said, "C'mon Donny, we're outta here." To which I raised my hands in self-defense and uttered, "You are on your *own*, my friend."

Americans can be ugly to each other. I have a friend who claims he was once stopped for speeding by a Georgia state trooper. Rolling down his window, he heard the officer drawl, "Son, nobody drives through Georgia that fast." To which my friend replied, in his finest New England accent, "Sherman did."[4]

YUKON CROSSING TO CARMACKS

Thursday, March 6

Sitting around the campfire, Anderson and Parsons finishing up MacKenzie's Forty Pounder for breakfast. Millar claims yesterday will be the day to remember. Anderson tells of his machine rolling on him, Hogan recounts his accident to those who haven't heard.

Light snow falls from an overcast sky. We climb out of the Yukon River basin on a narrow, harrowing trail up a shelf in the bluff, emerging

---

4 This is not a recommended approach to southern law enforcement. My friend was able to continue his journey within a few days.

onto fairly level ground and eventually a road. Everyone is excited about the prospects awaiting us in Carmacks. Today, I am told, is a short run, which is also welcome. My body, sore beyond imagination, is exhausted, and more than a few are voicing impatience with our journey, imagining the comforts we will enjoy once we get through Whitehorse, and onto the ferry.

Hogan told McRae and I that today would be a good day to try mushing, as the roads are relatively level. I spoke to Craig about swapping, but end up running into Riopel and he agrees, somewhat reluctantly, to allow me to run his team of Frank Turner dogs. I receive a ten second lesson in mushing. Gee and haw. Ride the brake going down-hill so the lines don't slacken, the dogs don't get tangled and hurt. And whatever you do, don't let go of the sled. That was it. All in broken English I strain to understand. I grab the curved handles of the sled as the dogs sit looking back, askance.

"Mush!" I call, and the dogs jerk out of our place in the snow. I quickly see how difficult this art of dog mushing truly is. It is not a ride where you lay back and relax, enjoying the scenery. You must work the team, occasionally shouting instructions, "Gee!" "Haw!" But worse you can feel the dogs strain on the inclines, and you must jump from the runners and run, your hands on the handles, up through the snow with them, which proves another exhausting endeavor, draped as we are in wilderness clothing. The declines are worse, you must ride the brake, slowing down the sled.

But this is the Yukon! Between the hills, when you ride the runners away from the noise of the snow machines, the aura of isolated beauty envelops. A tin clangs lightly in the sled as I bump along, accompanied by the gentle patter of thirty-two booted paws tapping the snow. Every so often a bootie flies off into the air, settling beside the trail. The dogs are intelligent. They do not recognize this new voice urging them on, and constantly turn their heads back to look at me as they run, as if to say, *"Who's the new guy?"*

I develop greater respect for the mushers. They are an individual breed. Ask five mushers about rests and food, and you'll get five different answers. Or, if Cowboy is along, four. Generally this is their routine: they rise earlier than the rest to feed the dogs. The junk is a horrible sight, a frozen mixture of dry dog food, fish, and, if I got this right, something called Electrolyte Replacement Powder. Sometimes eggs. After feeding the dogs, they harness them and roll up the picket line. Then they boot the dogs, saving those that bite them off for last. Two or three times a day, depending on the scheduled miles, they must stop and rest, and feed the dogs salmon snacks. When they arrive in camp, the real work begins. They pull out huge kettles and defrost the frozen junk, then take care of all the little duties, unharness the dogs and put them on the picket, pulling off booties, checking each dog's condition as they go. Food bowls out for each dog, checking dog feces for problems. Building a bed of spruce boughs or straw when in town. Tending traces and harnesses, sorting out useless booties and drying the good ones, attending injuries that may be afflicting the animals, all before thinking of their own comfort and giving new meaning to the expression, "dog tired." All in a Yukon cold that brutalizes the senses. Hogan emphasizes their burden at the morning campfire.

"Last night that Patrice guy was sleeping next to me, and I woke up in the middle of the night, and that Patrice guy had scooched down and he had his feet right against the heater and his bag was smoking. And I'm shaking him, 'Hey Patrice *wake up wake up!*' No fucking way, he's dead, eh? So I grab him in the bag, haul him back up and throw a little snow on the end of his bag, and the little fucker never woke up, eh?"

A few miles of dog-sledding are enough for me, and I gladly reclaim my snow machine. On the trail I pass Hogan mushing Cowboy Smith's dog team, waving as I fly by. Concern: Hogan and Flynn are normally in the lead. And although today we are on a road, there are other roads, and I do not want to be the point man on this journey. Too dangerous. I turn a bend in the road to see Cowboy Smith leaning, arms folded, against Hogan's snow machine. I pull up next to Smith and shut down my machine.

"Who's ahead, Larry, anyone?" I ask. The legendary Iditarod and Yukon Quest dog-racing veteran looks at Hogan's machine, looks down at my sled, then places his hands about a foot apart.

"You're this far from the lead."

We pause on the outskirts of Carmacks, waiting for all to catch up so that we can enter the village as a team. Locals had hailed us with a sign posted on the trail before town, "Carmacks Welcomes the Dawson Nuggets." We are three hours early, and when the last of the dog teams arrive, we begin our triumphant entry. No one greets us, and we mill about in sheepish embarrassment before the locked doors of the Community Center.

Word passes that Earl MacKenzie, true to his Dawson benefactor reputation, is paying for the entire team to refill each of our two five-gallon Jerry cans at the local gas station. We finally gain entry to the Community Center and dump our bags on the floor, staking out our turf. McRae immediately sits at a table to work on his column and I join him to make my daily journal entry.

"I come up to the Deranged Whacko," he says to me, "and I ask him, 'So Larry, what brought you to the Yukon in the first place?' And he looks at me and says, 'That's fucking classified.'"

Several lay about on their sleeping bags, Flynn, Farr, Millar. The rest, led by the Wild Bunch of Anderson, Peterson, and Parsons, are off to the local barroom. A dinner sponsored by Carmacks Youth Hockey is planned for 5:30, and a road hockey game afterward on the community rink. I finish up my journal entry and decide to join those at the bar. McRae waves off an invitation, busy scribbling away. Duffee does likewise, and the Indians won't drink.

The Goldrush Lounge lies at one end of a long, ramshackle building, part of the last standing original roadhouse on the Whitehorse-Dawson Overland Trail. I marvel that, though I have no definitive proof, the original Dawson team probably stayed overnight in this very building in 1904. Inside are two pool tables and a jukebox, a small dance floor, and a series of tables and chairs looking like something out of the 1940's. The barroom is low and dark, the bar manned by a solid looking, middle-aged woman named Shirley Tracy. She carries a no-nonsense, I've-seen-it-all demeanor daring to be messed with. Cowboy

Smith and MacKenzie are leaning against the bar. I am late; MacKenzie had held an open bar for the entire team for the first hour.

We have a few drinks, then filter back out and attend dinner. While the team plays their road hockey game against the local kids, I wander back to the Goldrush Lounge and rejoin Smith and MacKenzie at the bar. Stories fly, whiskey is bought, and upside-down glasses signaling paid drinks ahead start to accumulate. Shirley Tracy is not one to shy from a good story.

"We had this guy in here one night—Cowboy was here—and this guy was a hippie," she says. "And one thing led to another—we probably drank too much—and one thing led to another, and this other fellow got awfully mad at the hippie, and told everyone he was gonna kill him. He pulls out his pistol, but he's got no bullets, so he runs outside to his truck to get his bullets!" As Shirley tells this story, I see Smith grinning sheepishly.

"I'm a freakin' mess, I run to the door and this guy is trying to get back in, the hippie is scared shit, and I'm holding the door against this guy who's waving his pistol in one hand and his box of cartridges in the other, and finally he forces himself in. I grabbed that box of bullets right out of his hand before he could load his gun, thank God." Shirley Tracy looks at Cowboy now. *"And no one would help me!"* A wide grin covers Cowboy Smith's face as he lifts his whiskey and shrugs.

"I wanted to see him shoot the fucking hippie."

After the road hockey game, the team crowds the bar like sailors fresh in port after toiling long at sea. There is a sense that this most romantic part of our adventure is coming to an end, with only one night in the wilderness left before Whitehorse. Hundreds of dollars dropped, toasts, laughter, our team cheer, "One, two, three—*Nuggets!*" resounds through the ancient tavern. Supporters of the team arrive, Aedes Scheer once again, Wendy Burns of Yukon Anniversaries up from Whitehorse, Elizabeth Connellan down from Dawson. Sandy Sippola, Cowboy's on-again, off-again girlfriend, leans against the bar. She is as reticent as Shirley Tracy is bold. When she tells me of her relationship with the Deranged Whacko I stare at her, wondering of the stories she could tell.

Shirley Tracy, when told I'm the author of *Dawson City Seven*, gives me a present, a white tee-shirt covered with fornicating green fish. It is too small for me, and when I pull it on over my shirt it rips at the seams, and Shirley begins a game of attacking it with a large butcher knife she grabs from her cook, Kung Fu. Others join in the fun, Doc Parsons particularly enjoying the game. I am the good sport, remaining calm as staggering, screaming Yukoners slash at me with a knife that would do *Paul* Hogan proud, until the tee-shirt hangs in threads from my body.

The players soberly discuss word that the last stretch from Carmacks to Lake Laberge will be the most difficult yet, with almost eighty-five miles of tortuous trail. It is along this route, we are told, that most of the dog injuries occurred during the recent Yukon Quest race. The leaders determine that our five dog teams will not engage it, but be trucked down to Braeburn where they will run a road in and meet up with us at our last camp on Lake Laberge.

Rounds are bought, dancing begins, and I stand, one foot on the rail, next to Cowboy and MacKenzie, downing drinks with Shirley Tracy. It is a marvelous sight, exhilarating in that I have survived the wilderness part of our trip, and will make it into Whitehorse in one piece. A sense of hard-earned accomplishment. Bundled-up emotions are let loose, the frustration, toil, and isolation of the trail released, and the tavern descends into a politically incorrect nightmare for those striving to suppress any ill-advised behavior of the Dawson City Nuggets. We partied long and hard into the night, dancing, drinking, celebrating nothing less than a great adventure in this speck of light village, lost in the middle of the sprawling Yukon wilderness. The next day I heard that the party continued very late indeed, culminating with several of the Dawson Nuggets dancing on the tables at 5:00 A.M. I'm pretty sure I wasn't one of them.

CHAPTER SEVEN

"It is worthy of mention that minute specks of gold have been found by some of the Hudson Bay Company's men in the Yukon, but not in quantities to warrant a 'rush' to the locality."

— Frederick Whymper,
Travels in Alaska and on the Yukon, 1869

"Almost all the large streams which have been prospected in the Yukon basin have been found to yield placer gold in greater or less quantity...Discoveries...may be expected to occur at any time in the Yukon district...there can be no reasonable doubt that such deposits exist."

— George Mercer Dawson, *1887*
Exploration Report

To tackle a book on the Yukon, you immerse yourself in the literature. One of the more disconcerting aspects of the investigation is the discovery of errors likely missed by a more pedestrian reading public. Perhaps most egregious, because of his reputation as well as its mean-spiritedness, is the following from James Mitchener's *Alaska:* "Robert W. Service would immortalize the sourdough with poems that may have been no more than jingles...He misspelled Lake Laberge in order to find an attractive rhyme..." He is referring to Service's most famous poem, *The Cremation of Sam McGee*, in which he has Lake Laberge rhyme with, "marge." Mitchener's words reek of condescension, and the fact is Mitchener—or more likely his staff—did not do their homework.[5]

Mike Labarge was an explorer for the Western Union Telegraph Company. Indians had told him about the only lake on the Yukon River, and he in turn had told others about it until it became known as Labarge's Lake in 1866. Labarge spelled his own name "Labarge." The lake immortalized in Robert Service's poem *The Cremation of Sam McGee* was officially named by William Dall, who worked with Labarge, and he spelled it "Labarge." George Dawson, in his *1887 Exploration Report: Yukon District, N.W.T. & Northern B.C.* spells the name "Labarge." The U.S. board of Geographic Names adopted that spelling in 1890, but when Canada set up its own Name Board in 1897 they changed the spelling to Laberge, noting that they had consulted Labarge's home town church in Chateauguay, Quebec, which they claimed had recorded the name as "Laberge." Tappan Adney's seminal *The Klondike Stampede*, published in 1900, spells the name "Labarge." In the literature the lake is referred to as Laberge, Labarge, Leberge, and Lebarge. In an era rife with marginal reading and writing skills, words were often spelled phonetically. Mike Labarge's last name, whatever its correct spelling, most certainly rhymed with "marge."

Ann Cook, in her book *Running North* on the Yukon Quest dog race, gives this description of Dawson City's origin: "Once an obscure fishing camp…Dawson was not prepared for its sudden popularity…" Dawson didn't even exist before the gold discoveries on Rabbit Creek, but was laid out five months later by Joseph Ladue in January of '97, and was initially referred to as Harper & Ladue's Town Site. Only when William Ogilvie surveyed the town was the site named Dawson City at Ogilvie's insistence, "for the greatest man I know." Ogilvie may have had another motivation for his demand; Dawson had previously named the valley in which lies Lake Laberge, "Ogilvie Valley."

---

5 To appreciate Service's influence on modern American poetry, I would direct those who disparage Service to read his 1911 poem *The Lone Trail*, and compare it to Robert Frost's famous 1920 poem, *The Road Not Taken*.

Jack London biographer Alex Kershaw confuses the Dead Horse Trail with the Chilkoot Pass. To the casual reader this may not seem like much of a mistake, but to the student of the Yukon it is significant. He also wrote of Dawson City, "According to Frank Canton, a U.S. Marshal sent to keep the peace in Dawson, the town was 'a wild, picturesque, lawless mining camp. The like had never been known, never would be seen again. It was a picture of blood and glittering gold dust, starvation and death...If a man could not get the woman he wanted, the man who did get her had to fight for her life.'" Contrast that with this, from Ken Coates' introduction to Adney's book, "...the presence of the North-West Mounted Police, the quintessential expression of the Canadian ethos, extended the national commitment to 'peace, order, and good government' into the far northwest corner of the Dominion, a stark and intriguing contrast to the libertarian, lawless mining frontier of the American West." Coates goes on to state, "Separating truth from fiction, reality from self-interested promotion, honest accounts from the hyperbole of adventure stories, proved to be extremely difficult. The exaggerations were often more interesting than the actual situation—although the Klondike experience was suitably intriguing and captivating on its own. Americans, in particular, were quick to project the historical experiences of the American mining frontier on to the Canadian northwest, and assumed that the same pattern of lawlessness and vigilante justice would apply to the Yukon..."

Errors in logic exist. T. Ann Brennan in her book *The Real Klondike Kate* states, "Canadians were appalled by the wanton thievery and the roaming cut-throats they encountered at Skagway and Wrangell." Fleeced Americans weren't?

Peter L. Bernstein in *The Power of Gold* commits a staggering error. He discusses the Klondike gold rush, summarizing, "For all the hoopla, all the gold mined in Alaska since 1880 has amounted to less than 10 percent of the gold mined in all the other parts of the United States over the same period of time." *Alaska*?

These errors are rather benign. But there is one legendary error that begs further inspection if the truth of the Klondike gold rush is to be respected. Robert Henderson is virtually co-credited with the great

Klondike gold discovery. Only through careful reading of the existing history can one glean a glimmer of the long-lost truth.

The best prime source material on the Klondike gold rush is Adney's book *The Klondike Stampede*. Adney was a thirty-year-old journalist dispatched by both *Harper's Weekly* and the *London Chronicle* to participate in and report back on the gold rush of 1898. He was interested particularly in the sequence of events leading to the initial discovery, and sought out individuals involved, including Henderson himself. The following is a summary of Adney's account.

In 1890 Joe Ladue, in partnership with Arthur Harper, built a trading post at the mouth of the Sixty-Mile River. Ladue was of the breed that saw profit not in the back-breaking labor of the wandering prospector, but in outfitting the same. He felt his best chance of success was in growing with a new gold area, and encouraged those he supplied to begin prospecting the rivers and streams near his new post. Four years later, Robert Henderson, recently of the mines of Aspen, Colorado, arrived at Ladue's post. He arranged a grubstake with Ladue, with the understanding that he would prospect the Indian River area. Henderson made his way up the Indian River working surface bars, scraping together just enough color to lure him further. He returned to Indian River the following spring, pushing on to a fork in the river, and continued up Australia Creek. Here he found "leaf" gold, an encouraging find. And here the alleged bad luck of Robert Henderson began, for had he taken the other fork he would have found himself on what later became known as Dominion and Sulphur Creeks, which were to produce millions of dollars in gold in the ensuing years.[6]

Henderson wintered on Quartz Creek, from which he took $500. In the spring of 1896 Henderson turned his sights on the

---

6 This is not to suggest Henderson would necessarily have found it. William Ogilvie, in a newspaper article appearing in the *Victoria Colonist*, November 6, 1897, states: "The Klondike was prospected for forty miles up in 1887, without anything being found, and again in 1893, with a similar lack of result." Forty years earlier James Marshall, after discovering gold at Sutter's Mill, spent the ensuing months prospecting the Deer Creek area near Nevada City. He gave up on the site, which a year later would be worked over by 5,000 men, eventually yielding over $387,000,000 in gold.

ridge above this creek, a thin line of low hills separating it from the watershed of the Klondike River. He crossed the ridge and discovered "wages" in a small, north-running creek. Returning to the Indian River, Henderson persuaded Ed Munson, Frank Swanson, and Albert Dalton, three of about twenty men working the area, to return with him. These men staked a claim on a creek they named Gold Bottom, and by August had garnered $750. Running short of provisions, Henderson then left his partners, and struck out for Ladue's post back on the Sixty-Mile.

When Henderson arrived he found several prospectors, and convinced a few bound for the Stewart River to instead return with him to the Indian River area, "telling them they would have to look for it, whereas he had found it." Ladue, anxious for a major discovery in his new territory—or even the appearance of one—sent two horses overland loaded with goods, while Henderson returned in his boat. Because the water was low on the Indian River, Henderson chose to return to Gold Bottom Creek by traveling up the Klondike River.

At the mouth of the Klondike he found a band of Han Indians at a seasonal salmon fishing camp. Across the river from them was another party, consisting of a white man and several Indians. Henderson spied them and thought to himself, "There is a poor devil who hasn't struck it." He introduced himself to George Washington Carmack, known along the Yukon also as "McCormick," and found that his party included his Indian wife and two brothers-in-law, Skookum Jim and Tagish Charlie.

Henderson urged Carmack to join his group up on Gold Bottom. Carmack was interested, but only if he could bring along not only his extended family, but the Indians fishing across the river as well. Henderson balked, telling Carmack, "I don't intend to stake the whole Siwash tribe. I want to give preference to my old Sixtymile friends." Adney states that Henderson "may have said something not complimentary about 'Siwashes' in general," and opines that it may have had some effect on Carmack's later actions.

The next morning Henderson ascended the Klondike to the mouth of Hunker Creek, while Carmack and his family opted to ascend the nearer Rabbit Creek, which they would follow to its end and cross over the low hills as a short-cut to the Gold Bottom camp. On the way up Rabbit Creek the trio tested the gravel, finding colors which Carmack showed Henderson once they had arrived.

The Carmack group prospected Gold Bottom Creek, all three men staking claims on the new site. When they prepared to leave, Henderson asked if they were going to prospect on their way out through the Rabbit Creek route. When Carmack indicated that they were, Henderson asked to get word to him if they struck anything worthwhile. Carmack is said to have agreed, and thus was set the circumstances around which controversy would swirl for the next hundred years.

Carmack, Skookum Jim, and Tagish Charley made their way back over the small hills into the Rabbit Creek watershed. A few miles into the densely wooded valley, the men stopped to rest. Adney states, "They had been panning here and there. Carmack, it is said, went to sleep; Skookum Jim, taking the pan, went to the rim of the valley at the foot of a birch tree and filled it with dirt. Washing it in the creek, he found a large showing of gold." Thus was the initial Klondike strike made on the cool, late summer day of August 16, 1896.

What happened next fired Adney with Victorian outrage: "After staking, they hastened to Forty-Mile, forgetting their promise to Henderson, who by every moral right was entitled to a claim near the rich ground they undoubtedly had discovered." On their way they notified everyone they met that they had made a significant strike. But they did not know how big a strike it was, and neither did the men who raced onto the river to see for themselves what Carmack had found. Gold rushes were common in the early Yukon days, men hanging on the perimeter waiting for someone to make a discovery, then hustling in to stake their claims. When Carmack reached Forty-Mile he told Joe Ladue, who immediately spread the word to anyone who would listen. The rush was on.

Henderson learned of the strike when prospectors George Wilson and James MacNamee made their way over the low hills and down into Henderson's Gold Bottom camp, probably in September. When Henderson asked where they were from, they told him Bonanza Creek. Not wanting to appear unknowledgeable about the territory in which he had spent the last three years prospecting, Henderson refrained from asking where Bonanza Creek was until his curiosity finally got the better of him. The miners indicated it was just over the hills.

"Rabbit Creek?" Henderson asked. "What have you got there?"

"We have the biggest thing in the world!"

"Who found it?"

"McCormick."

Henderson reportedly threw his shovel to the ground and sat by the creek, unable to speak. In his interview with Adney a few years later, not only would Henderson convey his dismay with Carmack for not sending word back to him, but confessed the next stream he intended to prospect was Rabbit Creek.

These are the facts as we know them. Adney became an early proponent of Henderson's cause. In his book he states, "Canada owes not less to Henderson than California Marshall the discoverer of gold at Sutter's Mill." Adney believed that Carmack had forsaken Henderson by not sending word back to him about the strike. Both were members of the Yukon Order of Pioneers, one of whose tenets required that information on all gold discoveries be shared with all other YOOP members. Yet Carmack had spread the word to everyone he had met on his way to file his claim at Forty-Mile. How much responsibility did he have to go back to Gold Bottom Creek and personally alert Henderson? Carmack defended himself in his memoir, *My Experiences in the Yukon*. He argued that by showing Henderson the colors his party had found on the way in to Gold Bottom Creek, he had alerted Henderson to the prospect. He claimed he even urged Henderson to prospect there, but that the miner demurred, indicating that colors could be found anywhere. And what of the alleged racial remarks Henderson had made to Carmack? Did they play a part? Adney suspects they may have.

These were racist times. In the foreword to Adney's book, Ken Coates states, "Tappan Adney was a man of the late nineteenth century and, as such, his account carries the perspective and values of that generation. This is particularly the case in his harsh and unflattering descriptions of the native peoples...He describes the facial make-up of the Chilkoot as leaving the women with 'a hideous, repulsive expression.' The Chilkoot packers, who were actually shrewd businessmen, were to Adney, 'not trustworthy, and are wholly unscrupulous.' After a difficult trading experience near Little Salmon River, Adney suggested that 'these Indians, pilfering thieves that they are, doubtless are only practicing on the white men what the Chilcats have taught them.'"

It would not take a leap of faith, then, to suspect that Adney might harbor disgust for a white man who would intermarry with such creatures, as Carmack had done.[7] Nor would it surprise if Adney found the great Klondike gold discovery attributed to a "Squaw Man" unsettling. A close look at Adney's words indicates his condescension of Carmack, a man he never met. He states, "…Carmack, it is said, fell asleep." Who said this? The only eye-witnesses were Skookum Jim and Tagish Charley. If one of them in fact said this, this might be the only time Adney believed the word of an Indian. Adney subtly infers that Carmack, like Indians, is lazy, slothful. He states that "they were certainly not miners," yet acknowledges Carmack was outfitted by Harper at Fort Selkirk, staked claims on Gold Bottom, prospected Rabbit Creek and discovered the greatest concentration of placer gold ever found on the face of the earth. In fact, Carmack was the son of a California gold rush 49er, had been prospecting on and off since his arrival in the Yukon in 1885, and would spend the rest of his life developing mines in Washington and California.

Adney, in support of his position, quotes Ogilvie, who wrote in 1897, "…the difference is seen when the right course is taken, and this was led up to by Robert Henderson. This man is a born prospector, and you could not persuade him to stay on even the richest claim on Bonanza. He started up in a small boat to spend this summer and win-

---

7 Time in the wilderness tempered Victorian disgust for this practice. Clarence Berry, who would take $1.5 million in gold from Eldorado Creek during the winter of '96–'97, recorded in his memoirs that at Forty-Mile in 1895 all forty of the sourdoughs there had native wives, while none of the Cheechakos (newcomers) did. William Ogilvie, in his book *Early Days on the Yukon*, described the situation with typical Victorian discretion: "Carmack lived in closer association with the natives than the miners found acceptable."

ter on Stewart River prospecting. This is the stuff the true prospector is made of, and I am proud to say he is a Canadian." This statement, more than any other, sheds light on the attempt to rewrite history.

Henderson was the son of a lighthouse keeper on Big Island, Pictou County, Nova Scotia. Carmack was an American, from San Francisco. Three of the most prominent names in early Yukon history were all American. Leroy Napoleon "Jack" McQuesten, who organized the Yukon Order of Pioneers at Circle City, was born in New Hampshire and grew up in Maine. Alfred Mayo was from Kentucky, and Arthur Harper, born in Antrim, Ireland in 1832, emigrated to New York City in 1850. Other significant Yukon pioneers were American. Jack Dalton, responsible for laying the Dalton Trail into the Yukon, was from Oklahoma. Joe Ladue, who laid out the original Dawson town site, was from Plattsburg, New York. It's apparent that anti-American feelings in the Klondike were responsible to a degree in the deification of the Henderson legend. There were so many Americans in the Yukon that in 1894 William Ogilvie appealed to Ottawa to send Mounties as a show of force. That Canada was apprehensive about Americans on their territory is evident in what occurred in 1898 to the south. When gold was discovered in British Columbia, the province immediately passed an alien law, preventing none but Canadians from staking claims there.

Canada's fear was well-founded. At this stage in the history of North American expansion, possession was a powerful claim on territorial lands. Over 300,000 American farmers would homestead the plains of Alberta, Saskatchewan, and Manitoba in the next twenty years alone. From alien claim laws to Name Boards to a show of force with the arrival of the Mounties, Canada reacted quickly to the perceived American threat. The support for Henderson as discoverer of Klondike gold seems, from all testimony, to be an extension of this Canadian reaction.

Surveyor William Ogilvie, in his book *Early Days on the Yukon*, documents a thorough investigation of the Klondike gold rush's origin. He interviewed Henderson, Carmack, Skookum Jim, and Tagish Charlie. "I have had long interviews with both Jim and Charlie, and some of the others camped with them on the Klondike at that time, and reduced the purport of our talks to writing," Ogilvie reports. "I took the precaution to interview them separately and afterwards get them all together and criticize and discuss the narrative of each in committee of the whole..." Ogilvie's assessment, despite Adney's out-of-context quote, is that Skookum Jim was the actual discoverer of gold on what became known as Bonanza Creek.

"After satisfying themselves that they had the best spot," Ogilvie wrote, "and deciding to stake and record there, they got into a dispute as to who should stake discovery claim, Jim claiming it by right of discovery, and Carmack claiming it, Jim says, on the ground that an Indian would not be allowed to record it. Jim says the difficulty was finally settled by agreeing that Carmack was to stake and to record discovery claim, and assign half of it, or a half-interest in it, to Jim, so on the morning of August 17th, 1896, Carmack staked discovery claim..."[8] Ogilvie's account stresses that Carmack and his Indian brothers-in-law were insulted not only when Henderson balked at leading them to the gold site, but also, when on Gold Bottom, by his refusing to sell the two Indians any tobacco. Carmack, Ogilvie notes, emphasized these points when expressing his view.

Skookum Jim was the actual discoverer of the historic Klondike gold. That Canada had an urgent interest in promoting Henderson the Canadian over Carmack the American as discoverer eclipsed any possibility of a First Nation individual receiving credit. Henderson had as much to do with the Klondike gold rush as the man who sent Marshall to build his sawmill on the south fork of the American River had to do with the California gold rush. Nevertheless, the Canadian government awarded Henderson a yearly pension to help validate its position. And today, if you search "Dawson City" on the internet, one of the first available sites is "Bell's Alaska, Yukon, & British Columbia

---

8 There is controversy over which date, August 16 or 17, 1896, the Klondike strike was made. Considering the time involved in traversing hills, pausing for rest, discovering gold, "satisfying themselves they had the best spot," discussion on how to claim, and then staking claim on the morning of the 17th, it seems reasonable to conclude the actual strike was made the previous day.

Guide." Under the history link, the first words are, "It all began with Robert Henderson..."

CARMACKS TO LAKE LABERGE

Friday, March 7

Before leaving for the Yukon, I vowed never to complain about anything while on the trail. I remind myself of this pledge now, outside the Community Center at 8:00 A.M. Parsons grins at me, a French Foreign Legion-style havelock hanging down from under the back of his fur cap. It is white, with fornicating green fish on it.

Leaving Carmacks, we are immediately challenged by a steep, burned-out hill which takes pains to mount. We bog down completely when confronted by a more difficult obstacle. Hogan and I stop and judge how best to make it over this sudden, twisted rise in the trail. It is a steep double hill with a shelf half way, upon which the trail veers to the right. To make it over one must gun his machine up to the step, somehow turn mid-air, and quickly accelerate again to make the second. Hogan mounts his machine, face determined, and makes it up and over on his first try. I do not succeed, don't even reach the first step. Hogan tries to run my snow machine up and over, and also fails. Others arrive and likewise try in vain. Several make the first hill, only to fly into the branches of the trees instead of managing the right turn. We decide to haul up the machines by rope, with four, five of us pulling while two or three push. It is an enormous amount of work at this stage of the trip, but we manage to pull the entire troop through.

Onward we churn through the woods. Behind Hogan and Flynn, traveling alone, I come upon a slight rise in the trail and veer too much to the right catching untrod snow, which collapses. Over my machine rolls, pitching me headlong into the snow several feet down the side of the hill, the machine rolling after me until jamming against a tree, preventing it from landing on top of me. I rise dazed as Suzuki appears, jumps off his machine, and begins filming the scene.

"Tell me what happened, Don," he says, film rolling, and I stand there pointing, "I almost bought the farm." Hogan appears, and dismounts.

"I told myself Don was gonna have trouble here!" he says, and so had decided to return. We pull my machine back up with difficulty, and again my respect for wilderness snowmobiling increases. We are lucky that no one has been injured, but this day has just begun. We remind ourselves that this is the part of the trail that the Quest mushers had warned about.

Pulling over the rise, we enter a wonderful run, one of the easier and more scenic we have experienced, crossing a series of broad, open spaces called the Chain-of-Lakes. They are small lakes separated by short stretches of wood, thirty miles of nice running through crisp air and bright sunshine. There is a degree of concern, however, for we are all aware that Bruce Johnson, one-time Yukon Quest winner, broke through the ice on Little Atlin Lake with eight dogs and drowned while training for the '94 Quest race.

Hogan and Flynn lead McRae and I into a heavily wooded area, and we come upon a clearing. Nestled beside the trail, deep here in the wilderness, lies a log cabin, smoke drifting from its chimney. We stop, and McRae and I wait as the leaders get off their machines and stomp through the snow up to the cabin and enter. We wait so long that we turn off our machines.

"What are they doing," McRae finally complains, "getting directions?"

"I don't know."

A minute later, "Jesus Christ I'm freezing my ass off, what are they doing?"

A minute later, "Jesus Christ, what are they doing?"

A minute later, "I have a vicious injury on the end of my nose."

"What's it matter?"

Ten minutes later they emerge, mount their machines and buzz off without a word of explanation. Back at it we go, entering a stretch that taxes us all. This is a bad twenty-five miles where several accidents occur. Peterson's machine suffers over a thousand dollars in damage; Duffee, driving Gudmundson's machine, slices off the trail sideways into the trees, stripping off the windshield. That he escapes uninjured is remarkable. McRae and Anderson both run head-on into trees in this section of woods. Onward we plow, separated by different lengths of yards and miles, most unaware of the misfortunes of the others.

I find myself alone for a very long time, rising and falling through rugged terrain. I traverse long runs of bush land where the path is so twisted it must be engaged at a frustratingly slow gait. A seemingly endless, slow wriggling. The depression in the snow narrow, unforgiving, the day late and diminishing into long-cast shadows as the sun brushes the horizon. The trail becomes too long, as though fate decreed that this last, interminable day must be the most hard-earned, the most trying. Long after it seems too long, it continues. And continues. I'm frustrated not knowing how far we've traveled, nor how far we still have to go. Eighty-five miles without signs, or odometers. Hours alone, not a soul with whom to pause, and commiserate.

Onward, thoughts crowd my mind, that it is good this is the last night out, that tomorrow we will make the easy run across Lake Laberge and up the Yukon River into Whitehorse. Exhilaration that the wilderness has been conquered, that the cold has been endured, that even though there is not a soul among us who can use his right hand, we are all alive and well. Through the darkening woods I plod, through vast fields of bushes, up and over small hills, the whine of the machine maddening now after seven long days. I run up one long, gentle slope and top a hill. Finally the expanse of lake materializes through the trees. I hear dogs hacking and men swearing, settling into our last camp on the shores of Lake Laberge.

CHAPTER EIGHT

"There are strange things done in the midnight sun
By the men who moil for gold;
The arctic trails have their secret tales
That would make your blood run cold;
The Northern Lights have seen queer sights,
But the queerest they ever did see
Was the night on the marge of Lake Lebarge
I cremated Sam McGee."

— ROBERT SERVICE, *THE CREMATION OF SAM MCGEE*

The man was a bum and failure, harboring a self-described "aversion to strenuous forms of toil." He left Scotland in 1896 and wandered the western United States and Canada, surviving on an assortment of menial jobs. His most colorful was that of a troubadour, singing his way across Arizona, Colorado, and Nevada until he lost his guitar in California's Tehachapi Mountains. He was turned away from the most base work, fired from jobs, and walked away from others. He reached a low point outside Los Angeles when he snuck out of a make-shift hut after being joined by a bum he suspected was the thief and killer then terrorizing local railroad lines. After sleeping on a hillside of dried leaves, he met a fellow Scot who invited him to meet his parents. Disheveled, poverty stricken, and without prospects, he was too embarrassed to do so. Yet he refused offers that would have improved his situation. He had sunk into the dregs of society, considered little more than a bum to be scorned. Looking back forty years later with hindsight colored by his enormous ensuing success, Robert Service dismissed this period of his life as, "the romance of destiny."

The path leading Service from degradation to the heights of literary fame was studded with coincidence and luck. Despite proximity to departure points to the Yukon gold rush, Service had ignored the opportunity. He did not like the cold. He worked as a laborer, an orange picker, a tunneler, a tutor, a hayer, a cow-milker, and finally determined that he would not be a victim of endless toil. Fate intervened in Victoria, British Columbia when, upon leaving a store where he had been refused a job as an office boy, Service stopped to chat with a salesman who suggested he apply for a clerk's job across the street at the Canadian Bank of Commerce.

Service was accepted at this post in October, 1903, and transferred to Kamloops nine months later. There he quickly assimilated into the white collar society so much more agreeable to his delicate temperament. Shortly thereafter, he was informed that he had once again been transferred. On November 8, 1904, Service boarded a steamer north, bound for his new post in Whitehorse, Yukon Territory.[9]

The future Bard of the North was quickly accepted into Whitehorse society. Encouraged with his fortuitous escape from poverty, he avoided the town's lower echelons. Instead he immersed himself in the dances, dinners, and winter carnivals of the higher classes, and reveled in his long walks through the silent beauty of the Yukon wilderness.

During the autumn of 1906 a literary breakthrough occurred. Service joined an amateur theatrical group, reciting such ballads as *Casey at the Bat* and *Gunga Din*. He sent some verse to the *Whitehorse Star* newspaper, whose editor in turn requested that Service provide a piece with a more local flavor for an upcoming church social. The budding poet responded with *The Shooting of Dan McGrew*. Considered a bit too bawdy for the church social, it was not performed. But the encouragement fired Service with ambition, and a month later luck again presented itself.

---

9 This means that Service was in Whitehorse for the arrival of the Dawson Klondiker hockey team in December of '04. As the team enjoyed great notoriety and was stranded in Whitehorse for several days, it is likely Service had contact with the group.

Service relates that he was attending a social gathering uninvited when a "big mining man from Dawson, smoking a big cigar with a gilt band" told the story of a miner who cremated his partner. Service later wrote that he immediately recognized the potential of the story, and walked outside and began composing the poem. The next morning he arose and committed the words to *The Cremation of Sam McGee* to paper. He then tossed the manuscript into his desk drawer among a growing assortment of poems in various stages of completion. Granted a one hundred dollar Christmas bonus, Service decided to publish a small volume of verse he intended to give to friends. He sent the manuscript to his father, who with his mother had emigrated to Toronto. His father carried the work to William Briggs of Methodist Church Publishing, and thus was another source created to disseminate the growing Yukon legend for generations to come.

LAKE LABERGE TO WHITEHORSE

Saturday, March 8

Sitting on a stump over a morning fire on the shores of Lake Laberge. Warm, maybe not even below zero Fahrenheit. I marvel at how quickly one acclimates to the cold. *Warm, maybe not even below zero...* Anderson wears neither coat nor gloves. All of our campsites have been beautiful, but this is the best of all. Hogan picked a point of flat land jutting into the lake, and here we made camp after our tortuous day yesterday. The lake, originally called by the Tagish Tloo-tat-sai, is ringed with limestone mountains, the larger on the eastern shore, toward the southern end. There was a long lead of open water forty yards out that we walked to last night for some easy water; it is now lightly frozen over, a mist rising from the spot.

There is excitement as the wilderness portion of our journey is coming to an end. It is thirty miles over the lake, twenty up the Yukon River to Whitehorse, an easy run compared to all we have done. Millar cooks sausages on the fire, Duffee walks up to sit and chat for a bit.

The topic of Millar's gold claim arises.

"My father started in 1974," the rough-hewn figure tells me, "came to Dawson on his honeymoon. My father died and then I took over."

"What did you do before?" I ask.

"As little as possible. Costs me $250,000 a year to run my operation, and I make about $20,000. I tell people I make $700 an hour, but I don't tell 'em I only work a hundred hours a year..."

I recall McRae mentioning that Troy Suzuki's father might be famous. I turn to Duffee, who had once roomed with Suzuki.

"Hey, is Troy's father someone famous?"

"I don't know," Duffee replies, shrugging his shoulders. "I never asked him."

We stage some humorous photos; McRae lies prone on his hog, I hold Parson's chainsaw over his neck while Hogan signals "thumbs down" next to us. Anderson puts a log through the holes in the front skis of his snow machine, and with the help of Parsons on one end of the log and Farr on the other, lifts it as if doing curls while he barks, "Step right up! Step right up and buy your ticket to see Brad Marsh and the Senators meet their doom!"

Ready with my sled packed and tied down, I enjoy a few moments by the campfire. Amidst a swirl of packing, I pull out my paperback copy of *The Best of Robert Service* and turn to its most renown entry. I once wondered if Service chose the name "McGee" on purpose, in retaliation for what Frank McGee had done to the Dawson Klondikers in Ottawa the previous year. But I learned that Service had selected the name from a bank ledger while composing his poem.[10] I reread the poem in its entirety, fully cognizant of where I am. I have always loved experiences in their natural setting; watching the Bruins in Boston Garden, eating Cajun crawfish in Louisiana, seeing Jerry Jeff Walker perform in Luckenback, Texas, and now reading *The Cremation of Sam McGee* here, on the frozen marge of Lake Laberge. I finish and look up, savoring the moment. I retrieve a pen from my pack, and write in my book at the end of the poem, "Read campfire-side on a point jutting into Lake

---

10 The real Sam McGee, a copper miner and road builder, posted a sign before his Whitehorse shack, "Have a cup of tea with the ghost of Sam McGee," thus capitalizing on his new-found fame. He died in Beiseker, Alberta, in 1940

Labarge, Saturday, March 8, 1997. Two dog teams just slid by, others wailing down the shore, ready to go. The lake mist covered, beautiful."

The players are coming more into focus as individuals. Duffee and Farr are quiet souls, Farr keeping a sort of journal of his own on small, yellow scraps of paper. Anderson, Parsons, and Peterson are the Wild Bunch, the raucous, hard-drinking core of the Dawson Nuggets. Flynn and Hogan are similar; they are the leaders, sober, intelligent, intent on pulling us through. Flynn possesses a signature laugh and a sing-song voice. But once in the bush, this man raised in fish camps along the banks of the Yukon River is all business, casting a weathered, discerning eye on all around him. Hogan a mass of conflicting qualities; he is eloquent and intelligent, sober and serious yet capable of that Irish gleam in the eye that exposes a wild interior. Great storyteller, a mesmerizing quality to his voice. Millar is something of an enigma; he is quick-tempered and frequently in a bad mood, not conducive to small talk. The men running the dogs, Craig and Gudmundson remain obscure to me, separated as we are at the moment. Suzuki is reserved, harboring razor-sharp intelligence. A self-described fish-out-of-water amongst the Dawson crowd, he constantly peers about for camera fodder. Also packed and ready to go, he joins me on the log before the dwindling fire. I ask how he came to live in the Yukon.

"I was looking after my grandfather for the last two years of his life, and he died and I was rattling around numb for a year," the filmmaker tells me. "I'd finished Art School but I was preoccupied with family. I needed a break, and I had a friend in Dawson who kept trying to get me up, so I came. The country here reminds me of B.C. when I was a kid. That wilderness is getting pushed to this little corner, so I felt honored to be here. It's not gonna last forever. I came up in '86 maybe, '85.

"I'm kinda, well, I guess I'm feeling a little more settled. I wasn't used to the fish bowl thing, not an inch of anonymity. In Vancouver I was an artsy closet hoser, here I'm a closet artsy. I'm feeling more comfortable here. I'd have dinners at first and serve Japanese food, exotic food, curries and sushi, and people didn't get it. And last year I had a moose dinner and carrots and everyone raved, 'Man you can cook all right!' I guess you gotta give people what they want. Dawson's lost a lot of character people, lots have died. They've been replaced by urban kids—kids like me. They don't have the character, and that's a shame. I think I caught the tail end of the rough and tumble wild west era.

"Look at Dawson, it's pretty tacky. I like the buildings, but this obsession with the gold rush and Robert Service, and everyone's trying to be a Yukon legend. There's life now, there's life in any town you're in. That's what I'm interested in, the expression of life. Most of the guys on this trip aren't rah-rah gold rush guys. They're just tremendous. I think Dawson would be better off taking care of its people instead of trying to drive the tourism."

We jump up when we see Hogan and Flynn mount their hogs. Flynn is concerned, warning all to stay on his tracks as we cross the vast lake. It is far more dangerous here, he explains, than the smaller lakes we had crossed. The open water off-shore is testament to that. We begin our run across the white expanse, but I soon fall behind and become confused. I'm following a set of tracks toward the western shore, and stop when I see this trail winding up into some cottages. I turn about and spot what I believe is a contingent of our expedition, a mile or so away. Running hard after them across virgin snow against Flynn's advice, I catch up when they stop for a break in the middle of the long lake.

Anderson takes a swig from his whiskey bottle and passes it around. McRae pesters him with questions, wondering if by gathering so many so close we will all fall through the ice and die. Anderson, typical Yukon gleam in his eye, reassures by saying to me, "Imagine, Dangerous Don, you're six inches away from *instant death*."

We continue, reaching the southern end of the lake and running several miles along shore, looking for the inlet of the Yukon River. The leaders stop and stand up on their machines, scouring the shoreline. We finally spot wooden piles of a ruined dock and drive for it. Turning the point, we are back on the Yukon River, closing fast on our goal.

Here the river is 200 yards wide, white cliffs riddled with bank swallow holes rising above. We come to a low bridge and file one by one under it, ducking our heads as we go. Here Cowboy Smith plays his final joke on the rookie dog mushers Riopel and Christianson by running up off the ice, then carefully backtracking down. He knows they follow his trail, and will take the bait...

We stop to regroup so that we can enter Whitehorse as a unit. We begin the wait for the dog teams, which take much more time to cover the fifty miles from camp. Our excitement erodes into impatience, as most of us just want to get into town and take a long, hot shower. We wait more than an hour in the cold before entering the capital of the Yukon Territory. The reception is less than expected with only the CBC film crew, Deb Belinsky and Jim Nicol, and the Whitehorse Oldtimer Hockey Club there to meet us.

We load our snowmobiles into MacKenzie's Whitehorse Freightliner trucks, which will haul them back to Dawson. I am one of the first to check into the Gold Rush Inn. I dump my bags in my room and go down to the bar where players are filtering in. I see Duffee, order two beers and sit with him at one of the tables. When Millar strolls by, still in wilderness gear, he pauses, then grabs my beer off the table and proceeds to guzzle the entire bottle in one fell swoop. He slams it back down and walks off. I laugh, but Duffee does not.

"That's an insult up here, you know."

"Aw c'mon, he's just screwing around."

"No, that's an insult. I saw someone do the very same thing to him a few weeks ago, and he was bullshit."

Duffee is staying in town at a friend's house, and when he finishes his beer excuses himself. I see Margo Anderson and Earl MacKenzie at the bar, and join them. We marvel that the first, hardest portion of our journey is actually over.

"I am so proud of you!" Margo gushes, and I admit I am happy to have finished. I tell them it was much harder than I had envisioned.

"If we hadn't hit Pelly Crossing," MacKenzie agrees, "I would have packed it in." I find solace in that the Yukoners have also had a difficult time. MacKenzie buys me a beer, turns and says, "Don, it's been a privilege meeting you," shakes my hand and wanders off. I make small talk with Margo, asking her how Kevin and she ended up in the Yukon.

"I was originally from High River, Alberta," she tells me. "I met

Kevin in B.C., I was the only girl on a crew of eighty-five building hydro towers in B.C. I picked him. We met in '84, we married in '85. Spent six months in Australia camping for our honeymoon.

"Kevin had worked in Dawson the previous year, and he wanted to go back when we returned from Australia. When we got back we were broke, and we knew you could make lots of money up in Dawson. It wasn't well known then, there were tons of jobs available. I managed the Gold Poke, in '89 I got a job with the Yukon government. Kevin started painting for someone else and then started his own business. Kevin is a perfectionist, he does perfect jobs. Impeccable reputation for work."

Dale Kulych steps into the vacated spot next to me. Kulych is a member of the team, a short, stocky guy with harsh, demanding eyes. He has not done the wilderness part of the trip. Living in Whitehorse, he had driven to Dawson to see us off, and is now rejoining the group for the rest of the journey as are Budd Docken, Chester Kelly, Joe Mason, and team fiddler Willie Gordon. Kulych orders a beer, then interrupts Margo and I.

"Well Don," he begins, "did you pull your weight?"

"Huh?"

"Did you pull your weight?"

"On the trip?"

"Yes or no! Did you pull your weight in the bush?"

"Well…" I begin to respond, wanting to explain how unprepared I was, how green—

"Yes or no!"

"Well—" Kulych leans close.

"I'm gonna get you. I'm gonna harass the fuck out of you, I'm gonna be your worst fucking nightmare, pal."

"C'mon…"

"I'm gonna get you, pal!"

"What is your problem!"

"Aha! I struck the nerve!" he says, and walks away.

Pent-up emotions evident in Carmacks resurface in Whitehorse tonight, fueled with the knowledge that the first, most romantic and difficult leg of our reenactment is over. This fact is not met without a degree of relief. The members of the team disperse in numerous directions, some spending the night with relatives, some with friends, many holed up in the Gold Rush Inn. One direction is common: we are all celebrating.

Walking the streets of Whitehorse, into the Blue Moon Saloon and the 202's Sam McGee's Lounge I roam, and then the irresistible sound of country music draws me into a tavern whose name I never discovered. I am met by a grinning Cowboy Smith leaning against the bar, who takes one look at me and declares, "You're banned from this place."

I see several members of the Wild Bunch, Parsons, Peterson, and MacKenzie seated at a booth, drinking. Dave Millar walks in. I lean against the bar with Cowboy. His appearance is stunning, and in vast contrast to his silent, brooding image on the trail. No longer bundled in well-worn Yukon garb, he is now in boots and jeans, his signature Stetson on his head, his eyes alive, drinking, talking.

"You earned your right to the Yukon the night you matched Shirley Tracy drink-for-drink in Carmacks," he tells me. "Someday you got no cash, you got no plastic, you got a place to come to. You earned your right to the Yukon on this trip."

We laugh rehashing the night in Carmacks; I am told the team dropped over $700 in the Goldrush Lounge. We are interrupted by a small, dark, Eskimo woman. Cowboy excuses himself, leans down and listens to her for a moment, then pulls his wallet out and hands her a twenty dollar bill.

"That doesn't even begin to repay that woman for what she did for me when I was green," he says as she shuffles away.

I notice Millar staring. When I walk toward the men's room I pass the gold miner walking in the opposite direction. He utters something under his breath.

"Hey," I say stopping, Duffee's admonishment fresh in my mind, as well as Kulych's words. Millar stops and turns toward me.

"You got a problem?"

"Yeah," he replies, squaring himself to me, his feet apart, his hands going to his hips.

"Well, what's your problem?"

"You."

"Me? What's your problem with me?"

"You're trying too hard. This isn't about you."

Ouch.

To be honest, I am in a difficult position. I sense some resentment, but I do not know what to do about it. I am an author, invited to participate in a great adventure. When I arrived in Dawson City, I found myself treated like a celebrity. As soon as I stepped foot in town the CBC camera crew followed me everywhere I went. They are making a documentary on the trip, and have chosen John Flynn, Dawson City First Nation member of the team, and Don Reddick, outsider/ writer, as the vehicle through which to portray the Dawson reenactment experience.

The local radio station was reading *Dawson City Seven* a chapter a day on the air, and the afternoon before we left I was invited to read one myself. The first evening in town I attended the final hockey game of the Dawson league season. Flynn and I sat together, trying to ignore the cameramen who sat two rows below us, filming our every move. Afterward we retired to Dick Van Nostrand's Downtown Hotel for libations. The large barroom was crowded with hockey players from all the Dawson teams, many of them pointing, whispering about the author now among them.

Here I first met Millar as I sat at one of the tables. He tilted back in his chair from an adjacent table and said, "I didn't like your book." He proceeded to explain how ludicrous it was to tell the Dawson story from the point of view of an American protagonist, though the word "protagonist" was certainly not one he used. Millar continued, telling me he had once been a member of some elite Canadian military group, whose training and abilities "would make the United States Marines look like babies." This is the Dave Millar I face now, challenged that this trip is somehow about me.

"What does *that* mean?" I protested. "Why would you say that?"

"Relax, you're trying too hard."

"What do you mean?"

"You just think of yourself—you ate your Cup-O-Soup on the trail while the rest of us threw in together with the meals—"

"*What?*"

"You—" but I do not let him finish, but tell him he has been difficult the entire trip. When I say this, he turns to the Wild Bunch, witnessing the scene, and asks, "Have I been being an asshole?" To which, to my complete relief, they all nod in unison. Millar turns back at me, infuriated. But my primordial interest in informing him as impolitely as possible that I will not be taking any more of his grief comes from me in a torrent of abuse. I am careful to be as indelicate as possible, lest my message be misunderstood. Beard touching beard, I inform him in no uncertain terms that he can shove his attitude up a place not mentioned on any map of the Yukon. He informs me in no uncertain terms that I can shove my attitude up a place not mentioned on any map of Massachusetts. When I suggest we step outside and settle it, the others jump in and break it up. I stomp away back to Cowboy Smith, who by his bemused grin I know has enjoyed the scene.

Smith opens up, talking of his years in the bush, his entire demeanor a remarkable metamorphosis from the hardened, bitter legend into an utterly charming, not unsophisticated character.

"My grandfather was from Texas," the musher tells me. "Born 1880, called him H. P. Smith. Nobody knew what his name was, so he called himself Horse Power. Horse Power Smith. He's buried under a rock up on the banks of the Saskatchewan River. Came across the border with his horses and they said 'What's your name?' Said his name was Smith and they said, 'Good.' They're still talking about him. I don't know what part of Texas he's from, don't know where his parents were from. All I know is he hated Englishmen.

"I don't hate reporters, it's just that I get focused. I'm a sharp shooter that doesn't let the green pit viper distract me. My eye is on the prize. I'm not a smart man, I can't walk and chew gum at the same time. I need to focus on what I'm doing, and why these people come asking questions, it breaks my focus. I was on the Iditarod, and I was going over a hill, and you can't see beyond the hill, which way the trail goes, and I see this photographer so I figure he's beside the trail, so you know how it is when you turn a semi, it's a wide turn—or you know how they train you in bayoneting, to put your foot up at the same time to push the guy to pull it back out—so I go over the hill and just level this guy with my foot, with his cameras, just for the hell of it. That's why they say I don't like reporters and photographers.

"I'm not a smart man. That's why I can get by on four hours sleep, there's nothing else going on up there. Hell, I can't even read or write. And I'll tell you, mean isn't tough. Patience is tough, perseverance is tough. You're wet on the side of the riverbank and got to get warm, mean won't get you warm. These black guys in the ghetto, they're not tough. They're mean.

"I had a bad trip with you guys, my back went out. It's either in or out, by Carmacks it got a little better. By the end of Lake Laberge I was OK.

"I don't need to talk to anyone. You know, a guy does what he does, that should be enough. You don't need to go out and try to make money because of it, hell, there's guys out there that done a lot more than me. Why should anyone be interested in me, when these guys are out there? It's enough to do what you do. Millar is a gold miner, Parsons is a doctor. That's enough. I'm gonna go out of this world with what I came into it with. You never saw a Brinks truck following a hearse to the cemetery, and let me tell you, you meet a guy who never made a mistake, there's one cocksucker who never tried to do anything in his life. It's enough to be who you are.

"I have guys out on the trail. I'm a guide. Some you get along with, some you don't. I got this guy, every two hours he asks me what time it is. I tell him. He asks me again two hours later. Finally, I says, 'Don't you have a fucking watch?' He gets riled like this, he says sure, I got a Rolex.

"'Well *wear* it.' I called in. Said get a chopper in to get this guy out. They say it's three days short, there's no chopper available. I says, 'You either get a chopper or a body bag.' I had one guy—you ask if they wanna cut the meat up. We got a sheep, and I got three knives. I ask but they usually say no, you do it. I got this guy who says you do it, then he's standing over me, saying this and that. So you know when you cut open a sheep you got those big globs of white fat hanging from the guts? I just grab one of them and eat it, and then I get my space."

I mention to Cowboy that McRae has nick-named him the Deranged Whacko. The famous musher grins.

"You tell that little reporter to come back to see me if he wants to know what tough is." I ask if he might continue on with the team to Ottawa, and he grins again and doesn't answer. Smith salts his words with references to Vietnam. He tells me that his favorite country singer is Tom Russell, "the guy who wrote *Navajo Rug*. He wrote the definitive Vietnam song. I can't remember the name of it, hell, it's about Jimmy McGrew…"[11] When I pick up on the Vietnam reference and broach the subject directly, I receive his standard issue: "That's classified information."

Millar walks back up to us. I learned long ago that bullies are essentially cowards, and need to be confronted as soon as possible. It is disconcerting that Millar genuinely believes he has a grievance with me, and certainly does not now appear to be a coward. He says something that triggers my anger, and I tear into him once more. My words are emphatic, loud, and obscene. Every effort made to convince him that I am not just some *writer*. Millar sticks a finger in my face.

"You just embarrassed me in front of my friends," he seethes. "I came over here to apologize to you, and you just give me more shit. You are on my list, my friend. *Watch out.*" He stomps away, leaving me wondering what words of apology he had uttered.

I bar-hop a bit more, then wander into a Chinese restaurant where Doc Parsons sits with a few others I do not know. I sit alone, simmering over the treatment some of these guys are giving me. Parsons waves me to join his group but I decline. I've had enough Yukon hospitality for one night. When I finish my fried rice I walk out of the restaurant and into the cold Yukon night.

---

11 The song referred to is *Veteran's Day*, by Tom Russell.

CHAPTER NINE

"Accursed thirst for gold! What dost thou not compel mortals to do?"

— VERGIL, *THE AENEID* , 70–19 B.C.

fter Columbus waded ashore on the Bahamas in 1492, it was three hundred fifty more years before a white man laid eyes on this land. The Spanish plundering of Central and South America, the establishment of English, French, and Dutch colonies on the eastern seaboard, the eventual triumph of the English over the French and the ensuing American Revolution, followed by the relentless conquering of the continent's wilderness all occurred unbeknownst to the aboriginal inhabitants of the Yukon Territory.

Guarded by a phalanx of mountains and the sheer bulge of an unexplored Alaska from the Pacific coast, a ridge of the northern Rockies from the Mackenzie River watershed, to the north by the frozen Beaufort Sea and to the south by fifteen hundred desolate, mountainous miles, the Yukon is the lost corner of North America. In 1789 Alexander MacKenzie of the Canadian North West Company descended the river which came to carry his name, and was told of an even greater river on the other side of the mountains. MacKenzie's journal alerted the leaders of Russian America, and they searched for it. But the great river, which provides the easiest access into the interior, proved elusive. Three of the greatest northern explorers, James Cook in 1778, Joseph Billings in 1790–93, and Otto Von Kotzebue in 1815–18 all sailed past the Yukon River delta without recognizing it.

The region's geographic isolation is abetted by a climate so severe that only those driven hard by profit even thought of going there. It was the profit in fur trapping that provided the initial impetus. George Mercer Dawson, in his *1887 Exploration Report*, provides in fascinating detail how the fur trade worked: "At the time of the establishment of Forts Yukon and Selkirk, and for many years afterwards, the 'returns' from these furthest stations reached the market only after seven years, the course of trade being as follows: Goods—1st year, reach York Factory; 2nd year, Norway House; 3rd year Peel River, and were hauled during the winter across the mountains to La Pierre's House; 4th year, reach Fort Yukon. Returns—5th year, reach La Pierre's House and are hauled across to Peel River; 6th year, reach depot at Fort Simpson; 7th year, reach market." All of which is an arduous way to make money, but it was well worth the trouble. William Dall mentions that a $5 musket bartered at Fort Yukon got twenty beaver, or forty martin skins in return, worth $150, a three-thousand percent return on money invested.[12]

The Hudson Bay Company sent John Bell northward in 1840, based on the reports of Sir John Franklin, who in 1825 had touched Herschel Island during his Arctic forays. Bell founded a trading post he named Ft. McPherson on the MacKenzie River delta. The following year Hudson Bay employee Robert Campbell crossed the divide from the MacKenzie River watershed, becoming the first white man to lay eyes on the Yukon interior.

At the same time, the pressures of gold exploration were slowly, methodically wending their way northward. The great 1848 discovery at Sutter's Mill on the south fork of the American River was the watershed event in North American gold exploration. Within ten years the world's total amount of stored gold, accumulated over thousands of years, doubled. It took approximately two hundred fifty years to settle Spanish Florida to the Ohio valley, a distance of about eight hundred

---

12 The Indian trade produced remarkably consistent returns for investors. Ray Allen Billington's *Westward Expansion* states that one hundred and fifty years earlier in 1668, 19,000 British pounds worth of furs were obtained for 650 pounds in trade goods, *exactly* the same ratio of return. Normally left unexamined in such histories, however, is the nefarious rate of return.

miles. The discovery of gold outside Sacramento accelerated the exploration of the remaining two thousand miles of the North American continent in less than fifty years. The best way to illustrate the steady progression is simply to provide the list of gold-discovery dates:

1848: Sutter's Mill, California
1855: Upper Columbia River, Washington
1857: Fraser River, British Columbia
1859: Pikes Peak, Colorado
1860: Orofino Creek, Idaho
1860: Caribou, British Columbia
1861: Wrangell, Alaska Panhandle
1861: Stikine River, British Columbia
1863: Helena, Montana
1874: Black Hills, South Dakota
1874: Cassiar, British Columbia
1880: Stewart River, Yukon Territory
1881: Juneau, Alaska Panhandle
1886: Fortymile, Yukon Territory
1893: Birch Creek, Yukon Territory
1896: Klondike River, Yukon Territory

In context of this incremental northward advance, the Klondike strike of 1896 was virtually predestined. Who actually discovered the gold becomes irrelevant. Had it not been one of the greatest concentrations of placer gold ever discovered in one of the most romantic locations imaginable, George Carmack, Skookum Jim, and Tagish Charlie would be as memorable as Thibert, McCullough, French Pete, McConky, Poplin, Marx, Beach, Franklin, Madison, Pitka, Sorresco, Choquette, Barker, Boswell, O'Riley, or McLaughlin, discoverers of historic placer gold all.

Contemporary views on the effect of the Klondike strike on the world-wide gold economy held it insignificant. It was dwarfed by the California strike in both size and production. The Klondike is said to have produced between 250 and 300 million dollars in gold.

California yielded over 500 million between 1848 and 1857 alone. On the Klondike River, gold was found in a twenty-five by thirty mile square. There was nothing on the entire north bank of the river, only the bottom fifth of the south bank held any treasure. The California gold fields stretched some two hundred miles long by sixty miles wide along the western slope of the Sierra Nevada.

I have not yet read the account that satisfactorily explains gold's great metamorphosis. Thousands of years ago it was discovered that this malleable substance was useful in fashioning adornments worn by primitive people. How this transformed into the Gold Standard of the twentieth century, which pegged the world's currencies directly to this natural element, is as fascinating as it is unfathomable. It is essentially worthless as an industrial metal; it is too soft, and so scarce that industrial uses are few. There are scarcer elements, yet gold reigns supreme.

So much of our culture is grounded in gold. Academy Award statues are gold. The highest Olympic medal is gold. We have Gold Medal Flour, Solid Gold Dancers, the Golden Globe Awards. Credit cards with higher limits are Gold Cards. Our vernacular includes "good as gold," and "we're golden." Old music is called "solid gold." Seniors enjoy their "golden years." We have gold diggers, golden opportunities, even advice drawn from the Bible admonishes that, "all that glitters is not gold." Traditionally people retire to a gold watch. There is a vernacular-by-association; things do or don't "pan out." You hit the "mother lode." One "strikes a vein." A current country song laments, "she got the gold, and I got the shaft." Gold is mentioned by the second page of the Bible.

Information on gold appears unexpectedly. On a flight from Toronto to Fredericton during my book tour across Canada, an elderly woman named Anna Gallagher sat next to me and struck up a conversation. "My father went to the Klondike," she told me, and pulled a necklace from under her blouse. "He gave me this." It was a gold nugget on a chain. On a flight to California I sat beside a well-dressed, polite, thirty-year-old man returning from a vacation in France. It was my 1,345th flight. Slumped in my seat, staring out the window, I avoided his attempts at conversation. The flight from Boston to LA is six hours long. I managed to elude the man for five of them, until pressed by a need to exhibit a modicum of civility, I asked him what he did for a living.

"I'm a geologist," David Orta replied, and I sat straight up.

"Tell me everything you know about gold."

"What do you want to know?"

"Everything, why it's found where it is, why it's so valuable. What it actually is—*everything*."

"Well, it was discovered in antiquity. Its original value is probably the sum of several inherent qualities. It is very malleable, hence useful in the fashioning of jewelry. It has a luster, a glitter, a color that is pleasing to the eye. It is scarce, a condition all societies have correlated with value, and yet accessible. It is inviolate in nature, you cannot tarnish it, burn it, destroy it in any way. It does not rust, nor does it react with any other element.

"Do you realize that all the gold ever found on this earth would fit into one container ship? I have a friend who is also a geologist, his theory is that the mother load is in Nevada. He has a pickup truck outfitted as a gold dredge. He won't tell me where he goes, but he's made some significant discoveries. Gold is an element, I won't bore you with the numbers and signs, but it takes an incredible amount of heat to form any element. Matter is neither created nor destroyed, except at intense heat. Every element on this earth was created in the sun.

"Gold has some qualities other elements do not have. It is extremely malleable. I've read that an ounce of gold can be stretched into a forty-mile-long piece of wiring. I don't know if that's exactly true, but it is an indication of its malleability. It is extremely dense and heavy, which is why it is relatively easy to find. And by that I mean if it were of some more ordinary density, it would never have collected in placer locations the way it does. See, gold is heavier than anything else on a mountain. When erosion carries away all the host material, the gold merely settles to the lowest common denominator. It seeks bedrock. It seeks the lowest cracks and folds of a river or stream. It is very hard for water to carry. It collects in identifiable locations. It is not only located in mountainous areas. It's simply that the mountains have created the opportunity for it to settle in quantity through the process of erosion. Gold is probably located everywhere." Our plane landed at LAX and I waved goodbye to David Orta, chastising myself for the nearly lost opportunity.

It is ironic that here in the Yukon, under the aurora borealis, was found this mass of gold. The chemical symbol for gold, Au, is from the Latin *aurora*, which means "shining dawn." Gold continues to dominate life in the Yukon. Of the team, John Flynn has supervised gold operations for years, Poncho Rudniski once worked for him. Roy Johnson worked for Viceroy, and Bruce Duffee, a heavy machinery operator, has worked in the mines. Budd Docken is a mine supervisor. Steve Craig has worked on Dave Millar's gold mine out on Hunker Creek, though the word "mine" is misleading. Today most Yukon gold mining is a process of shearing off top soil to expose the bedrock-hugging "pay steak," and separating what gold is found from remaining detritus. Millar came up to me one day in the bush and said, "Hey, you wanna see something?" He pulled a flat nugget from his pocket that must have been three inches long, and two inches wide.

"It's my gold card."

WHITEHORSE

Sunday, March 9

As I stroll into the Gold Rush Inn restaurant for breakfast, McRae rises from his table and frantically waves me over.

"You're a legend!" he gushes. "Last anyone heard of you, you were walking out of a Chinese restaurant at three A.M.! You're a fucken Yukon legend! What happened, you had it out with Millar!"

"I went straight to bed from the restaurant."

"What happened?"

I sheepishly tell McRae all that had occurred. I am not feeling like a Yukon legend, but an embarrassed, conflicted novelist from the south. I don't want to rock any boats, I want to get along with everyone. I'm conscious of Millar sitting nearby. When we finish breakfast, I make a point of stopping by his table and placing my hand on his shoulder as I joke with the others. I'm anxious to forgive and forget. Millar gives no indication of his thoughts.

Today's big event is the widely publicized road hockey game against the Whitehorse oldtimer hockey team. I arrive at the game concerned with the attention directed toward me. The morning's newspaper contained a block ad for the event, my name in bold print. A young woman comes up to me, a copy of *Dawson City Seven* in hand.

"I can't believe you're here!" she says. "My brother lives in Quebec, and he sent me his copy of your book when he heard of the reenactment of the trip and asked me to get all the players to autograph it. He won't believe you're here!" I sign her copy, but all I can think of is attracting too much attention, aggravating certain fellow travelers.

The game is well attended. Before it begins, a line of wild looking guys, some with long hair and beards, run onto the "ice" dressed in red union suits and skirts. They perform a can-can show. In a quintessential display of northern eccentricity, a tuba player appears and performs *O Canada*. A loudspeaker blares that Yukon M.P. Audrey McLaughlin is playing, along with Yukon Premier Piers McDonald and the author of *Dawson City Seven*, Don Reddick.

One of the rules is that if the ref blows his whistle at any time, all the players must immediately hug one another. I play, shuffling up and down the iced roadway, barely keeping my balance. I cause the crowd to groan when I spin and fire the ball—only to strike the special education teenager playing on the other side smack in the face. He shrugs it off, and we hug. Anderson feigns a fight with one of his buddies on the other team, and they fall to the ground grappling. Flynn plays it up as goaltender; after every save he turns to the crowd, raises his arms and jumps up and down. Little kids carry signs "Yea-hooray" and "Boo-hiss" around the crowd, getting everyone to chant the slogans when they raise them up. No one keeps score of the game. It is very cold and we are relieved when it ends, so we can put on our coats.

After the game there is a signing at the local book store for both myself and Yukon artist Chris Caldwell, who has drawn the official poster for the Dawson City Challenge of the Century. Inside the store

I ask Chris to sign my copy of *Dawson City Seven*, and she replies that she must sign it on a certain page.

"Here it is," she says, turning to the page in the novel where the Dawson team barges out onto the ice in Ottawa, the crowd going wild. "I've read this page a thousand times trying to visualize it, I used this page as a mental blueprint for the poster." She then inscribes, "Memorized & Visualized!!" along with a sketch of a sled dog's head. John Flynn leads an old man up to me, introduces me to Fred Cook. Cook says, "I knew Jim Johnstone in 1943." This is a remarkable moment; it is the first time I have met anyone, other than family members, who personally knew an original Dawson player.

I sell three books. When I stand with the owner at the end expecting to be paid for them, he suggests I take payment in the form of credit on other books. I pick out three books on Yukon history, then head for a saloon where the team has been promised a free drink. When I arrive, only Budd Docken is present. We receive our beer and sit at a wooden table, awaiting our teammates. When Docken rises to go to the men's room, he walks two steps then hesitates, turns back to me.

"Dangerous Don," he says, "can you watch that for a minute?" He points to a black bag that looks like an old-time house-calling doctor's bag, on the floor under the table.

"Sure, no problem." Other players filter in and line the bar. The Yukon has the characteristics of a small town laid out over a huge area. Everyone seems to know one another, and the tavern noise increases with the arrival of more teammates. Later, when we are leaving, I notice Docken reach down for his black bag.

"What's in the bag, anyway?" I ask.

"Oh, it's the $25,000 in gold for the game."

Jim Nicol agrees to drive me back to the Gold Rush Inn, but tells me he has to stop by Dale Kulych's house first. Once there, we find ourselves with Hogan, Anderson, Docken, John Flynn and his wife Jennifer and kids Melissa and J.J. We are all invited to stay for dinner, which proves a marvelous feast of chicken, hamburgers, perogies, and pasta salad. A huge meal we all gobble until we can eat no more.

Kulych displays none of his vitriol toward me as host with his wife present. When we lean back from the meal, Docken dumps the contents of his black bag onto a coffee table. Vials of gold, plastic zip-lock bags of gold, nuggets, dust, every conceivable size and shape of the element is spread before us. Most have little white notes stuck inside the packages, identifying both contributor and creek of origin. It is the prize for the game in Ottawa; the winner then to donate the gold to the two charities involved, the Heart Fund and Special Olympics.

I stare at the pile shining up at me. Gold is mesmerizing. I am nervous touching it, examining it. I am surprised by its actual color, uncertain whether I would recognize the element had I found it myself. I think of the miners who donated it, and realize one of the more selfless, admirable aspects of this whole adventure.

"We'd been playing hockey and Johnny took a puck in the face, we went to the nursing station," Pat Hogan tells me. "The next day I'm on a plane flying south on business, and he's on the same plane going down to get some medical attention, and we start shooting the shit talking about 1905 and John says, 'We can do that,' and I said 'Yeah, that's a great idea we should do that.' That was about '94 or '95, so we kinda pushed a little bit, but didn't push too hard, and didn't get very far. At one point Doc Parsons was going to Ottawa, and we gave him a nugget the size of your thumb. Give this to Bruce Firestone—the owner of the Ottawa Senators—tell him look, no strings attached, this is to show that we're earnest, that we'll raise a bunch of gold to put up as a prize, and have a non-profit hockey game with the Dawson City Nuggets recreating the 1905 hockey challenge. And he couldn't even get past the secretary, wouldn't even let him in the door.

"We wouldn't stop. We started bugging 'em and bugging 'em and bugging 'em. And we got Brad Marsh's name, and Marie Olney's name, and we kept bugging them. We got the support of the Yukon government. Audrey McLaughlin is our representative in our federal Parliament, and she is also the leader of the NDP, and she was on our side. We started getting people to say, 'Hey...' And we started talking to Audrey, and she said, 'That's a great idea!' Kevin went to see Piers McDonald, who is the leader of the Yukon Territorial government, and

Piers got all excited and said to his tourism minister, 'You gotta hear this!' We wanted twenty-five grand to hire Debra Belinsky of DCB, and he came through. And very soon after, we had a meeting in Whitehorse, and Marie Olney flew up for that. She is with the Ottawa Senators, she flew up, and that gave us the idea that they were in earnest.

"Olney was OK to deal with. There was some impediments, some roadblocks that she created as much as she paved the way through. She got involved in local politics to some extent. It was a bit tortuous wending our way through and saying, 'C'mon you guys, this is what we're going to do. We won't give up. We will persevere. There's no way you're gonna hear the last of us, until we do it.' And that's what really broke through, we won't take no for an answer. We said, 'Hey, we're doing it.'

"That was the general consensus, look, we're gonna do this thing. Kevin is a ball of energy, eh? I fed off his energy, for sure. He was really a great guy to have. Johnny's a really smart guy, he has a lot of wisdom. He has a very considered opinion. Another guy whose opinion was always worthwhile to listen to was Bob Sutherland. Bob Sutherland, you know sometimes he was pretty negative, but he was always very realistic.

"I can't say enough about Audrey McLaughlin and how she supported us. She liked the idea, she became instantly committed to the idea when she saw we were in earnest. And when we started showing them gold, they knew it was happening! I think I trotted out thirty or forty ounces of gold at the one meeting when we had representatives of the Ottawa Senators and Debra Belinsky and they could see it. When you look at the gold you can see it is one ounce, and two ounces, it is people who said, 'Yeah, I'll support this. I'm in.' It wasn't people who were rich. It was people who said OK I'll make a donation 'cuz I believe in this, and I believe in what you guys are doing. And they represent us. Johnny Flynn was in charge of getting the gold. John's a gold miner. And Dave Millar helped out a lot on that too, he's a gold miner as well. He served a term as a member of the legislative assembly, which is our territorial Parliament if you will, and had some connections as a miner as well. And people kicked in, Earl MacKenzie was a major sponsor, he'd sit in on some of the meetings, it was kind of open. We made up a list of people who might be interested here and across the territory and asked them, and different people followed up. Greg Hakonson helped us out a lot. He made up a shortfall, I think it was five or six ounces. He had already put in a couple ounces. We had a five-ounce medallion poured by Viceroy.

"One guy over in Mayo gave us a whole bunch of gold, too. He's going to Ottawa, too. I'm trying to remember his name, but I can't. He told a great story. He told a story about going through the ice on Mayo Lake. He said he'd done that before, he'd dropped his snow machine before, he'd dropped it through the water and remembered that you had to follow the bubbles up. But don't bail out until you're at the bottom, and he was over forty feet down when he left that Cat at the bottom, and he popped out and was lucky because he hit the hole in the ice. And he crawled out onto the ice. He had some great stories, he was an oldtimer. Guy from Mayo, from the Mayo area. Johnny, what was his name? But it was that meeting when we showed them all this gold, that things started to happen."

I stare at the mound of gold. I understand why the Ottawa representatives were impressed. The evening at the Kulych's winds down, the gold is packed up. When I return to the Gold Rush Inn this evening's variation of the Wild Bunch is preparing for another night out on the town. Respectfully declining their invitation, I go up to my room. And stay there.

CHAPTER TEN

"He that seeks trouble always finds it."

— English Proverb

"By God, trouble is what I'm looking for."

— Soapy Smith, July 8, 1898

Open any book on the history of the Klondike gold rush, and one is regaled with the legend of Jefferson Randolf "Soapy" Smith. Like many northern legends, the truth is both more complicated and docile than the oft-repeated mantra.

The quickest route into the Yukon interior was the last broached by white men. The Lynn Canal is a fiord reaching deep into the rugged coastline, at the end of which lie two ancient trails that became known as the Chilkoot and White Passes. These passes were closely guarded by Chilkat Indians, who provided a conduit between foreign traders and interior Athabascan tribes.

The Chilkat had conducted business with white men for generations. John Muir reported in his 1867 account that the Indians shook hands "Boston fashion," having learned it from whalers out of Nantucket, Massachusetts. Robert Campbell of the Hudson Bay Company reported that as early as 1851 white diseases had devastated the coastal Indian population. Close association with the French, English, and Russians is evidenced by the intricate language the natives had evolved. Coastal dialects were unusually rich, the largest sound inventories occurring in areas where bilingualism was most common.

The assimilation of European languages was accompanied by the development of an astute business sense among the Chilkat. They fully understood their position as guardians of the inland passages, and were hostile to those who threatened it. Mounting gold discoveries along the Alaskan panhandle, however, pressured the Indians' coveted position. That white men seemed more interested in chasing useless rocks than interfering with their fur trade, as well as the burgeoning business of guiding and packing, seems to have eased aboriginal fears. George Mercer Dawson records that the first white man allowed to cross from the coast into the Yukon interior was George Holt via Dyea Pass, as the Chilkoot Pass was then called, in 1878. A dribble of gold miners as well as a succession of Canadian and U.S. government sponsored expeditions soon followed, the most prominent headed by Dawson himself.

In 1887 the Canadian government directed Dawson to lead a three-pronged expedition into the Yukon wilderness. Dawson led one group via the Liard River in the Northwest Territories, crossing over the mountains into the Yukon basin. R. G. McConnell was entrusted with another that traveled up British Columbia's Stikine River and into the region, while the third group, led by surveyor William Ogilvie, crossed the Chilkoot Pass and descended the Yukon River. During his assessment of the Chilkoot Pass, Ogilvie heard of an alternate route which he sent Captain William Moore to investigate. Ogilvie named this route the White Pass, in recognition of the Honorable Thomas White, a former Minister of the Interior. This pass proved an easier though longer route into the interior, conducive to road or railway if either were to be deemed desirable.

Moore understood the implications of this discovery. He staked a town site at the end of the Lynn Canal, and named it Mooresville. The mounting influx of miners and their promising gold discoveries convinced many that a great strike was imminent. This notion attracted the more sophisticated who understood the infrastructure of a gold rush. The relatively recent California gold rush had taught many that greater fortunes were to be realized in supplying those frenzied in a rush, whether by providing goods, transportation, or information, than by the back-breaking labor of gold mining itself. When word of the great Klondike gold strike emerged from the wilderness in the spring of 1897, it appeared Moore's prescience would be greatly rewarded.

Frank Reid, a former county official from Oregon who had been acquitted of a murder charge there, was the leader of a group of surveyors who arrived in Mooresville on July 29, 1897. This group intended to plot a town site at the terminus of the water route to the Klondike. They promptly renamed Mooresville "Skagway," and began surveying house lots to be put up for sale. The new group was intent on swindling Mooresville from Moore; indeed Moore would be in court several years fighting to regain the profits from his stolen town.

As word of the great strike spread across the world in the summer of '97, the region braced for the inevitable onslaught. Tappan Adney described the scene in 1898: "As we steamed slowly into the little bay the white streak resolved itself into tents, a city of tents, stretched across a plain barely a quarter of a mile wide, level, and presenting a straight front to the harbor...I go ashore—and such a scene as meets the eye! It is simply bewildering, it is all so strange. There are great crowds of men rowing in boats to the beach, then clambering out in rubber boots and packing the stuff, and setting it down in little piles out of reach of the tide. Here are little groups of men resting with their outfits. Horses are tethered out singly and in groups. Tents there are of every size and kind, and men cooking over large sheet-iron stoves set up outside. Behind are more tents and men, and piles of merchandise and hay, bacon smoking, men loading bags and bales of hay upon horses and starting off, leading from one to three animals along a sort of lane in the direction of a grove of small cottonwoods, beyond which lies the trail towards White Pass. Everybody is on the move, excepting those just arrived, and each is intent upon his own business. There are said to be twenty-five hundred people along the road between the bay and the summit, who have come on the *Mexico, Willamette, Queen*, etc. There are not over one hundred tents at Skagway, and there may be five hundred persons actually in the town."

The inundation of adventurers turned the muddy streets of this tent town into a blast furnace of activity. Ships discharged huge amounts of goods upon the shoreline. Men crowded shops and saloons searching for information, assistance in crossing the pass, as well as other, less productive endeavors. Laying in wait for them was a battery of high-waymen under the control of Soapy Smith.

Smith was a thirty-eight-year-old from Georgia. He had married a woman in St. Louis and fathered six children before honing his noto-rious trade in the mining camps of the American west. He arrived in Skagway in October of 1897, quickly establishing himself as the leader of a group of men who creatively relieved gold seekers of their money. From shell games to outright thievery, the gang operated with Skagway's indifference, careful to assault only the transient, and not the local population.

In a letter to his wife written March 31, 1898 from Dyea at the foot of the Chilkoot Pass, novice gold seeker Alfred McMichael of Detroit gives testimony to the common experience: "I have not seen a drunken man since I came to town, but I struck two 'sure-thing' men today. I was coming up the sands from Skaguay when a gentleman strolled up to me and asked if I was 'going in.' I told him yes...we had talked a few minutes...when No. 2 came up and asked if either of us wanted to buy a dog. He had just come out from Dawson and wanted to sell his dog. Then he began telling No. 1 about his Dawson experience. We asked if he brought out any 'stuff.' He pulled out a great roll of bills from one pocket. It must have been two or three thousand. Then he pulled out a hand full of $20 gold pieces, then a bottle of gold dust from another pocket and said he has 'dropped' $1,800 in Dawson. No. 1 asked how he did it. He was ashamed to tell, he said, but it was by a little game. Said he paid up like a man and then told the fellow he would give $50 if he would show him how to do the trick.

"So it went on for a few minutes and soon he was showing No. 1 how the 'Black Jack' trick was done and they played 'just for fun.' Finally they got playing in earnest and No. 1 won five $40 gold pieces. He tried for fun again, and this time he lost. Then No. 1 wanted me to pick out the card, and as he had turned up the corner previously while

No. 2's back was turned for a minute, I had no difficulty in picking the right one, which he bet me $500 I could not do. Well, I picked 'Black Jack' all right and he counted $500 into my hands.

"This was the time for me to quit the game and go, but I did not. I said, 'Here old man, you two play this game. I don't want any more of it—nor your money.' So I handed back the $500 and walked away. No. 1 protested that I had won it fair and it was mine.

"It was worked pretty slick and would have taken lots of fellows in. For some time I did not suspect what was up. They had lots of money, which no doubt they had skinned out of some poor devils. These fellows are thick here and up the trail as well. Men are losing their money every day. The boat that came up behind us stopped at Wrangell and the sharpers took over $900 away from some of the boys. I did not hear of any of our boys being caught..."

Smith was a cunning operator. He gave back to the town, donating to various charities exorbitant sums of his ill-got gain. He wrote offering to raise a company of volunteer rough riders for the war effort against Spain, and used the returned refusal letter as proof that he was in contact with major officials in Washington. Shortly before his confrontation with Reid, Smith was offered the position of Marshall for the town of Skagway by the governor of Alaska Territory, which he declined. He was cited in the newspapers for his charity and goodwill toward the town. All was well in Soapy Smith's Skagway world, the pickings easy and his criminal activities tolerated under the aforementioned agreement. According to Judge James Wickersham in his book, *Old Yukon,* this arrangement was violated when Soapy's men began robbing those returning from the goldfields. As word spread of the lawlessness, successful argonauts began favoring the longer but safer route out of the Klondike via the Yukon River to St. Michael, thus bypassing Skagway. Once the implications of this was realized by local businessmen, their indifference ceased.

In the first days of July, a notice was posted stating that a meeting was planned to promote law and order in the town. It was signed "Committee of 101," also known as the Vigilantes. Smith allegedly posted his own notice, signed "Law and Order Committee 303," intimidating the group. But on July 7th an incident occurred which rendered the tenuous understanding between Smith and the local businessmen untenable.

A miner named Stewart, returning from Dawson City with a poke worth $2,700, was approached by Smith's cohorts and escorted into one of their saloons where he was quickly cheated out of his gold, and thrown back out onto the street. Stewart complained to the Vigilantes, who promptly held a meeting and agreed that Smith had gone too far. Smith was asked to return the unfortunate's poke, to which Smith replied that he would not, that the man had lost the gold fair and square.

A Vigilante meeting was announced for the evening of July 8th, to be held at the Sylvester dock warehouse on the town wharf. During the day Smith heard of the meeting, and began drinking heavily. He was quoted as stating, "By God, trouble is what I'm looking for." When the meeting was underway Smith, cradling a .45 caliber Winchester rifle, and several henchmen approached the dock and confronted four sentries, one of whom was Frank Reid. What happened next is unclear. With an appreciation that often the first observation is most accurate, I defer to the following day's newspaper account: "Smith approached Reid and three others guarding a meeting on the wharf, and when he raised his rifle Reid grabbed the barrel and pushed it down, when Smith pulled the trigger, wounding him in the groin. Reid fired three or four shots, hitting Smith in the heart and killing him instantly."

Both men were hit by second shots, both in the leg. Wickersham states that Smith's henchmen drew their weapons and advanced upon the guards, but were driven back by a man named Murphy, who had picked up Smith's Winchester. The gunfire alerted the men in the meeting and they then ran out onto the wharf, "calling as they came 'Get your guns, men and kill them!'"

The Vigilantes' reaction was swift and decisive. Determining that current Deputy Marshall Taylor "by his affiliation with the Smith crowd was not the proper man," they swore in J. M. Tanner as Deputy Marshall, as well as twenty-five others. All businesses were closed, all wharves guarded, while hundreds of local men—"most with

Winchesters"—patrolled the streets and sought out Smith's known associates. Men were sent to Lake Bennett to search for three men believed to be in possession of Stewart's poke, as well as to guard the surrounding passes to prevent any escapes.

The following day's newspaper ran banner headlines of the gun battle, and detailed the fallout. "Although there was not a single person in Skagway who appeared to do honor to the man who yesterday was a popular hero and is today but a dead highwayman...it gives one pause to know that Smith had just received a letter of photos of his wife and six children from St. Louis..." The article told of Reid's wounds. The first shot entered Reid "two inches above the groin on the right side and making its exit an inch to the right of the point of the spinal column. The ball made a compound comminuted fracture of the pelvic bone, several fragments of this were removed at the time of examination. It needs no words to tell the agonizing pain attending this operation. Mr. Reid showed the same Spartan coolness and endurance which he has exhibited since first struck by the rifle of 'Soapy Smith.' Before the doctors began the examination and operations he asked for a cigar which he calmly smoked while the shattered fragments of his anatomy were removed."

Smith's cohorts were quickly brought to justice. Top lieutenants were dealt with harshly. Turner Jackson received ten years in the Sitka penitentiary, George Wilder seven. Several gang members received from one to three years, while a full thirty-five others were deported to Seattle, where all were arrested upon debarkation.

This is the basis for the legend of Soapy Smith. Like many northern legends, his Skagway reign of terror is exaggerated. Smith landed in Skagway in October of '97, and was dead by the following July. The gold rush had barely begun before he was gone. Skagway's image as a town out of control is inaccurate, considering the number of men who came to the Vigilantes' assistance once the shooting began, and how quickly the problems were resolved.

More intriguing are the various and suspect motives before the altercation on the wharf. How could Smith, openly known to be a criminal, have been offered a marshalship by the governor of Alaska? Implicit in this offer is the understanding that it would have enabled Smith to entirely control the town, and yet he turned it down. Contemporary Skagway historians believe it was an attempt to remove Smith without a confrontation, assuming he would "go straight." And why would a populace who knew the man to be a criminal cite him for his good works for the town? Alas, the entire truth of the legend of Soapy Smith will probably never be known.

Frank Reid, a man caught in the wrong place at the wrong time, languished in agony for twelve days before succumbing to his wounds. Accused murderer, town site jumper, and now martyred hero, he was laid to rest a short distance from his notorious killer. Grateful Skagway citizens had inscribed upon his monument, "He gave his Life for the Honor of Skagway."

WHITEHORSE TO SKAGWAY

Monday, March 10

We mill about waiting to board the bus. CBC cameraman Brendan McEwen has asked me to accompany him on the three hour, one hundred twenty mile drive through the mountains to Skagway. When Hogan announces that we must team-up in twos in the ferry berths, McRae approaches and asks to room with me. I invite him to join me in McEwen's car.

"We'll miss the ferry, I know we'll miss the ferry if we drive. We can't miss the ferry."

"We won't miss the ferry."

"We'll miss the boat. I know we'll miss the gawdam boat."

Sure enough, twenty minutes into our ride, with McEwen chatting famously of his life in Canada after leaving his native England, I notice signs for Watson Lake. I frown, but say nothing. I assume the guy knows what he's doing, but when another sign indicating we're heading east appears, I mention that Watson Lake is in the opposite direction from Skagway. I see McEwen's face contort in sudden realization.

"We're going the wrong way!" he exclaims.

"We're gonna miss the boat, I knew it! We're gonna miss the gawdam boat!"

"We're not gonna miss the gawdam boat."

"I told you we were gonna miss the boat!"

We race as fast as Brendan dares toward the snow-covered height of land separating Alaska from the Yukon. We pass through the ancient aboriginal village of Caribou Crossing, now known as Carcross. Through vast fields of gloomy, white reaches barren of life we ride. The mountain scenery here turns spectacular, great snow-laden lakes snuggled within the cold folds of towering masses of earth reaching high into the clouds, white into white, over white. Now and then the cut of the White Pass and Yukon Railway is glimpsed on the mountainsides to our left. When we catch up to the bus at American customs, McRae and I decide to rejoin the team.

The bus turns and twists down the long sloping mountain road until it begins to level out. We glimpse the remains of a rotting gold dredge sinking into the Skagway River to our left, dwellings appear, and we finally roll onto the ice-encrusted gravel streets of an isolated, nearly deserted Skagway, Alaska.

The team is treated to a sandwich buffet by the local Chamber of Commerce. Afterward the guys head outside, with three hours to kill before the ferry departs. Some wander onto the pier, others along the refurbished frontier facades of Broad Street, but most trod the boardwalk to Moe's Frontier Bar, "Skagway's oldest operating Bar," on the corner of 5th Street, to take advantage of the free round offered to the Dawson City Nuggets hockey team. When told here that the ferry serves no alcohol, some quickly gulp their beer, then frantically seek out the local liquor store. I manage to collar Steve Halloran, Executive Director of the Skagway Convention and Visitors Bureau, and ask if he will escort me to the Skagway cemetery.

Skagway is a quintessential sub-arctic community, with its share of eccentricity and northern flavor. I had read in a guide book of the town's annual events, which include the Ducky Derby, where "1000 little plastic duckies pass through two culverts, under railroad tracks, always in danger of getting stuck along the way." They also hold a "chicken chuck," whatever that is, as well as an Ugly Animal Contest. We drive slowly through town, the seven block center of which has been designated the "Klondike Gold Rush National Historical Park-Skagway Historic District," featuring boardwalks and several restored buildings.

"Every July 8th we hold Soapy Smith's Wake, a dance at Eagles Hall," Halloran tells me. "We used to go to the cemetery to Smith's grave and drink and party there all night long, but, you know…grown-ups…political correctness…the powers-to-be toned things down when the tourism increased. Eagles Hall is the same building Soapy lived in, called the Mondamin Hotel at the time. Up behind the graves, there's Reid Falls."

We stop and walk into the cemetery, a disheveled, rocky hillside a stone's throw from the White Pass railway tracks and the gurgling waters of the Skagway River. We locate the famous graves of Reid and Smith. Ironically, it is Smith's that has remnants of roses scattered at the base of the newly painted wooden marker.

"The original stone was stolen long ago, and so many people steal these white markers we mass produce them," Halloran tells me.

I marvel at our society's penchant for the villain over the hero. Every July it is Soapy Smith's wake that is celebrated in Skagway, not Frank Reid's. We stand in the cool air, a full twenty degrees warmer than the land over the pass, and read the famous, "He Gave His Life for the Honor of Skagway," inscribed on Reid's obelisk-like monument.

As we leave I notice at the entrance to the cemetery a sign containing short synopses of some of the more interesting people interred within. One of them tells the story of a prostitute who had been strangled in the red-light district of Skagway. On her stone, in typical northern irreverence, is inscribed, "She gave her Honor for the Life of Skagway."

We board the ferry *Malaspina* and leave the Skagway pier at 4:00 P.M. Docken, Flynn, Kulych, Peterson, and I line the rail at the rear of the ship, leaning and waving in unison to the CBC camera below. Everyone is excited to finally be on the water. Despite a reprieve from the cold and toil of the trail in Whitehorse, the days there were filled with media, family, friends, and events. For the first time in ten days we now have a chance to wind down completely.

Most of the guys congregate in the observation room. It is a large, open room at the front of the ferry lined with rows of chairs, with floor-to-ceiling windows overlooking our slow, methodical progress. We arrive for a short stop in Haines two hours later. The boys are anticipating our arrival in Juneau at 11:30 this evening, where the Juneau Old Timers hockey club plans a barbecue in our honor on the wharf.

I sit with Bruce Duffee. We watch as our world morphs into a slow, steady progression through narrow, mountain-choked channels. We eat dinner with some teammates, and afterward attend a slide show on Denali Park. We both nod off to sleep at times and when it ends, decide to call it a night. I locate my cabin and find McRae sprawled across the bottom bunk fully clothed, and fast asleep. I climb into the top bunk and quickly fall asleep. I awake to a sense that the ferry is no longer moving, indicating our presence at Juneau. But nothing can entice me out of my bed and onto shore. I miss the shrimp, salmon, and champagne on the pier with the Juneau Old Timers. The next morning I hear that the Juneau police broke it up around 2:00 A.M.

CHAPTER ELEVEN

"Gazing from the deck of the steamer, one is borne smoothly over calm blue waters, through the midst of countless forest-clad islands...we seemed to float in true fairyland, each succeeding view seeming more and more beautiful, the one we chanced to have before us the most surprisingly beautiful of all. Never before this had I been embosomed in scenery so hopelessly beyond description... tracing shining ways through fiord and sound, past forests and waterfalls, islands and mountains and far azure headlands, it seems as surely we must at length reach the very paradise of poets, the abode of the blessed."

— JOHN MUIR, *TRAVELS IN ALASKA*, 1879

When I read the words above, I wonder how Muir wrote them. Was this a gift in the great man, an ability to translate easily and directly the wondrous surroundings? Or did he labor over them, writing and rewriting the words and sentences and paragraphs, carefully perfecting his prose? How does one write so well, describe so accurately? Is it an acquired skill, or a god-given blessing? I read and reread his description of this fairy tale land we bore through, braving a slight wind in cold air to lean on the railing and stare.

Muir's words intimidate me. I cannot fathom a stronger grasp of what an array of physical beauty such as this can do for a thoughtful soul. I do not want to even attempt to describe it better, more thoroughly than he already has. I stare as we slowly glide by islands and rivers, cloud-enshrouded ravines and valleys. I think of how I could describe it, what books I must scour to capture the ability of description, the cadence and rhythm of appreciation and wonder.

Walden, of course, and *A Sand County Almanac*. *The Outermost House*, by Henry Beston, the hand-written monuments of nature, of description, words somehow endowed with the magic quality of wisdom and knowledge strung together in a sequence so compelling, so irresistible, that you must follow them to the end, like a falling star in the hollow, cold night. How did these men do it, what was the day like when the idea first came to them, the day they sat down and faced empty pages and began filling them with a form of life that would endure long after their own? What is it in a man that truly creates a great writer, is it tragedy, or love, or hatred or fear or is it travel and experience and work and penance and loathing and responsibility or some mystical, or methodical melding of some, or all of these? Do you have to be different to describe things differently? Do you have to be lost to lose yourself so completely that you stare about in panic, desperate to escape, to relieve the great fears that impound your reason and pound your heart, until running, gasping for breath, you burst into the familiar, the found, having *written* yourself back to reality?

An unusual twist, an odd path of reason: I think of Irish music, of pipes haunting smoky Dublin pubs, how lonely and wistful the tin whistle sounds, how mesmerizing, the crowded faces all silent and staring in at one whose eyes are closed, his fingers roving, the simple ancient sound of thousand-year-old stone fences and fields, thatched-roofed cottages mired in a poverty-stricken countryside. Visions of big, bearded men hovering over a campfire in some lost valley, the storytellers in front, their hands waving and gesturing and pointing, their gap-toothed grins spinning tales of ten generations in the cool, hilly air. I wonder if I was one of them, because I feel I was. I wonder if I roamed the hills and valleys of England would I recognize my land, my valley, the place my European ancestors inhabited for a thousand generations before the world turned, and began to read and write. I wonder if I could smell it, or see it, somehow sense it in the wind, would I recognize the imprint, would I finally stand and stare, then drop to my haunches and realize *this was once mine...*

This scenery is so stunning that it stirs my imagination into these improbable, unrelated realms of thought. I think of Barry Lopez' masterpiece *Arctic Dreams,* the passages I dog-eared for their remarkable insight, his brilliant correlation of seemingly unrelated events, thoughts, and fact—and suddenly I am humbled before these men, these natural masters, and understand I cannot challenge Muir's vision, attempt to duplicate or expand. I realize I cannot describe this passage through these Alaskan waters ordinarily, in the traditional sense, but only through the thought it inspires in me. I marvel at it all, smile to myself, grab the railing hard and laugh out loud *it's happening*! I go inside to the restaurant to buy a cup of coffee, sit with others, and listen to their stories.

TO SITKA, AND PETERSBURG

Tuesday, March 11

"Work is an abomination on man's soul. I hate work, and the times in my life when I've had the least money were the best times of my life. We're not here to work, we're here to learn and have fun."

Steve Craig and I sit at a table against a wall in the observation room. It is just after dusk. Most of the others have wandered back to their rooms, preparing for dinner. But now Craig leans toward me, an earnest, intense man with long hair, wire-rimmed glasses, and a beard.

"If one does something he enjoys and gets paid, I don't call that work. When one does something he doesn't enjoy, to get paid, just to survive, then to me that is work and that idea I hate. I try to work to live, not live to work. Everyone thinks I'm a hippie, but I'm not. I don't drink much and I don't do drugs. I worked on a gold mine for a summer, and I never had more money in my entire life, but I was never more miserable. And I swore I'd never, *never* get caught up like that again.

"When I was twenty-one I took a year off University and began roaming. I spent sixteen months in New Zealand and Australia, which was the beginning of my lifestyle of work and travel and play. When I was sixteen I had an inspiration to harvest wheat in Saskatchewan. I don't know where it came from, but it was very strong. I had no connection to farming. I think I farmed wheat in southern Saskatchewan in a past life. From the first time I crossed into Saskatchewan it was like I was home and when I am there harvesting, it is like something that is a part of me or something I was meant to do. I did eleven harvests for the same people until 1996. Though I hate work, harvest isn't work in that sense. It is a lot of work, but I love doing it. What is it you wrote in your book, the part about the difference between a hobo, tramp, and a bum. I liked the idea he was a hobo—he was willing to work. I would be happy with that label. I travel and work to pay my way. I'm not a tramp or a bum.

"Hockey was my very reason for existence when I was a kid. Until I was twenty-one, it was the center of my life. Nothing and nobody came before hockey. I played Junior B in Victoria. I don't know the guys up here that well, I'm a defenseman. I wasn't initially chosen to go on this trip, I only got to go when Wes Peterson gave up his player spot to be the coach, just for me. Ever since I first heard about the idea of doing the 1905 trip, it was a dream for me. So I owe thanks beyond thanks to Wes.

"The biggest influence in my life was the deaths of three friends. The first was a teammate of mine, we were eighteen-years-old. It was a Junior B teammate. We had won the B.C. championship the previous year and had nearly the same team back. It was like a family. We were playing in the B.C.'s again, and during the first game of a best-of-three series my teammate felt quite sick. After the game he didn't go out drinking with us, which was most unusual. Later an ambulance came and took him to hospital for observation. About four or five A.M. a couple guys woke everybody up saying he had died. All I could think of was what a sick joke that was, but it was true. It turned out that Brent had had a heart attack during the game and then had another at hospital early in the morning. He had just turned twenty-one and was probably the strongest skater on the team. That was a huge thing for everyone.

"The second one was when I was about twenty-three in New

Zealand. I met this guy, also twenty-three and Canadian. He was cycling and we met four times while traveling. Then I read in the newspaper that he fell off a cliff while hiking. That blew me away because I had been in a situation the same day where I could have easily fallen off a cliff and had thought that if I did I would likely have died. I also felt then that it was crazy because I rarely felt as alive as when I was traveling, so to go all the way to New Zealand to die while being so alive was nuts. Now I think that's one of the best ways to die. But at the time it had a very large impact on me.

"The third I was about twenty-seven and it was another teammate from hockey since my very first practice and we also graduated from high school together. He had a brain aneurysm during a rec league hockey game. He was skating behind the net, he was dead before he hit the ice. These three deaths convinced me that life can end at any moment, and must be lived for the day. So I try to live in the now. All we have for sure is here and now. People say to me, you're almost forty-years-old, you have no career, you have no future, what are you going to do when you're sixty? Hell, how do they know I'll *be* here when I'm sixty?

"I'd never done, oh, more than twenty miles in a day and had never run more than eight dogs. Mostly I had run four, a few times six, and only a couple of times eight. For me to mush to Whitehorse was my own dream within the dream of coming to Ottawa. A week before we left I was introduced to Cowboy. I certainly knew who he was but had never been introduced. In the conversation, I said how I wanted to mush to Whitehorse. The next day I get a message to call Sandy Sippola. I did and she says Cowboy said I wanted to mush so she offers me ten dogs of hers and Larry's to run. Two times that week I ran ten dogs for about twenty-five miles and then I'm running ten dogs for four hundred-plus miles on the Yukon Quest trail over eight days. I had no idea how tough it would be, but I had a lot of help with Cowboy doing the dog food and Kevin, Gerard, and Wes doing the camp. I have never been so physically exhausted in my life. I pretty much fell asleep in the shower in Whitehorse.

"The day into Pelly Farm was the toughest. Over sixty-five miles and twelve hours with a couple of rests. We were told it was sixty miles for that day. We had a good long stop about mid-way, in the sun, with the other teams and several skidoo guys. Late in the day I stopped to help Gerard with his machine. The dogs didn't want to go after several warm miles, after Gerard left. So I gave them a break. Once the sun went down they came to life. We cruised into the darkness. I had a good idea of when sixty miles were done and there was no sign of camp. I started to wonder if I had missed it somehow or where it was. It was well into the evening and there I was, from Victoria, behind ten dogs on a sled in the middle of total Yukon wilderness, in the dark, thirty-something below zero, alone and feeling quite alone, wondering if I was lost.

"For a while I was a bit uncomfortable. But then I thought, here I am, from Victoria, behind ten dogs on a sled in the middle of total Yukon wilderness, in the dark, in the cold, as part of this incredible 1905 Stanley Cup Challenge re-creation, the only sound that of the dogs running, really cruising in the cold of the night, and the sled on the snow, a starry sky above. It became exhilarating. I gave my trust to the dogs to follow the right trail and reveled in the night travel. I had the dogs, had my sleeping bag. I wouldn't freeze to death. The trail went to Pelly Crossing, eventually. So I figured that I would be OK. After sixty-six miles and over twelve hours on the trail I saw headlamps and the dogs pulled me into camp.

"Learning each dog was an individual and how to deal with them was interesting. Some needed to be watched a lot to keep them pulling, others were low maintenance. On and off the runners, weight on one runner then the other, or ride them both or running behind and pushing to help the dogs or pumping. Rarely could I stand on the back and just look around like a tourist. The dogs would let you know if you weren't working, too. They turn and look at you as if to say, 'Hello. You want to help, too?' It really is a team and you may be the top dog but you are still a part of the team. If you take care of your dogs then they'll take care of you.

"The whole relationship with the dog team and the dogs individually is a big part of the attraction of mushing for me. This trip had an extra challenge for me in that I didn't know the dogs and they didn't know me. The other guys all knew their dogs. Both I and my dogs had to learn about each other as we went and that in itself was an interesting experience. After three or four days I felt I knew them pretty well, and by the end it was great to see them individually and have some understanding of their individuality. Probably the biggest thing for me was that I got them to Whitehorse in good health and that at the end of each day they were still ready to go. I find it interesting that mushing is a meeting of very individual people and dogs, who must come together and work as a very strong team, to make it happen. Mushing to Whitehorse as part of this whole Nugget journey was a dream realized for me. It was physically exhausting but one of the best experiences of my life. I would have liked to have kept going to Skagway by dog sled.

"It wasn't tougher than I imagined, because I didn't imagine. I had no idea. I was a novice recreational musher. When it was over people asked me, 'Are you going to do the Quest? Are you a professional musher now?' Are you kidding? My answer was that I was a novice musher before the trip and now I was a much better novice musher. That's how I feel.

"With Larry, he was definitely intimidating. He is the Cowboy. And I had some of his dogs and was on a pretty large learning curve. But I was looking to learn. On the trip I didn't see much of him apart from arriving at night and hooking up in the morning. And there was the hippie thing. The morning after we got to Whitehorse I was walking through the hotel dining room for breakfast and Chester Kelly was standing with Cowboy. Chester asked me how I did, and Cowboy says, 'Not bad for a hippie.'"

Steve Craig leans back and smiles.

"I was pretty happy with that."

Back in our cabin, McRae is irritated. He paces back and forth in the three-step confinement between the bunk beds and the sink, his hands clasped behind his back. He has also spoken with Craig. I sense my willingness to accept Craig's unconventional views originates in my being a son of the sixties, where McRae is definitely a son of the fifties. Craig speaks with so much conviction, he's a strong-willed individual and you respect him because he's sincere and intelligent and likable. But his philosophy McRae cannot accept.

"How can you live that way?" McRae rants, now waving his hands, pulling his words from the air. "It's unreasonable. You can't do it—what if you have a family? Most of us normal people have families, we have to work. Most of us *normal* people. Jesus Christ… I can't wait to get home. Deal with these guys on my own turf. You know what I mean? I felt so stupid in the bush. Like a little kid who has to have his skates tied for him. Jesus *Christ*…"

McRae's had a long day. He's as exhausted as the rest of us, but still must produce his column for the *Ottawa Sun*. Even I lean on him; this morning I've already eaten but sit with him in the dining room. I stare at his breakfast.

"Hey Earl, are you gonna eat all that? Are you gonna eat all your sausage?" He moves his plate away from me.

"Hey Earl, are you gonna eat all your salt?"

"Get the hell out of here."

"Hey Earl, are you gonna eat all the onions in your potatoes?" McRae stops and stares at me, then resumes eating.

"Hey Earl, are you gonna eat all your yolks?"

"Jesus fucken Christ, *here*!" he yells, and throws a sausage off my chest.

During the afternoon there is heavy drinking in Hogan's berth, though he is not partaking. There is the Wild Bunch, and Earl MacKenzie. Doc Parsons shows everyone a bizarre, seven-diamond studded ring that he says was a gift from a Dawson patient of his, shortly before the man committed suicide. He says it's estimated to be worth $50,000.

"Hey Doc," I ask, "isn't that one of the recognized warning signs of suicide, to give away your most prized possessions?"

"It's what first interested me in medicinal psychology," he admits.

I leave them to monitor our progress in the observation room. I sit next to a young woman named Eileen. When I mention Parson's ring, she tells me of strange happenings in the Aleutian Islands, where herds of walrus are apparently committing suicide by jumping off cliffs. I mention an incident recounted in Adney's book, where a man told of witnessing a horse intentionally walking off a cliff on the Dead Horse Pass. Eileen is moving lock, stock, and barrel out of Alaska, and heading for Seattle. She is relocating, she tells me, to improve her social life.

"But doesn't Alaska have the best ratio of men to women in the entire country?"

"When it comes to the ratio of men to women in Alaska," she replies, "the odds are good, but the goods are odd."

Eileen's best story: "I used to live in Sitka, which is dominated by Mount Edgecumbe, a big, extinct, Fuji-like volcano. On April Fool's Day some millionaire hired a helicopter, and just before dawn flew up a couple barrels of oil and dumped it in the volcano and lit it on fire. So everyone in Sitka wakes up to an active volcano..."

We dock in Petersburg, and get a chance to walk the streets. Several of the fellows are attempting to stay in a modicum of shape for our game in Ottawa, and, led by John Flynn and Chester Kelly, take off jogging. I stroll the town with one who is becoming one of my better friends on the team.

Bruce Duffee is about fifty years old and acquiring that gnarled, driftwood look of the true outdoorsman. He has blue eyes, receding sandy hair, and glasses. Meticulous in his approach to everything, with thirty years in the Yukon he seems to have determined that there is only one way to do anything—his way. This has led many to roll their eyes. He admits he's "a pain in the ass," and has been described by others as "a mother hen," and "steady Eddy." But all acknowledge he knows what he's doing in the bush. The man harbors great grudges and resentments. He proclaims a strong belief in a Protestant work ethic.

"I have no use for doctors or lawyers," Duffee says to me as we walk. "This caused a great argument with my wife. There's nothing to a doctor, he works four hours a day and has something to fall back on. A farmer, a gold miner out here, he puts everything on the line, and usually with an eighth-grade education. I admire guys who have mastered the bush. Jack Smith is a good example, an eighth-grade education, and he can do anything. He's not a stupid man. He guides, has horses, farms, there's always an emergency at his place in Mayo, a horse sick or machinery to fix. I respect anyone who can do something really well."

Duffee tells me of his arrival in the Yukon.

"In the spring of 1970 I found myself unemployed in the springtime and took off hitchhiking up through central B.C. and ended up in Dawson Creek. Spent a little while and heard about the barges that operate out of Ft. Nelson. I was curious about hitchhiking up there and seeing what the barges were like. I couldn't imagine barges on rivers. I'd never seen anything like that before. So I started hitchhiking north and an old Alaskan prospector picked me up in an old van, and this guy started telling stories. Story after story after story, and after we got to Ft. Nelson, he suggested I go farther north. So I figured sure, why not.

"So I traveled, and when we got to Watson Lake he suggested I get a job in Cassiar, the mine in Cassiar, but when we got to Watson Lake he said, 'Well, you know, since you got this far, you ought to see Dawson City.' I didn't know where the Yukon was. I had no idea, I was pretty ignorant of my own geography. Got to Watson Lake and turned north on the Campbell Highway which bypasses Whitehorse. But the stories got richer and more interesting, and I traveled to Dawson City with him. To be honest, I didn't know where Dawson City was. In Dawson he said, 'Well why don't you come over to Fairbanks?' But at that point I thought I was almost out of my range, and decided to stay put.

"I had intended to turn around and head south again. But as I turned south I stopped between Carmacks and Faro where there's a highway lodge on a lake called Little Salmon Lake. Beautiful, beautiful lake. I got waylaid by an old Austrian lodge owner, and he was a crook amongst crooks and I found myself working for him for five dollars a day and my room and board. This old Austrian, Tony Fritz is his name, one of the most colorful people that's ever been in the North. Said he'd pay me five dollars a day plus my room and board, and I worked there for thirty-five days before I asked him for money. And he brought out his little account book and he said, 'Wal, there war a few days dere'— I can't remember, there was eight or ten days there where I worked over twelve hours a day. If I worked over twelve hours a day I got five dollars. If I worked under twelve hours a day I just got the room and board. As it turned out I never got paid anything, so it was a moot point. And so by that time I moved on, and there was a mine in Faro to the east, and I went there to work.

"I hung around in Dawson with that Alaskan prospector for three weeks I guess, something like that. I had turned around headed south back to country I knew, but I never made it. So I worked in the mine, and then I went down south as far as Panama, and spent the winter in Panama. And that's basically how I came to the Yukon."

I open up to Duffee, tell him it seems as though some of the players are becoming rather cool toward me. He etches the familiar, edge-turned-up grin on his face and says, "Some of them didn't like you grabbing the women in Carmacks."

Grabbing the women! *Grabbing the women?*

"I didn't grab any women!" I protest. "We were just dancing, for chrissakes. I didn't do *anything!*" Duffee shrugs, as if he doesn't quite believe me, nor cares one way or the other.

But now, as I walk along the street with Duffee, I unload my frustration. I repeat in detail the insults of Millar, the challenge by Kulych, and the argument with Millar in Whitehorse. I tell him my problem is I'm essentially a nice guy and want to be friends with everyone. Duffee silently takes it all in, the corner of his mouth turning up in that wry smile of his. When I finish my tirade by repeating Kulych's, "I'm gonna get you, *I'm gonna be your worst fucking nightmare,*" he turns to me.

"The consensus is you're a bit sensitive," he says.

CHAPTER TWELVE

"We are very tired, but we are on schedule."

— Dr. Randy McLennan, on the
Dawson team's arrival at Whitehorse

There is no known written account of the original Dawson odyssey. What we know today can only be pieced together from newspaper reports of the day.[13] The dog sleds and bicycles followed the Overland Trail, which had been completed in 1902 between Dawson and Whitehorse. This road followed not the Yukon River, but a more direct route, cutting a full seventy miles from the journey. Tri-weekly horse-drawn carriage or sleigh service, depending upon the season, traveled the line.

Along this route were fourteen roadhouses, spaced roughly twenty-four miles apart. The first report from the wilderness was from Albert Forrest advising of his arrival at Yukon Crossing on the 26th. As this was his eighth day on the trail, and Yukon Crossing was the eighth roadhouse and approximately one hundred eighty-five miles south of Dawson, it is probable that the team stayed at these inns. It indicates an average of twenty-three miles a day, corresponding closely to the average distance between roadhouses. The next

---

13 Historians must evaluate these newspaper reports carefully. Referring sometimes to the team as "wanderers," the Dawson Daily News of Feb. 13, 1905, a month after the Ottawa Cup games and five days after the Klondikers played the Montreal Montagnards, ran banner headlines: KLONDIKERS AGAIN BEATEN BY 4 TO 2. A description of a game never played followed. They had mistaken Ottawa's 4–2 victory over the Montreal Wanderers for an Ottawa–Dawson rematch.

day Forrest reported back to Dawson that his bicycle broke down at Yukon Crossing, and that he planned on boarding a carriage for the remainder of the trip into Whitehorse. That he mentioned only himself suggests that team members were strung out along the Overland Trail. As newspapers reported that the team arrived in Whitehorse on Thursday, December 29th, and the following news article mentions a "coach sleigh," it is possible that all the argonauts abandoned their bicycles and dog sleds at some point, made arrangements for their delivery back to Dawson, and crowded one of the scheduled carriages.

The *Yukon World*, in an article dated January 20, 1905 advances a ludicrous view of their journey, allegedly related by one of the players:

> "HOW THEY MUSHED IT.
> Told By One Of Them
> Life On The Overland Trail In The Snow
> As Told By Dawson Boys"

"The men started out on their record-breaking journey with the idea of keeping in the finest possible physical condition, for hockey, be it known, is rougher than football or lacrosse, and is no game for children or girls. With that idea in view, these men left Dawson to walk to Whitehorse, 400 miles distant.

"They had with them a big coach sleigh, on which was piled their baggage, but the men walked and ran alongside and behind the horses. These hardy northerners rolled and tumbled in the snow like kittens at play all along the long journey, stopping occasionally for a snowball battle. If they failed to reach a roadhouse at night, they slept in the sleigh, so that the tramp was one long picnic for them."

This cannot be accurate. Lacking any first-person account, we do have evidence of a harsher truth. When the team arrived in Whitehorse, newly elected Captain Randy McLennan wired Dawson that, "We are very tired, but we are on schedule." The *Ottawa Citizen* in its reporting after the first game stated, "One of the Dawson players said he felt as though he had walked forty miles in his dreams."

A poem published by the *Yukon Sun* on January 22, 1905 begins:
"Seven brave Klondike boys
Started for the Cup
They traveled many a weary mile
Till they were 'most done up"

Another hint lies in *The Whitehorse Star*'s account of the team's return in April: "The boys are all returning in fine health…they will start tomorrow morning on foot to cover the 320 miles that lie exposed to the climate to Dawson. They walked out from Dawson in December and…will take chances on 'that tired feeling' and reel off the distance one step at a time."

The team was certainly tired, but did not remain on schedule for long. Immediately after arriving in Whitehorse, a snowstorm shut down the narrow-gauge railway to Skagway with as many as seventeen snow slides. McLennan wired the Captain of the steamship *Amur* to wait for them, but upon arrival on the coast they found that the ship had departed. The wanderers then arranged berths on the steamer *Romano*, further complicating their timetable because this would deliver them not to Vancouver, but Seattle. Weary, anxious, and now seriously in danger of arriving in Ottawa too late to play the first game, the Dawson hockeyists could do little more than board their ship and slowly descend the inside passage.

Information on early Dawson hockey is contained in a document in the Yukon Archives written by Emil Forrest, younger brother of goalie Albert Forrest. It is undated, but written after 1941, for in it he mentions not the Great War, but World War One. It is included here only slightly edited, and we will forgive Emil for never meeting a comma he did not like, or a paragraph he did. It illuminates not only Dawson's formative hockey years, but the milieu of the gold rush as well.

Emil Forrest: "The big news of the fabulous gold find in the Klondike came to Grass Valley Calif. where my dad was Foreman at a small gold mine on the edge of town. The main topics in the news at the time was the McKinley–W. J. Bryan campaign over the Silver Issue, the blowing up of the U.S. battleship Maine in Havana harbor and the recent panic of 1897. So with the reports of gold by the ton or in lesser quantities, according to your luck, by the sack or bucket full, dad couldn't get started quick enough with a bundle of sacks to try his luck, he joined the rush out of San Francisco, mother, sister and I left for the east, Three Rivers P. Q. where my two brothers, Paul and Albert were in school, to await the bullion by the sack full as we fully expected to be shipping out to us, however, no bullion arrived but dad did well enough to come east for the winter, and returned in the spring of '99 with brother Paul, Paul in relating his experiences said dad had a sled and two dogs, he was the wheel dog, while at school in the east, naturally I learnt to skate, mother, Albert and I joined dad and Paul at Dawson in July 1901, that fall as soon as there was enough ice to skate on I found I could lord it over the kids in town as few of them had learnt to skate, most or all had come from the coast cities, Seattle, Tacoma, Portland, and San Francisco and were just beginning to learn. Among the grownup specially the government and Bank employees the town supported three hockey teams and a lot of enthusiasm, the fall of 1901 saw four open rinks set up on the river ice, the Mamoth, out in the middle of the river surrounded by a circular canvass wall and tents for dressing rooms, N. C. Co. rink in front of the N. C. block, the Civil Service rink built on shore ice surrounded by a wooden fence and benches for the hockey games but when the water dropped, the ice settled uneven, in fact four feet high on the shore side A D was useless, the fourth was a free rink maintained at the foot of George Street by the Standard Oil Co. dubbed the Tin Can Rink for beginners, all games and practices for three teams, N. C. Civil Service and Town were held on the N. C. Rink, as I was a pretty good skater, I was the only kid allowed on the ice during the practices, mostly with the N. C. Team.

"As the open air rinks were not a success, owing to cold, wind and snow, the Dawson Amateur Athletic Association was formed the summer of 1902, by fall the D.A.A.A., a three story 100 by 40 ft. club house with a then amateur regulation hockey rink and two sheet curling rink, then the first enclosed hockey and curling rinks west of Winnipeg, Cyclone Taylor and the Vancouver covered hockey and curling rink (1920) not withstanding. Unfortunately for Dawson, the club house, the gymnasium used as a movie theater was destroyed by

fire, however the rink was saved and is still used. The opening of the
D.A.A.A. stimulated the interest in hockey with four teams, skating
with a band in attendance, with steam heated dressing room for ladies
and gents, a well appointed lounge room, not to mention the private
club upstairs with a modern bar, where the post mortem arguments of
the curlers could be settled over a wee Dock an Doris. The D.A.A.A.
was the center of attraction, with hockey, skating, carnivals with costume skating parties, and sports festivals, races of all kinds, 3, 2 &1
mile speed, backwards, three legged, wheel barrow, egg, potato, snow
shoe, arm in arm ladies & gents a novelty Chillcoot Pass & Turkey race
which consisted of several turkeys hanging to be located blindfolded,
after the blindfolds were applied several other obstacles as old shoes
and stuff socks were dropped to add the amusement, needless to say
with 20,000 people to draw from, sometimes standing room was at
a premium, the first sports festival being held without any previous
records, and the Forrest boys eligible to enter most events, I quote from
a clipping, 'In all of the contests the brothers Forrest, Paul, Albert &
Emil seem to be the favorites' 'One of the prizes one that was keenly
struggled for, was a box of apples, it was won by Albert Forrest, it is
an odd coincidence that four different years on sports night, one of
the prizes was a box of apples, and on every one these four occasions
Albert Forrest has been the winner.' He won the first speed skating
race and retained that honor winning cups and medals up to the time
he left the Yukon in 1908.[14] Having won prizes in most of the events,
we did glean some worthwhile souvenirs, engraved gold medals, nugget
chains and fobs, with an organized club and an arena, the management
found itself in the usual position of community centers, 'with apolo-
gies to our Civic Center,' the headaches to make ends meet financially,
in order to alleviate these growing pains, prize fighters were imported

---

14 Race results printed in the *Dawson Daily News* give an opportunity to evaluate
the Klondike skaters. In *Skating*, by George A. Meagher, 1900, is stated: "First Class,
or Highest Badge shall be awarded to any skater who shall skate a mile with not less
than three turns in 3 minutes and 30 seconds." Albert Forrest won the one mile race
in 3 minutes, 44 seconds. The world record at the time for the one mile was 2:36, by
J. Nilsson, 1895.

for bouts with the local middle heavy weight, Nick Burley, three fights were staged one each year, with Joe Cohinske (1903 colored) Tommy Burns (1904), and Philadelphia Jack O'Brien (1905), these were great drawing cards and created much local interest, and was well covered in the sports sections of the outside papers, accompanied with pictures of the visitors being handed their earnings in the form of a shining engraved gold brick. The crowning event of the early sports, 1905, was the effort to make the Yukon a permanent home for the Stanley Cup, the fall of 1904 the late Col. J. W. Boyle of Yukon and World War One fame undertook to manage and help finance the local team for the purpose, with exhibition games as well as dances, funds were raised to deter expenses, brother Albert was chosen as goalie and won the distinction of being the youngest player ever to compete in a Stanley Cup game, age 18, yours truly brother Emil played goal for the local exhibition games, quite young to be playing with men who expected to return with the Stanley Cup age 16, when the boys got back, without the Cup of course, which is another story."

I have the opportunity on the ferry to contrast Dawson's formative hockey days with its more recent. I am surprised to learn the original rink has been used by many here in their youth.

"I didn't start skating till peewee age," John Flynn tells me. "They had the original rink with a wooden balcony and galvanized tin for the sides. We used to watch hockey through the cracks in the wall. My cousin Joe Mason first took me down to the rink. Never been on skates before I was twelve.

"It was a big league, peewee, midgets division sponsored by companies around town. Joe was already a skater. Actually I was a goaltender, because I couldn't skate. And went from there to defenseman, and once I found I could skate I moved to center. Played senior hockey, we played some really tough hockey out in the mining camps. Faro, Elsa, and Clinton Creek. Those camps had some pretty nasty guys playing hockey. Back then they had a great rivalry, and if you could play hockey you could get a job anywhere. Every other game was bench-clearing brawls, any age from sixteen to forty. Late sixties. My nose was broken five times. In a game against Clinton Creek I fractured my wrist. I caught a blind pass at center ice and a defenseman lined me up and nailed me. Well, the only doctor in Clinton Creek was playing on the other side and wouldn't leave the game to see me. This was the first period, he got into a fight in the third period and got kicked out of the game, and it was only then he came to see me.

"Joe Mason played, Fred Farr, Chester Kelly now and then, Chuckie Barber. Chuckie was a ferocious player. Saw him throw a check one time, I think against Clinton Creek, he left his feet in the faceoff circle and elbowed a guy on the boards!

"I had a chance to try out with the Edmonton Oilers of the old WHA, I paid my own way to hockey school and won the best forward award. They asked me to come back and teach, but you know, I was young and into partying…no regrets. No regrets.

"The Generals were sponsored by the General Store. There are guys still talking about playing for the Generals, they have an alumni. Whenever we traveled we traveled as the Dawson Generals. Even now we'll go as the Generals. In later years Gerard Parsons, Wes Peterson, Mike Fraser, Kevin Anderson, Troy and Pat would travel to Alaska, we played a tournament in Fairbanks once. We made it to the finals, we played and won a game, we had to wait for another game to play their winner, and I think we drank ten cases of beer before the second game. We had these guys who couldn't even tie their skates! We had guys who put the beer cases on their heads when they went on the ice. It was a close game, I scored the tying goal, assisted on the winner by Mike Fraser. Four or five of us didn't drink—I didn't drink—but we won the game.

"Those games in Elsa, it was an outside rink. They had lights swung across, if you shot at goal from far away the goalie couldn't see it. Poncho, happened to him one night. You sat in a snow bank for the penalty box. It would be twenty below, fifteen below.

"We were playing an oldtimers game, and Wes Peterson high-sticked me and broke my nose. Next day they flew me out of Dawson to Whitehorse in a plane and I was sitting right next to Pat Hogan. Same flight. Things always happen for a reason. If I hadn't broke my nose, we'd never have done it. I probably said let's reenact this trip, the original Dawson Stanley Cup trip. We'd talked about it before, but we didn't know how to do it. I suggested we follow the Quest trail, just after they run it because then it's all marked. And it lit a fire in Pat, you could see it in his eyes. You know how people get that look when they're excited. Then he got it in his head, and he just worked it. He never gave up, he had every reason to say the hell with it, he was ruthless, wouldn't take no for an answer from anybody. And the rest is history."

TO WRANGELL, AND KETCHIKAN

Wednesday, March 12

The team descends into a dreamlike state on the ferry. The exhaustion, the bitter cold, the whirl of activity in Whitehorse all seem distant, as though we wonder if any of it actually occurred. There is nothing but time here. I am asked to compare our current journey with the original, but other than weariness upon our Whitehorse arrival, I see few similarities. Dawson City has changed, as has Whitehorse. Our mode of transportation has changed, though we traveled virtually the same trail. We bus into Skagway, and do not take the narrow-gauge train. But here, in our slow motion odyssey through the inside passage, I sense for the first time a complete and utter bond with the original voyagers.

Nothing has changed out here. The long, thin arm of water leaving Skagway, snug between towering, snow-capped peaks, is exactly as it was at the turn of the century. I lean against the rail and marvel at the scene, and again experience a sudden flash of thought: It's happening! We tend to lose ourselves in the day-to-day struggle through the mountains, in repeated interviews, day after day uttering word-for-word the same sentiments for the press, by rote. We get lost in so much detail, yet suddenly, after so much time, so much work and preparation—and several of the guys have mentioned this to me—you realize, *it's happening!*

And what is happening is so much larger than life, so exciting it is difficult to put into perspective. I've always wanted to travel the inside passage, to travel across Canada on a train. I'd never even dreamed of eight days through the Yukon wilderness. To be doing it all in context of re-creating the greatest hockey legend of all time is a wild honor. We line the rail, pointing, laughing, fully appreciating an experience so unusual, so exceptional, a marvelous, short-lived existence for a bunch of guys unused to the limelight. Everything we do, everything we say, everywhere we travel, is heard on the radio, seen on TV, and written about in the papers. We stop at Ketchikan and disembark to waiting TV camera crews. John Flynn and Kevin Anderson are immediately approached by a local blonde newscaster.

"Nothing against Marsh," Anderson says into the woman's microphone, camera rolling. "He's a nice guy, but I can't wait to go at him. I have Marshmares at night just thinking about what I'm gonna do to that big, overweight marshmallow with a capital M. Marsh is the right name for him, because that's where he's gonna wind up. In some marsh. He looks like he needs about three months of hard labor in the Yukon to get back in shape. Except Yukon labor would probably kill him."

Flynn is interviewed, returns to the throng of Nugget onlookers, leans close and whispers, "Too much makeup."

McRae needs to find the local newspaper office. He knows from experience he'll be allowed, as a fellow journalist, to use their fax machine to relay his latest column to Ottawa. We make our way uphill through winding streets, finally locating the offices of the *Ketchikan Daily News.* We talk up our trip to the staff inside, and sports editor Richard Larson arranges to meet us in a local tavern for an interview. I wander outside while McRae faxes his article. When he appears back outside he pulls up his collar to the damp, cool air.

"What's the matter with you?" he asks. He pulls a cigarette from his pocket and sticks it in his mouth, cups his hand around a match to light it. I look out over the distant waterfront without answering. The truth is that despite all the excitement, there is something wrong. There is so much behind the scenes, so much untold and untellable, so many losses and faults and omissions, the things men leave behind in ordinary conversation, but which permeate every word they utter. I know Freddy Farr has no money, and carries the eternal burden of his brother's death with him wherever he goes. I would discover that as a teenager Doc

Parsons suffered the loss of his closest brother to a brain tumor, and that he never told this to a soul in Dawson. Dave Millar's triplets are all sick, and none of us would appreciate the degree of difficulty Margo and Kevin Anderson were enduring in their marriage until the trip was finally over. I know the guy standing next to me on this Ketchikan street once dedicated a book to a woman who is no longer his wife. I shrug, unable to shake my reticence. But I want to, because there is an honesty to it, a necessary catharsis, and I stare down at my boots.

"I've got problems at home," I say. Earl blows out some smoke and looks away, out over the waterfront. With his scraggly beard, his wounded nose, a cigarette dangling from his lip and pulled-up collar, he is the image of experience itself, grimly nodding his head.

"I've been there."

"No, not that," I say, and Earl looks at me. "It's my youngest daughter. I almost didn't make this trip. I spent the whole day before I left getting her out of a psychiatric hospital. The Commonwealth of Massachusetts remanded her without my consent. Terrible scene in the hospital when I realized what they were doing. Deemed her a threat to herself. Worst thing I've ever been through."

"Jesus…"

We stood in the cold, two fish out of water, two silent friends.

"Is she all right?"

"I don't know," I shrug. "We got her out the day before I flew up. I never knew the state could do that, just take them like that." Earl listens, his entire demeanor a gargoyle of concern. And that's all I ever said about it on the trip, and all I'll say about it now.

CHAPTER THIRTEEN

"I wouldn't write about myself so much if there were anyone else I knew as well."

— HENRY DAVID THOREAU,
WALDEN, OR LIFE IN THE WOODS, 1854

Norwood, Massachusetts is a town of thirty thousand people located fifteen miles southwest of Boston. It is an Irish enclave, many of its residents descendant from County Cork immigrants. Despite its proximity to The Hub of the Universe, growing up in Norwood in the late fifties and early sixties was very much a rural experience. There were no video games to play, no malls to cruise, and precious little TV. Saturday morning was a structured time of *The Three Stooges, Cinema Seven,* and then out the door to argue endless games of baseball in the "first field" during the summer, or play street hockey during the winter. I can still see the faces of Crestwood Circle, Dickie and Kevin Donovan, Kenny and Neil Higgins, the Sortevic and Maloney brothers, Bobby Connor, Dave Early and my big brothers Ken and Gordie Reddick, as well as the tough Hebner brothers, Richie and Dennis, from around the corner on Nahatan Street.

In 1960 I remember everyone excited with a visitor to my next door neighbor, Mrs. Terrangio. Her cousin was in town, and I stood in line in Mrs. Terrangio's kitchen as we all got his autograph. When I received mine I looked down and read, "Jim Kaat." I recall following these same kids one evening to the Higgins' home, where we crowded a basement window and peeked in at Mr. Higgins at his work bench.

Mr. Higgins was a plumber and his youngest son Neil a goalie, and, dismayed with the exorbitant cost as well as poor quality of the masks he had to buy, Mr. Higgins had decided to mold his own with plaster. These masks turned out so well that he eventually supplied the first molded masks ever used in the NHL. The Crestwood Circle gang was then astounded to witness the arrival of the likes of Jacques Plante, Cesar Maniago, Eddie Johnston, and Jerry Cheevers at the Higgins household, to be fitted with their new masks.

As the sixties progressed, Richie Hebner became a hockey legend. Hebner went on to play seventeen seasons of major league baseball, but when he was a Nahatan Street kid in Norwood he was best known for his hockey talent. At a time when Boston's Tommy Williams was the only American playing in the NHL, Richie was offered a contract by the Boston Bruins which he, in retrospect, sensibly declined. I delivered the *Patriot Ledger* to the Hebner household, and one day during Richie's rookie season encountered Mr. Hebner swearing, leaning over the engine of his car.

"Hey Mr. Hebner," I said, "that's somethin' about Richie, isn't it?"

"Ahh, *fuggit*" he spit out, dismissing the thought with a wave of a blackened hand. "He could have played with Bobby Orr..."

The first time I ever entered Boston Garden was in 1965 to see Richie Hebner's team lose the Massachusetts State Final game, 1–0 to Walpole. Two years later, with my brother Ken the leading scorer,[15] I again visited the Garden to watch Norwood lose the State Finals, this time to Arlington High School, 2–1. In 1968 Norwood again made the Finals, but despite the play of Norwood's new all-time leading scorer Dick Donovan and two goals in the last minute of play to tie the game by his wing Dennis Hebner, Arlington scored in overtime

---

15 In 1967 when Norwood's first line of Reddick, Oberlander, and Graham faced off against Framingham South's Kimball, Anderson, and Dowd, I was not the only younger sibling harboring literary aspirations in the crowd. Across the arena sat Nancy Dowd, who would pen the immortal *Slapshot*. Ned Dowd, who played Ogie Oglethorpe in the movie, played hockey with Crestwood Circle's Dick Donovan at Bowdoin. Vancouver native Michael Ontkean, a University of New Hampshire Hall of Fame hockey star, played Ned Braden in the movie, and played hockey against Ken Reddick at the University of Massachusetts.

against three-time All-Scholastic goalie Neil Higgins to win its second consecutive state title.

Norwood had become hockey mad. The obsession in my hometown was fueled further by one of the more colorful teams in NHL history. The Big, Bad, Bruins, led by Bobby Orr and Phil Esposito, accompanied by such colorful characters as Derek Sanderson and Johnny McKenzie, took New England by storm with their brawling, overconfident swagger. Boston became Hockeytown, idolizing these athletes in an era before the American obsession with political correctness. A time when conquering athletes drank freely and openly, apologized for nothing, and conducted their lives on and off the ice as if there were no tomorrow. I witnessed one of their more outrageous acts after the '70 Cup win, when during a frenzied celebration at City Hall, Pie McKenzie poured a pitcher of beer over the head of Boston Mayor Kevin White as he addressed the crowd.

That same year as a fifteen-year-old sophomore I first stepped out on the ice for Norwood to line up against Needham High School's Robbie Ftorek.[16] The following year I made my first trip into Boston Garden to play in a State Final game. In those days, before the Catholic schools began to recruit and dominate, there was tremendous interest in the high school tournament. Four teams were seeded each year, and a team had to win its first two games in Boston Arena to reach the quarterfinals, semis, and finals, all of which were held in Boston Garden. As destiny would have it, we once again played Arlington High School before a sold-out crowd of 13,909 and once again lost, 3–0. For the fourth time in seven years, Norwood had lost the State Finals, the last three to its now arch-rival, Arlington. All of which led up to the finest night in my home town's history.

The 1972 Norwood team was a powerhouse, destined to be remembered as one of the finest Massachusetts high school teams of all time. We had five of the best players in the state. Every single player

---

16 The emergence of Robbie Ftorek raised the bar for U.S. bred players. For the first time our best American players actually believed they could play in the NHL. Ftorek scored *ten points* in the 1970 Massachusetts State Final game in Boston Garden.

on the team went on to play college hockey. David Katchpole was cut from the team, but won a Division Three College Player of the Week a year later. Louie Parker, the backup goalie, started for four years at the University of Connecticut and was selected Division Two All-American. Our Captain Peter Brown became an All-American at Boston University and is enshrined in its Hall of Fame. When his college career ended, Peter played two years on the U.S. National team and was drafted by the Atlanta Flames.

We went through the regular season undefeated, making our two-year record 42 wins, 1 loss, and 2 ties. The only loss, of course, the State Final game the previous year. In '72 we went 18–0–0 during the regular season, outscoring our opponents 102–22. Three quarters of the way through the season our leading scorer Mike Martin fractured his wrist, preventing him from breaking Dick Donovan's single season point record. That night, cementing in my mind how seriously my home town embraced this sport on ice, I saw Mrs. Donovan raise a glass in Mrs. Praino's kitchen during a post-game party on Crestwood Circle to toast the security of her son's record...

The team won every tournament game to reach the State Finals once again, and once again prepared to play Arlington High School for the Massachusetts championship in Boston Garden. Every heart and soul in the town of Norwood hung in the balance on the evening of March 13, 1972. One veteran, nearly apoplectic and entirely inebriated, burst into our dressing room to render his own Knute Rockne impression. Every player from four previous losing efforts either graced the stands, sat at home leaning in on his radio, or occupied a dormitory room, nervously waiting by a telephone. And I can remember skating in Boston Garden, the glare of the lights blinding with its reflection off the ice, the maddened, howling crowd hanging over every piece of glass, off every balcony, every nook and cranny of that old barn filled with screaming, delirious fans, the noise so overwhelming that it was difficult to skate, to shoot, to stickhandle, the game now 2–2 with time winding down. And I'll remember more than anything I'll ever remember in this life Ed King deflecting a short pass from Bill Clifford into the net with under two minutes to play, erupting that now departed, legendary building into a hysterical, pounding, raging explosion of dancing delirium. In its fifth try in eight seasons, Norwood had finally won its Massachusetts State Hockey Championship.

On the ferry today, twenty-five years later to the day, somewhere between Sitka and Petersburg, I meet a couple from Massachusetts. They ask about our journey, and when they hear the hockey story and hear I'm also from Massachusetts, the man looks at me and says, "My son played hockey for Acton-Boxborough back in the old days, won the State Championship."

"Really," I reply, genuinely interested. "What year did he win it?"

"1972."

"Oh, I don't think so…"

TOWARD BELLINGHAM

Thursday, March 13

The days blur together on the ferry. Most of my time is spent in the observation room watching the scenery slide by. Groups of people sit in the rows of chairs, reading, dozing, busy with binoculars scouring the water for whales. I see five or six eagles standing on a stony shore. Park rangers hold a trivia game, played by several Nuggets scattered throughout the crowd. Occasionally someone shouts and points, causing a rush toward that side of the boat. A fellow traveler, weary with days of false alarms, leans toward me and stage-whispers, "*Another* whale."

McRae and I have made a new friend. Skip Heine is on board with his mother. He is a sixty-year-old photographer bedecked in black leather, including a cowboy hat adorned with a large, colorful feather. He has a series of cameras and auxiliary equipment slung over his shoulders and dangling from his neck at all times. To suggest he looks normal would be to suggest McRae *is* normal. He is a character who tells us he has been nominated twice for Pulitzer Prizes in photography. When asked to join us he demurs, saying, "I'd give anything to be drinking with you guys, but I'm with mom and she stuck with me through my bad years without saying a word."

Skip has written two novels, and is trying to get them published.

"And they're just as good as Grisham's stuff," he tells me. I am somewhat wary of the man, especially after McRae shares his initial observations.

"The guy's certifiable," McRae tells me. "Another Deranged Whacko. Do you notice something strange about the way he talks? He, like, starts his thoughts mid-sentence…" But after a few days the man has become one with us. He matches McRae laugh-for-laugh, even pulling out of his wallet, after discovering McRae is founder and president of the Elvis Sighting Society in Ottawa, a picture of Elvis Presley on a drivers license with his name on it. Skip even teaches McRae and I something we did not know about ourselves.

"You're word dinks, you know," he tells us. "That's all writers are, is word dinks."

The Dawson City Nuggets put on something of a traveling show for our fellow passengers. Everyone dressed in either turn-of-the-century costume or game jersey, we stood before the crowd. Hogan and Flynn take center stage and tell the story of the original Dawson challenge of 1905, as well as our own. But the star of the show is Earl McRae.

"I was the one sacrificed by my newspaper…" he begins. The man is a talented stand-up comedian. He seems to revel in posturing as the proverbial fish out of water, relating the various trials and tribulations of the trail, causing great waves of laughter through the crowd. A self-described grizzly-phobist, he expresses his wide ranging paranoia in the most hilarious manner. The best response is caused by his ribald retelling of one of the distressing necessities endured in the bush. It is a variation of a familiar joke I'd heard expressed as fact by more than one of the Yukoners, where an unfortunate walks into the woods away from camp, removes his mittens, unties his hood, removes his hat, removes his great coat, removes his bib overalls, pulls down his pants, opens his union suit, pulls down his underwear, does his duty as quickly as humanly possible in -40 degree air, then quickly pulls up his underwear, pulls up his union suit, pulls up his pants, pulls on his bib overalls, puts his great coat back on, puts his hat back on, ties his hood, puts his mittens back on, then turns to do some housekeeping— *and finds nothing there!* The crowd roars… When the show is over, I sell a few copies of my book. Last in line is Skip Heine.

"I want one of your books but I don't want to pay for it," he says. "This is what we'll do. I got all these meal tickets left, and I'm not gonna use them all. I'll trade you, say, five meals for one book. Not a bad deal for a word dink. What do you say?"

"Well...okay..."

Later I sit alone in the observation room. It is late, perhaps ten-thirty. Something odd...I could swear I hear... McRae bursts into the room, frantic.

"Don! Don! C'mon! C'mon! There's a guy playing bagpipes up top!" We make our way outside and climb up to the top deck, beckoning to Hogan, Craig, and Willie Gordon to follow. We find a fellow named Ken MacRae standing under the awning, his bagpipes slung over his shoulder. He seems terribly embarrassed, and refuses to play for us.

"I was looking for a quiet place to practice," he protests. His face is weather-beaten, tired. He seems remarkably sad, and annoyed. The face of a man who's suffered a loss. He is cajoled into playing his pipes. It is a marvelous scene, here atop the ferry, the air crisp under a cloudless, sparkling sky, the whining of the pipes flowing out and away over the dark waves. Ken MacRae plays a bit then stops, again protesting that he only wanted to be left alone. Willie Gordon tells him he plays a fiddle and offers to get it, but MacRae shakes his head.

"Well then," Willie says to the man, "my grandfather was Scottish, and he played the bagpipes. Would you do one thing, would you play *Amazing Grace* for me? It reminds me of my grandfather." There is something disarming about Willie Gordon, and MacRae raises the pipe to his mouth and begins the haunting strains of that old standard. I watch as Willie sinks back against a post, removes his glasses and dangles them from his right hand by his side. As the pipes whine his chin drops to his chest, and I see him begin to weep. A moving moment of cultural curiosity, that he could do that so easily in front of others without a shadow of embarrassment. An unusual moment where once again I appreciate the wonder of experiencing so unique a scene on this grand adventure, now accompanied by a beguiling strain of music.

This afternoon I sit on deck and retell the Dawson story to yet another middle-aged couple. I am overheard by Robin Ford, an Alaskan folk singer who is scheduled to play tonight.

"Are you a writer?" she asks, and we chat a bit about writing, and singing. "I'd like one of your books," Robin says. "Will you take one of my CD's in exchange?"

Later, most of the passengers assemble for Robin Ford's concert. Willie Gordon retrieves his fiddle and stands in with Robin and her guitar-playing boyfriend. Willie quickly has both staring at him as they play, Robin finally asking if he is available to come to Alaska to record with them. Our fiddler just smiles. The concert ends early, the rules prohibiting any noise after eight o'clock, but only after Willie rocks the boat with a foot-stomping rendition of *Orange Blossom Special.*

I return to my room to retrieve my Stanley Cup, and once again make the rounds through the corridors of the ferry, offering up a shot of Jack Daniels to every Dawson Nugget I can find. When I've found everyone I can, I go in search of McRae, who I know has secluded himself to write his column. I find him sitting at a folding table in a side room. He seems relieved to be visited, drops his pen and leans back in his chair. He takes the little cup brimming with whiskey, and downs it.

I was told of a reporter coming up from Ottawa just before my departure, and was somewhat disappointed with the news. A sense of not wanting to share this great adventure with anyone else who might write about it. The feeling was mutual, I found, when Wendy Burns of Yukon Anniversaries brought McRae and me out to dinner in Whitehorse the evening before we flew on to Dawson. As we sat down Earl excused himself and made a phone call, then returned to our table. When Wendy introduced me as the author of *Dawson City Seven*, he recoiled.

"Jesus fucken Christ," he blurted, waving his arms, "I just got off the phone telling my editor no one else was here and we'd *nailed* this— and you're the fucken *expert!*"

I look at McRae now, slumped in his folding chair, somewhere along Alaska's inside passage. He makes no bones about it that he's a city boy and this whole business is for the birds, yet he's loving every minute of it. I'm beginning to sense that he possesses a certain genius at playing the clown, the hapless, helpless city dude from the east. He's as dumb as a fox, and proud of his role, his job as a columnist. On the trail he wore a series of buttons on his jacket, "Ottawa Sun Press" embossed on them. It seemed wholly unnecessary, as everyone knew who he was and why he was there. But despite the harassment he got, Earl never removed them.

I marvel at his ability to extract information. In Pelly Crossing I stood in a circle with McRae and some others, and the columnist seemed to hinder the conversation with his direct, reporter-like questions. All business. I wanted to tell him to relax; now I see how seriously he takes his job, and understand better. This is not a vacation for him. I begin to see his mode of operation; he cultivates a keen eye for the human, touching moment, like Willie Gordon's tears, or Freddy Farr's guilt over his brother's death. The picture of dead Ronnie McPhee on Anderson's snowmobile. Making him all the more complex is his consummate paranoia, the lurking catastrophes at every turn, and truly believing that Elvis Presley lives in the rural town of Tweed, Ontario. Been on the Jerry Springer show twice, he tells me, with the Elvis thing. The self-professed, "four-eyed, lippy little shin-kicker." He complains constantly to anyone who'll listen. I throw him into fits of anxiety by following his every complaint with, "And if you think McRae's had it bad, I've had to *sleep* with him the last two weeks."

He has his detractors. Word has spread of the dishes incident in Pelly Crossing. Though no one has confronted him as they have me, there is a subtle dissatisfaction with what they perceive his view of them is. When I protest to one that McRae is pure, that his motive is simply the truth, the response is, "Yeah, six things are said, he picks a bit from each, and makes *that* his truth." There has been an effort to keep unfavorable information about the Ottawa Senators from him, for fear he might disparage them in his articles. *Don't tell McRae about this.* Now, in a side room on the ferry, we share our stories about the days activities, laughing hard at the idiosyncrasies of the Yukoners. But McRae has a deadline, pulls himself up and forward, and picks up his pen.

"Thanks," he says, looking at the bottle of Jack Daniels. "All right, one more…"

I go forward to the darkened observation room. Travelers without berths lay in sleeping bags along the rear wall. I join Steve Craig, Troy Suzuki, and Dale Kulych in the first row of seats. We had been told we would be traveling through an area called "the narrows," and were interested in seeing it. We stare soundlessly at the red and green guide lights along the shoreline, until it gets late. We struggle to remain awake. Craig calls it a night, Kulych follows soon after. Catching myself nodding off again, I finally rise and leave Suzuki alone, silently staring into the darkness.

CHAPTER FOURTEEN

*"Such are the trifles which produce quarrels on shipboard.
In fact we had been too long from port. We were getting
tired of one another, and were in an irritable state...
and a thousand little things, daily and almost hourly
occurring, which no one who has not himself been on
a long and tedious voyage can conceive of or properly
appreciate—little wars and rumors of wars—reports of
things said in the cabin—misunderstanding of words and
looks..."*

— RICHARD HENRY DANA,
TWO YEARS BEFORE THE MAST, 1840

We live in a culture enamored of its word dinks. From the murky depths of Anglo-Saxon history has emerged a reverence for the written word, and for those who scribble it. For most writers, getting published for the first time is a pinnacle as well as a defining moment in their lives. Their lives will change, some so much so that they lose all perspective. The worst case of this I've seen was that of a renown poet, who during a book tour stop in Boston actually had a list of rules printed in the *Boston Globe* governing her talk. The backlash was so severe that her publisher stepped forward and retracted the rules, wisely accepting all responsibility for the "confusion." Indeed, if you want to know what horses asses writers can be, read Michael Korda's book *Another Life*. If you want to see any romantic myth of alcohol in writing utterly smashed, read Donald

Newlove's, *Those Drinking Days: Myself and Other Writers*. All a writer need do to harness an errant ego is walk into any local library, pause, and look around at the thousands of books that preceded his.

The physical act of writing is as private as it is isolating; it's something you do late at night, in your room with the door closed, and no one knows unless you tell them. Or unless you get published. Those closest to you may be the most surprised. My high school football coach said, upon being handed my book, "What did *he* have to do with it?" A friend's father reacted, "Who helped him?" One family member responded, when asked his opinion, "Well, it isn't exactly *War and Peace*." Another cozied up to me one holiday and asked, "Well whaddaya think, Don, was it just *Reddick shit luck?*"

There is reason for some familial ambivalence. When your first novel is published, everyone is eager to ask about it. Initially you respond enthusiastically and at length, but with time the experience becomes tempered, until your eyes start to glaze over like baked hams whenever the subject is raised. You begin to respond in what I call "bookspeak," a rote reply covering all that you've experienced. And if you, as the author, are reduced to this, you can only imagine how those always around you come to view it. It actually becomes intrusive, and worse, embarrassing.

Another problem is the perception that strangers will create of you. They read your novel, but they do not know you. They do not understand that your words aren't necessarily an extension of your being, that you may not truly be as wise as your wise owl, or as good as your protagonist. In *Dawson City Seven* my main character Boston Mason is vehemently anti-drinking. That this same demeanor is expected of me is evident in some here, whose eyes betray their feelings when they see me spreading my charming self around these Yukon saloons. In my defense there was much to tempt me, a surprise party of friends in Massachusetts before I left, congratulatory drinks with co-workers, and then the celebrations in Dawson before the start of our trek. Suddenly withdrawn from all normal responsibilities, it is all too easy to succumb to the temptation of hearty laughs and endless mugs of cold beer.

I hate to disappoint. I want to get along with everybody, but in the end I can't bring myself to be anyone else but myself. Those that thought they were getting Boston Mason will have to settle for Don Reddick. I sense it in the eyes of one First Nation teammate whose Indian upbringing and family history of alcoholism I surmise may have enamored him of my fictional creation. I see it in the eyes of Yukon Anniversaries worker Wendy Burns, who fights a constant P.R. battle of the bottle. She does not want anyone to mention drinking during the trip, particularly to the media. I caught her evil eye in Whitehorse as I told newspaper reporter Adam Killick of the excesses on the trail. Wendy exchanged words with McRae on the subject.

"Hey," McRae argued, "don't tell me what to do. The truth is the truth. I'm not here to perpetuate any Yukon myths, I'm here to do a job and I'm gonna do it. You have your job, and I have mine."

ARRIVE AT BELLINGHAM, AND TO VANCOUVER

Friday, March 14

"It goes back to the focus of the attention," Pat Hogan tells me on deck. "Obviously, the Dawson City Nuggets and the story are the focus of the attention, not the Ottawa Senators, and certainly not Marie Olney. I had difficulty dealing with her. And I think there was a dynamic there that was a bit iffy. I found it increasing difficult to deal with Olney as things went on. I got pretty pissed off at one point, we were looking for sponsorships and wanted the local First Nation to be involved. And there are a lot of Indian guys on our club, they're as much a part of where we live and what we do as anything. So part of what I proposed is that they could sponsor us and they could partake in a cultural event to have dancers or singers or drummers, whatever, but I was getting a lot of resistance from Ottawa. They saw it as an unnecessary expense, they were worried about the bottom line and delivering sponsorship funding to the organizations of their choice, as opposed to this upstart club from the middle of nowhere who's gonna bring fifty ounces of gold that's gotta go back to the Yukon to things like minor hockey. Where the hell do we get anything out of that?

"So at one point I was in Whitehorse on business and phoning at five o'clock in the morning to catch them at their time from a hotel room, and they're saying we can hire some people to dress up as Indians, and I said, you know what? It's real easy for us to hire a bunch of hockey players like the Stars-On-Ice and dress them up as the Ottawa Senators. That's a bunch of horse shit! I got really pissed off, really pissed off. And I said that's enough of that, I got nothing more to say, I gotta go to work.

"And you know, the whole...there was at one point a debate over whether we should say, OK, fuck the Ottawa Senators. In reality, they are just a name. With what we're doing, we can play any club in Ottawa. Do we wanna go thirty miles outside of Ottawa and play in the Corel Center? Is that the focus that we want? We could just as easily hire the Stars-On-Ice, all the oldtimers who are a good hockey draw, lots of box office there, and rent the rink the Senators play in in downtown Ottawa, and charge eight bucks a ticket. And we'd probably fill the place. Because you don't have to go such a long way, it's not so expensive, you're gonna get families and their children coming to see this, that's the focus. Are we better off to do that? There was considerable debate that I brought to the table, and we went back and forth, and we decided no, we should go with the Ottawa Senators, that would be the best way to go.

"One of the biggest problems we had was marketing. Deb Belinsky and DCB came on board for advertising and production, but not marketing. We kept pressing her to do marketing, but she wasn't interested. So we picked up a local guy in Whitehorse, who turned out to be a real dud. Belinsky came up with a good marketing guy, Zoran Rajcic out of Winnipeg.

"Belinsky came up with doing pyrotechnics. We got shot down big time. And part of it was because it would have eclipsed the Ottawa Senators NHL game day production. And that's another issue in the background. You have to remember the context here, what we're proposing is something with the potential to be quite an event, more so than they could bring off on a normal basis. So there's some jealousy, some resistance there..."

We arrive at Bellingham, Washington slightly later than scheduled, around 8:00 A.M. Awaiting us on the large, wooden pier is the usual bank of TV cameras, and the boys waste no time in trashing the Ottawa alumni. In what has become the norm, we mill around waiting as Hogan, Flynn, and Anderson handle the interviews. I look around for Ken Forrest, but do not see him. As the grandson of original Dawson City Klondiker Albert Forrest, he is one of the more aware and interested family members that have been located. Living in nearby Marysville, he was readily accessible. When I ask Hogan if Forrest has been contacted, I am unhappy to hear that he has not.

In fact, this angers me. Ken Forrest was instrumental in my research. His name and phone number was one of several I gave to Belinsky and Hogan as individuals available to add to the trip. I begin to feel a bit naive...I think of Hogan's words about the background arguments with Ottawa, and realize that as bright and shiny and altruistic an endeavor we find ourselves engaged upon, there is a hard-core political side to it that's all business.

Deb Belinsky brings a sharp talent to the table for advertising and production, and her payback—besides $25,000—is she wants credit for it. Earl McRae brings exposure on a national scale, and his payback, besides his paycheck, is he's going to perpetuate his reputation by telling the truth no matter whose feelings he hurts. The Ottawa Senators bring their name and reputation to the table, and their payback is taking care of their corporate sponsors. Pat Hogan brings a hard-core, iron constitution to the table, and his payback is the satisfaction of seeing things through. Don Reddick brings a semblance of legitimacy, I suppose, as the historian of the subject, and all he asks is to promote his book, and maybe sell a few copies. But these politics, I realize, are not understood entirely by everybody. So you have Deb Belinsky complaining about others trying to run things, you have Hogan complaining about the Ottawa Senators, you have guys misunderstanding McRae, angry with Reddick, and you have everyone angry with the Ottawa Senators. There is all this anger because people pay attention only to the paybacks, and not the inputs.

Standing on the pier waiting for the bus, I suddenly have had it with the whole thing. A month with the "boys" is proving to be something of a trial. Too old for this shit. I am tempted to leave, and return home to my wife and kids. I feel like McRae did in the bush, that I have been too long out of my own element. I yearn for my recliner, and Peter Gammons' baseball column in the *Boston Globe*. I sullenly stare out the window as we bus across the border toward Vancouver.

We are scheduled for a press conference on the 28th floor of a downtown skyscraper, in some lawyer's office. We gather in a room off the main meeting area, the entire team bedecked in our turn-of-the-century suits, Yukon furs, and game shirts. Jim Nicol quiets us, then on cue we enter the meeting room, bulbs flashing, cameras rolling, and are introduced to the Vancouver media by Deb Belinsky. When a TV station asks for someone to give them a spot on the history of the original games, there is hesitation as Flynn and Hogan look at each other, and me. I step up and give as eloquent and engaging a briefing as I can muster. It is a good moment; it seems as though these guys respect someone who steps up, and delivers. My mood improves when I am approached by a singular looking man, fit, earrings in each ear, wearing a black turtleneck and sports coat.

"Are you Don Reddick?" Jeff Reinebold asks, offering me his hand. "I'm a friend of Deb Belinsky, she told me about the author who was living his own story. I had to meet you." Reinebold, it turns out, is the new head coach of the Winnipeg Blue Bombers of the Canadian Football League. He tells me he attended college at the University of Maine. When I tell him I'm from Norwood, Massachusetts, his eyes blow wide open.

"Do you know Johnny Chisolm, or Dennis Clifford?" he asks, and I laugh. He is referring to the younger brother of my former Norwood teammate Billy Clifford. We are astounded at this coincidence, and Reinebold invites me for cocktails afterwards. When he walks away, McRae approaches me.

"New head coach of the Winnipeg Blue Bombers," the columnist confides. "There's a lot that say he's an asshole."

"Doesn't seem like an asshole to me."

"You know, the bleached hair and earrings," McRae says, waving his hands around his hair, his ears. "Out of the mainstream, and there's a lot that don't like that shit. Had shoulder-length blonde hair last year, you know. We'll see how he does in his first year."

When the press conference breaks up, I accompany Reinebold, Belinsky, Nicol, and McRae across the street into the Hyatt Regency's lounge. Bruce Duffee joins us. As usual McRae has only one beer, then hustles elsewhere. I am intrigued by Reinebold, who is talking with a couple of lawyers, one of them, I am told, "the biggest lawyer in Winnipeg."

What impresses me is Reinebold's command of the situation. He is the newly hired head coach of a professional football team, and he is grilling these lawyers on how they choose their new, younger associates. It is clear he is looking for tips on how to hire his own coaching staff. He is intense, focused, impressive, and supremely confident. When he finishes, I lean toward him and tell him that I've been observing him, that I am interested in why he asked these particular questions. We warm to the subject, and he explains to me the process of hiring his new staff. He tells me his hero is Dick Vermeil, and relates anecdotes of the legendary football coach.

Reinebold is a movie buff; when I mention John Waters' *Pink Flamingos*, he says he's seen it, and we laugh. He tells me he loves Jimmy Buffett and the Florida Keys—I tell him my favorite song is *The Captain and the Kid* and we form a bond when he jumps up and recites the one haunting line from that song that I cherish more than any other: "He went from sailing ships, to raking mom's backyard..." A remarkable moment where two minds discover they are one. We stand and shake hands at the revelation. When the party breaks up, we agree to meet again for drinks in Ottawa, where Reinebold will be rejoining us for the game. As he leaves, several Nuggets follow and peak around a corner to see him walking hand-in-hand with Deb Belinsky, providing soap opera fodder galore for the inquiring minds on the team.

We line the hotel bar watching news reports on the arrival of the Dawson City Nuggets hockey team, on its way through Vancouver toward Ottawa. I look up and see myself on TV, the caption, "Hockey Expert," underneath. Everyone gets a good laugh, particularly me.

Seated at the bar is Kevin Anderson and his brother, sister, and mother. Vancouver proves an opportunity for several of the guys to visit with family. Bruce Duffee had a visit earlier from his ex-wife and two kids. I sat with them in the foyer of the hotel. As the kids rumbled around on the floor with some toys Bruce had brought, I watched his ex-wife. Something incongruent here; her eyes followed Bruce's every move with a look I would describe as adulation, not the severe, calculating, worn gaze normally associated with divorced individuals. After his family left, Duffee shook his head. "Can you imagine," he said, "all my life I figured I was the outdoorsman, the he-man type to go up and live in the Yukon, and both my kids turn out to be computer nerds..." He laughed out loud.

In the bar Anderson is reunited with his family. It is illuminating to see his mother matching him drink for drink, his brother staring into his two-hands-held glass of beer, and his sister laughing with the guys, beer in hand. I sit between Willie Gordon and an overweight, plain looking individual who tells me he used to play in a bluegrass band. He does not seem the type. I mention that Jerry Jeff Walker is my favorite singer, and am pleasantly surprised when they both claim to know who he is. "Wrote *Bojangles*," Willie assures me. But I'm unsure of the other guy.

"One of my other favorites is Doc Watson," I say to the man. This is a good test; Doc Watson is an American classic, a master bluegrass/folklore guitarist. The man claims he's familiar with him. Well, Doc Watson used to play with his son Merle, who was killed several years ago in a tractor accident on the family farm in the hills of Deep Gap, North Carolina. This is the ultimate test.

"Used to play with his son," I say, looking for the man's response.

"Yeah, Merle got killed a few years ago," he replies.

The team breaks up to pursue various interests during our sole evening in Vancouver. Some plan dinner with family, others, particularly First Nation members, anxiously eye nearby casinos, while the Wild Bunch prepares to experience the flashing, neon sign cultural opportunities beckoning close by. McRae informs me he is secluding himself in his room to work on his latest column, on our bag-piping

Ken MacRae. I join Joe Mason and Chester Kelly for an hour in a casino, Kelly telling me he's won five hundred dollars. I soon relent and make my way back, kicking along my mental can as I go, to the hotel alone.

CHAPTER FIFTEEN

"We did not think of the great open plains, the beautiful rolling hills and the winding streams with tangled growth as wild. Only to the white man was nature a wilderness and only to him was the land infested with wild animals and savage people. To us it was tame. Earth was bountiful and we were surrounded with the blessings of the Great Mystery."

— LUTHER STANDING BEAR,
LAND OF THE SPOTTED EAGLE, 1933

Linguists estimate that in 1492 there were approximately three hundred Indian languages spoken in North America. By 1962 two hundred remained, and many of those spoken only by a handful of elders. Of an estimated twenty million original inhabitants of the Americas in 1492, one hundred years later, due to the ravages of war, disease, forced labor, and starvation, less than twenty percent remained. Ray Allen Billington, in his seminal *Westward Expansion*, describes the effect of aboriginal interaction with white men: "They broke down Indian self-sufficiency accustoming red men to the guns, knives, and firewater of the white men's higher civilization. They weakened the natives by spreading diseases and vices among them."

Canadians have historically enjoyed better relations with native inhabitants than any other nation in the Americas. Predicated early on by a partnership with fur traders, the relationship was abetted by climate and terrain that discouraged mass settlement and its subsequent turmoil. So difficult was mere survival that natives embraced interaction with traders simply because it made their lives easier. These conditions, however, did not shield Canadian First Nation peoples from the more nefarious effects of this new intimacy.

Athabascan tribes populate the vast Yukon River watershed. Principle among them are sub-groups such as Tagish, Koyukon, Kutchin, Tutchone, Tanana, and, along the US–Canadian border in the Dawson area, the Han. All with distinct dialects, they speak a language closely related to the Navajo and Apache of the American Southwest, as well as tribes of the California coast, the Hopa, Kato, and Mattole. Robert Campbell reported to Hudson Bay Company superiors that by 1851 European disease had devastated the native population, the agent having been carried into the Yukon interior by unsuspecting Chilkat Indians after contact with coastal traders.

Native vulnerability to alien diseases is a well-known facet of European domination of the continent. A first person account of a 1635 smallpox outbreak was written by William Bradford in his memoirs of Plymouth Colony in Massachusetts. He makes clear the horror of the oft-mentioned, but seldom described, pestilence: "This spring, also, those Indians that lived about their trading house there fell sick of the small pox, and died most miserably; for a sorer disease cannot befall them; they fear it more than the plague; for usually they that have this disease have them in abundance, and for want of bedding and lining and other helps, they fall into a lamentable condition, as they lie on their hard mats, the pox breaking and mattering, and running one into another, their skin cleaving to the mats they lie on; when they turn them, a whole side will flea off at once, and they will be all of a gore blood, most fearful to behold; and then being very sore, what with cold and other distempers, they die like rotten sheep. The condition of this people was so lamentable, and they fell down so generally of this disease, as they were in the end not able to help one another; no, not to make a fire, nor to fetch a little water to drink, nor any to bury the dead; but would strive as long as they could, and when they could procure no other means to make fire, they would burn the wooden trays and dishes they ate their meat in, and their very bows and arrows; and some would crawl out on all four to get a little water, and sometimes die by the way, and not be able to get in again...very few of them escaped, notwithstanding they (the local English) did what they could for them, to the hazard of themselves. The chief sachem himself now died, and almost all his friends and kindred. But by the marvelous goodness and providence of God not one of the English was so much as sick, or in the least measure tainted with disease..."

Two hundred years later the scourge continued. This testimony is from the shores of a primitive 1835 California, as related by Richard Henry Dana in his classic, *Two Years Before The Mast*:

"It has been said, that the greatest curse to each of the South Sea islands, was the first man who discovered it; and every one who knows anything of the history of our commerce in those parts, knows how much truth there is in this; and that the white men, with their vices, have brought in diseases before unknown to the islanders, and which are now sweeping off the native population of the Sandwich Islands (Hawaii), at the rate of one fortieth of the entire population annually. They seem to be a doomed people...here, in this obscure place, lay two young islanders, whom I had left strong, active young men, in the vigor of health, wasting away under a disease, which they would never have known but for their intercourse with Christianized Mexico and people from Christian America. One of them was not so ill; and was moving about, smoking his pipe, and talking, and trying to keep up his spirits; but the other, who was my friend Hope...was the most dreadful object I had ever seen in my life; his eyes sunken and dead, his cheeks fallen in against his teeth, his hands looking like claws; a dreadful cough, which seemed to rack his whole shattered system, a hollow whispering voice, and an entire inability to move himself. There he lay, upon a mat, on the ground, which was the only floor...with no medicine, no comforts, and no one to care for, or help him...The sight of him made me sick, and faint. Poor fellow!

"Thinking, from my education, that I must have some knowledge of medicine, the Kanakas had insisted upon my examining him carefully; and it was not a sight to be forgotten. One of our crew, an old man-of-war's man, of twenty years' standing, who had seen sin and suffering in every shape, and whom I afterwards took to see Hope, said it was dreadfully worse than anything he had ever seen, or even dreamed of. He was horror-struck, as his countenance showed, yet he had been among the worst cases in our naval hospitals. I could not get the thought of the poor fellow out of my head all night; his horrible suffering, and his apparently inevitable, horrible end."

Three generations later, Yukon natives literally did not know what hit them, as illustrated in *Upper Yukon Native Customs and Folk Lore*, published by Dr. Ferdinand Schmitter in 1910: "About 500 Indians encamped in skin houses about a mile up Mission Creek were taken with smallpox and most of them died. The remnant of the band migrated to Fortymile, where they were attacked in 1897 by an epidemic of coughing and bleeding from the lungs, and many died in from four to six days. The Indians think that each of these epidemics was due to a bad medicine man from elsewhere sending an evil spirit amongst them. The evil spirit was supposed to enter the man's body in the form of an animal and, by moving about in him, produced sickness."

In his memoir of an 1867 expedition to coastal Alaska, John Muir described the oratory skills of a local sachem: "In all his gestures, and in the language in which he expressed himself, there was a noble simplicity and earnestness and majestic bearing which made the sermons and behavior of the three distinguished divinity doctors present seem commonplace in comparison." Muir went on to relate, "The most striking characteristic of these people is their serene dignity…the fine, strong, specious deliberation of Indians was well illustrated on this eventful trip. It was fresh every morning. They all behaved well, however, exerted themselves under tedious hardships without flinching for days or weeks at a time; never seemed in the least nonplused; were prompt to act in every exigency; good as servants, fellow travelers, and friends."

The horde of gold seekers soon to follow spoke in contrast. Most came from the United States bearing long-held prejudices. Advice such as this from a Texan to a 49er, related from Paula Mitchell Marks' *Precious Dust*, indicates the depth to which American–Indian relations had fallen: "Shoot every Indian you see and save them a life of misery in subsisting on snakes, lizards, skunks and other disgusting objects."

George Mercer Dawson himself wrote that the Kaska Indians were, "lazy and untrustworthy." Judge Wickersham quotes a man named Callbreath on the Tahl-tan Indians in *Old Yukon*, "Brain-capacity small...they seem to have no inherent good qualities which will overcome the vicious, and unnatural rules and customs of their tribe...gratitude and charity seem to be foreign to the natures of these people."

White condescension manifested itself in numerous ways, including this oft-told, demeaning episode, usually related as one of hilarity. Asked in 1905 to marry two Indians who had alienated themselves from their tribe's more common rituals, a man named Guy Lawrence related, "Bidding the two to stand up and hold hands I read them a recipe from the small cook book my mother had sent me."

Author Larry Pynn, in his book *The Forgotten Trail*, dispenses his view: "The history of white influence on Northern natives over the past century is filled with heartache: the introduction of smallpox and other diseases for which the natives had no immunity, the stripping away of their language and culture to be replaced by alcohol and satellite dishes, the evidence of cultural degradation is all around. The language is almost extinct except among a few elders. There is too much drinking, too much family violence, not enough focus on the old ways."

In contrast, Jon Krakauer has this to say in *Into Thin Air*, relating to aboriginal Himalayan tribes: "The transformation of the Khumbu culture is certainly not all for the best, but I didn't hear many Sherpas bemoaning the changes...it seems more than a little patronizing for Westerners to lament the loss of the good old days when life in the Khumbu was so much simpler and picturesque. Most of the people who live in this rugged country seem to have no desire to be severed from the modern world or the untidy flow of human progress. The last thing Sherpas want is to be preserved as specimens in an anthropological museum."

Alcohol became a problem of great magnitude. This remarkable passage from Muir documents the early ravages of the debilitating habit: "We arrived at the upper village about half-past one o'clock. Here we saw Hootsenoo Indians in a very different light from that which illuminated the lower village. While we were yet half a mile or more away, we heard sounds I had never before heard—a storm of strange howls, yells, and screams rising from a base of gasping, bellowing grunts and groans. Had I been alone, I should have fled as from a pack of fiends, but our Indians quietly recognized this awful sound, if such stuff could be called sound, simply as the 'whiskey howl' and pushed quietly on. As we approached the landing, the demoniac howling so increased I tried to dissuade Mr. Young from attempting to say a single word in the village…the whole village was afire with bad whiskey."

Yukon First Nation teammates John Flynn, Joe Mason, Chuck Barber, Richard Nagano, Freddy Farr, Chester Kelly, Willie Gordon, and Roy Johnson live with the remnants of this history today. When asked, they shrug off the topic in typical northern manner, the burden of their cultural heritage often veiled with humor such as this, expressed by one in Whitehorse, "You know, the nice thing about being half Indian and half white is that you can play cowboys and Indians by yourself."

DEPART VANCOUVER ON VIA RAIL

Saturday, March 15

Exiting the grand station building to make our 8:00 P.M. Via Rail departure we walk past a pile of suitcases and bags, and a hovering crowd of Japanese tourists.

"Look," Wes Peterson says, pointing. "Troy's family is here."

Five new members join our entourage, Glen Heinbigner, Mike Fraser, Poncho Rudniski, Roy Johnson, and our modern-day Diamond Tooth Gertie, Patricia Dahlquist. We board the train and are directed to our berths, my new roommate goalie Rudniski. The players are like kittens in a new home, tentatively poking about, glancing in doorways and down hallways, getting the lay of the land. Up front is the dining car, down back the car we will call the drink room, adjacent a room transformed for the next few days into the card room. Stairs from the drink room lead up to the dome car, where one can sit for a panoramic view of all we will pass through. As I wander around, McRae races up to me.

"Jesus Christ there's a gawdam gook in my room! Two weeks I'm in sleeping with the gawdam bears, I finally get my own room and there's a gawdam gook in there! I ask her why she's in my room and she can't speak English, all she says is 'Yayayayayaya!' Jesus *Christ...*"

When McRae calms we find a place to sit and rehash the latest rumors and stories. Making the rounds is a story about Anderson, who unwittingly had been led into a gay bar in Vancouver and had settled himself in on his barstool, completely oblivious to the clientele. Anderson is now, "the best two-way player on the team."

We are in closer proximity to one another. On the ferry there was room to escape, whether among other passengers in the observation room, outside on the cold decks, or in a vacant side room, as McRae often sought to churn out his column. The train offers no such refuge. Everything is tight, cramped. Our berths are boxes that attendants change from sleeping to living quarters each morning. In the drink room, or up in the dome car, there is little to do but read or chat with others.

"Back in those days we weren't allowed downtown by my father," John Flynn tells me. "My house was in the north end of Dawson, the north side of the Catholic church. The church was the dividing line, all the natives on one side, and on the other the white. On the north side of the church there was no running water, we had a community tap where people would get their water. In the fifties they used to ring a curfew bell in the evening and all the Indians had to go back to Moose Hide, the old Indian village. Bill Hakonson tells a story about my father, they came into Dawson on a dog team and he never saw such good looking Indian men, but he couldn't allow them in his bar. He built the Eldorado. Indians weren't allowed in the barrooms, for their own good.

"The native kids owe a lot to a guy named Art Fry. Art Fry was a dredge master, placer miner, and he was a pro boxer in his younger days. He ended up in the North, middle-aged guy, and it was mostly native kids that went to him. He was in our corner, nobody else would give us the time of day. Of course the best boxers were the native kids, because we just grew up fighting. We would be hauling wood, chopping wood, it was a tougher existence for us. We natives, we always got into trouble. I remember as a kid going downtown and walking home with a bag of groceries. I was stopped three times by an RCMP—three times!—asking me what I had in my bag. If anything happened, they'd come right after us. That's where the hate comes from for the RCMP's, and it still exists. Well, maybe 'hate' is too harsh a word. It's really hard... They've got a program now where they hire more natives, and these are the guys they send into the Indian communities. I mean, I remember being called a dirty Indian to my face. It changed in the mid to late seventies, I think just native people made the change, they got more involved in businesses, and the community. And some of the old school white families kind of disappeared, divorce and stuff.

"Fry ran the boxing club. Joe Mason was North American Champion, he fought Sean O'Sullivan. Joe was an incredible amateur fighter. He was a great guy, Fry, he started the Tagish Charley Club, got people to donate money for kids. He was always big on getting something happening for kids, not just hockey. I went to his hockey club, a lot. He always told people, 'John was always concerned with his looks, so he played ice hockey, not boxing.' And I go on to break my nose five times. I've separated my shoulder three times. I can't even tell you when he died."[17]

"The Indians, they grew up fighting," Troy Suzuki tells me later. "They could all have gone to the dark side, but they didn't. Those three, Johnny, Chester Kelly, and Joe Mason, they all married strong white women, and now they're the pillars of Dawson. They're a major part of turning that town around. That town was split down the middle. If you were white you didn't go to the north side, you got beat up. It's all changing now because of these guys."

The dark side, however, exists. Roy Johnson tells me, "I was born in Dawson and in the '50's I had tuberculosis and went to Edmonton for two years, and when I finished there I came back and government thought it best for me to go to Residential School in Carcross instead

17 Art Fry died June 24, 1994 at age eighty-one in Dawson City. He was inducted into the Yukon Hall of Fame as a boxing coach, joining his two prize students Chester Kelly and Joe Mason, elected in 1985 and 1990 respectively.

of back to Dawson. I did ten months of the year in school there and two in Dawson. I started in school about six years old. I lived in Carcross about nine years, ten months of the year, but I grew up in Lousetown, across the Klondike River. They called it Klondike City or Lousetown. My parents emigrated from Ft. Selkirk to Dawson. I don't know when.

"I never knew Art Fry that well. I spent most of my time across the river in Lousetown. When we moved over into Dawson I knew he had a boxing club, but I never got involved. We moved over in '63, '64. Around '65, I think. We stayed in a one-room shack, my grandma's place. There, ah, were four brothers and mom and dad. It was hard. It was not very good. In the summertime we had a tent set up in the back.

"Residential School wasn't that great, either. What do you call it, abuse. We took a lot of abuse from the principle and supervisors. Physical abuse. It was their policy, the way the church and the government chose to take the native culture and language away. If you spoke in your native tongue, you would have gotten punished for it. The strap, ah, ah, psychological mind...a lot of talk about religion. The native tongue was not recognized as the language. I guess they were, through the whole century, the government was watching the church, and ah, the government saw a different way to attack the native language and culture.

"My mother went to Residential School and then the kids went to Residential School, that's why you see the language and the culture disappearing. It is in danger of becoming extinct. Today I'm appalled... there are stories...I am a self-taught reader. When I left school I was illiterate, but I learned how to read, and as the legend goes, this white guy said when he first saw the Indians here, they were big, strong, but then his people, his European people...they saw an abundance of fur, these two companies got together, the Northwest Trading Company and Hudson Bay, and they used alcohol to get furs from the Indians. They know this liquor was, what do you call it, addictive. So the natives got addicted to it. The more they got addicted, the more they brought in their furs. For two beaver furs they got one pint of diluted liquor. They just kept it up. It's appalling. Historians kept these records.

"A writer from England, he sees this as a crime against humanity. He sees us as humanity. This writer came back and saw this, but his government saw something different. Through the whole century until they finally realized it was wrong. The human factor, the human rights factor, that we had rights too.

"There was a lot of friction in Dawson when I was growing up. I never spent my winters here, I spent them in Carcross. Then I went to Whitehorse to further my school. I was stuck in grade four for four years in Carcross. There was one teacher in grade three, it started OK, but he had a nicotine problem, so he'd go outside to smoke and didn't teach us anything in grade three. He passed everyone to grade four without any grade three education. We were lacking in fractions, I couldn't do fractions. So the fourth grade teacher kept keeping us back, keeping us back, keeping us back…

"It was hard for me because I was alcoholic for a while. I didn't understand alcohol. I was alcoholic for at least thirty years. I quit and kept up with sports. I also kept up my reading, and work, to make a living. I jogged a lot, I used to jog fourteen kilometers a day at one time. And people see this and they say, 'Why you run?' and I say it's healthy, it's for the health.

"I had my young son, he was six. I needed a better life for him, and I didn't want him to be an alcoholic like me. To understand alcohol I took a job at Preventive, Intervention of Alcohol. I worked as a carpenter for quite a while. I was working in the office and had the opportunity to go to Neechin—it is Institute for, ah, counseling course for…Neechin. To understand alcohol. I wanted to understand alcohol, what it does to a person. You can say I hit rock bottom. I didn't ask for help from anybody. I did it on my own. Residential School had a lot to do with it. People say, 'He has a strong will…' Anyway, one day my son was six years old, he said we're going up town, and he said, 'Dad, when you go up town, don't get drunk.' This was after six months of being sober. I said I promise I won't and I kept that promise. And to this day I'm sober."

It is McRae who draws out the most haunting story from amongst our First Nation teammates. Freddy Farr possesses a soft, high voice in contrast to his fierce, aboriginal face. He is a reserved, quiet soul content to hover in the background. He was capable, however, of outbursts; on the trail I witnessed him erupting at Duffee, uttering the ultimate insult, *"How long have you lived in the Yukon?"*

"He got mad at me in the tent," Duffee recalled, "because the boughs he cut he piled so high he was falling off of them, and I told him, spread 'em around. He looks at me and says, 'Do you want me to take a round out of you?'"

I first noticed Farr in the Downtown Hotel the night before we left Dawson. He was conspicuous because of his ragged old boots and pants, and a sweater with gaping holes in its back and elbows. On the ferry there had been whispers of a problem that McRae and I had trouble learning the details of, but eventually found that Farr had already run out of money, and was too proud to ask anyone for help. We understood it had been taken care of by Hogan and Flynn, but details were not forthcoming from this group of tight-lipped hockey players.

Somewhat intimidated by his look, I had asked others about him, and received an arrayed reply. One described him as kind, another as smoldering, while another, white input was a derogatory, "He's *Indian...* bordering on crazy." Agreed by all, however, is that Freddy Farr is one of the best hockey players in the Yukon.

Despite his hardened look and silent demeanor, I had found him quite friendly on the trail. When I had foolishly not brought enough fluids and was reduced to melting snow in my mouth for relief, he freely shared his limited stash of soft drinks. I suspect I had stumbled upon one of the grey areas of the Indian's co-existence when I had asked what tribe he was from, and Farr covered his mouth with the back of his hand and whispered the answer, adding, *"but don't tell anyone."* It was on the trail one evening that McRae got Farr talking of the tragedy that has haunted him for the past twenty years.

"I was one of fourteen kids growing up," Farr told us. "My mother was from the Northwest Territories, and my father Weldon was an Irish gold miner. My father worked in the mines, and one day after a twelve-hour shift, he was walking home. It was Discovery Day. He saw a crowd and knew the race was about to start. It was a mile-long race to the bridge and back again. People trained a long time for the race. My father didn't, but he got in the race and won. He was wearing his gumboots!" But then Farr's normally high, shy voice softened even more.

"I was at a party one night, and we were drinking. I was with my brother Dave. He was one year older than me. He was my hero. He was the best street fighter in Dawson, when Dave was around me, nobody bothered me. I started hockey at fifteen, I was twenty-one before I got my first gloves and pads. Borrowed skates, but I learned hockey from my brother Dave. And twenty years ago we were drinking outside of Dawson, and we were at the party, and there was some girls there I was interested in, and when Dave wanted to go I said no, you go ahead. I'm gonna stay here with the girls. And Dave went out, and he was drunk, and he climbed one of the big twin towers that conveyed asbestos over the Yukon, and he fell to his death."

Farr paused, and shook his head.

"I've always felt I could have stopped him, if only I hadn't stayed behind chasing the girls. I know I could have stopped him…"

As Freddy Farr concluded his tale, his face reflected that of another I had witnessed back when my book tour had brought me to Dawson City. Put up by John and Jennifer Flynn, we had stayed up late one evening discussing the First Nation aspects of Dawson. Flynn had sat on a couch opposite me, elbows on knees and hands clasped together, leaning forward, telling me of the alcohol problems of his own family. With Jennifer looking on, John had ended his tale with, "…and my own father, well, he died of alcoholism on our wedding day." And John Flynn had hung his head, and spoke no more.

CHAPTER SIXTEEN

"Let a few men with sticks and a ball make their appearance and begin to knock the ball about. Very soon others will join in, a side will be picked up, and the game will not only have been started but also established; for whoever has once tasted the delights of hockey becomes soon its devoted slave to the end of his active existence."

— C. G. Tebbutt, *Skating*, 1921

The dome car is crowded as we snake our way through the narrow passes of the Canadian Rockies. Gently chugging along we marvel at the ever-changing vista of jagged, raw mountains. I join Patty Dahlquist, our modern-day Diamond Tooth Gertie, pleased to see she is reading *Dawson City Seven* in the car.

"This is great," she says, "if I have any questions—I'll just ask you!"

Dahlquist, despite the involvement of a mushing legend and an award-winning columnist, is the most famous member of our entourage. With a long list of TV and stage credits, she is best known for her 1975 hit song, *Keep Our Love Alive*. This song spent seven weeks on the Canadian Top Forty, leading to her winning the 1976 Juno Award, for Most Promising Female Vocalist of the Year. I have a chance to chat with Diamond Tooth Gertie as we wind our way through the British Columbia–Alberta borderland.

"I love trains!" Patty tells me. "I lived in a little town in the interior of British Columbia named Kaslo, which is a little tiny beautiful town, and I lived right beside the railway tracks and I listened to the trains going by every night and loved it. So to get on a train and go across country is wonderful. Kaslo was one of the towns I grew up in in the Kootenay Valley, also lived in South Slocan, looks and is like the name suggests. Blink an eye and you'll miss it.

"I had a friend named Patricia Vezina, she was married to Larry Vezina. Larry was a hotshot poker player up in Dawson. We worked together and she came to me and said she was promoting a Diamond Tooth Gertie show, and she asked me if I would be Diamond Tooth Gertie and I said 'Yeah!' I was in Vancouver, she asked me for some pictures, and I had done a Barkerville show, I worked in theater. Have you been to Barkerville? It's a gold rush town in central B.C. Great shots in this sexy outfit, and they included them in their proposal to the Klondike Visitor Association. It didn't hurt that I had won the Juno award. I had done hundreds of musical theater shows.

"The Klondike Visitor Association is the governing body of whatever goes on in Dawson, particularly in bringing in tourists. This is '93, the proposal was accepted that fall, and by, ah, probably late March of '94 I was up in Dawson—no, maybe it was April—and I immediately fell in love with Dawson. I just loved it!

"It was quite extraordinary, on my first trip up I came up the inside passage, traveled up through Skagway and up to Whitehorse. I was reading Laura Berton's *I Married the Klondike*, so I got a feel for the times. I loved that book, then I read her son's book, Pierre Berton, *The Klondike Stampede*. I immediately went down to the bookstore in Whitehorse and chatted away and got a number of books including *Klondike Women*, *Gold at Fortymile Creek*, Michael Gates' book, couple of others on the gold rush. I just read the stories of the people and got a sense of the characters. I could only get snips of Diamond Tooth Gertie. By the time I got to Dawson I already had a sense of the history of the place and the various historical points in the city.

"Dawson, well, it was like Barkerville but it was four or five times the size. Where Barkerville had two streets, Dawson had seven. I lived the first year in a little house in the northern part of town, just beneath the Dome. There was myself, two of the can-can girls, and

Lloyd Nicholson, our piano player. We all lived in that house. The Eldorado was there, The Pit was there, the Downtowner, we'd go to the Westminster Hotel, mostly the Downtowner.

"It was six shows, no, three shows a night for six nights. They were only half hour shows. It was really easy, about an hour and a half between shows. We'd do the first at eight, and each show was different. But mainly it was turn-of-the-century, it was vaudeville, it was burlesque, and it was the old-time music. I got to wear some really beautiful costumes.

"I was up there for the summer and early fall of '94, I stayed in Whitehorse that winter. I did some teaching in Whitehorse, then I went up to Dawson and did an RCMP show and I went back up the following summer. And the third year I was in the Palace Grand. There was a deal where I couldn't do Diamond Tooth Gertie for over two years. But they liked me so much they put me in the Palace Grand for the third year. So I was involved in and around Dawson for three years, and I would have stayed there if they had offered me the job. I would have bought a house and stayed there. I just felt so good in the time period, I loved the music, I loved the town, I loved the people. I would have lived there.

"I actually fell in love and got engaged to a miner. He was just a very cute, hot guy! We had a wonderful summer of '94 together, I went to Whitehorse and stayed with him, but I quickly realized I wasn't cut out for the lifestyle. To spend the winter you need to be a certain type of person. I was scared silly, I knew if my car died on the side of the road I could die. Even though I was brought up in the Kootenay Valley, I knew I wasn't cut out for this. You know, the guys that really take the winter on are just great. I knew I wasn't cut out to do that. Too many easy years…it's a hard life, but it's a life that a guy takes on with such gusto. I think people that take on that environment are true characters…"

We emerge swaying from the train in the wide-open spaces of Jasper, Alberta. Stepping over the tracks toward a row of restaurants and tourist shops, I pause and stare south toward the mountains, and wonder at what they have brought me.

I vividly recall shivering on Noble and Greenough's outdoor rink on a bank of the Charles River back home, being lectured by our Junior Varsity coach Jim Gormley. Gormley is an educated, insightful, thoughtful man who loves the game of hockey, and who tried to impart some sense of this to a group of fourteen-year-olds. He told us that hockey was better than football, better than baseball, because of the sheer joy of skating, the sheer exhilaration of movement across the ice. Hockey was the best sport ever devised simply because it was so much fun, Gormley told us, and his thoughts resonate here in Jasper, thirty years later.

Lost amidst our traveling turmoil is the simple, overwhelming love of hockey. Caught up in the day-to-day schedule, interviews, and personal problems, we forget the essence of this whole adventure, that a group of guys could so love a game, be so enamored of its history that they would drop everything in their lives for a month just to reenact one game. I think of this as I stare at the line of mountains and their Icefield Parkway, winding its way down through the passes and valleys toward the lake.

I am a Mountain Man. I have spent much time in the quaint, rolling White and Green Mountains of my native New England, and have driven the length of the Skyline Drive atop the Blue Ridge Mountains. I have worried through a flat tire 10,000 feet high on a dirt pass in Utah's Wasatch Range, and driven half a dozen times out of Estes Park and over the majestic, awe-inspiring Colorado spine. I have driven what I consider the thirty most beautiful miles in North America on Montana's Road to the Sun Highway in Glacier National Park. I have paused high above Los Angeles in the San Gabriel Mountains, completely alone amidst stunning grandeur, only to gaze upon the lights of twenty million people below, wondering why on earth none of them—not one!—was up there with me. I have driven north out of Santiago, Chile and viewed Aconcagua. But nothing has so moved me, nothing has so inspired my wonder and appreciation of natural beauty more than the moment I walked through the tall pines and emerged onto the shoreline of Alberta's Lake Louise.

The lake instantly came to represent all that I appreciate in the outdoors, all that I love in physical, raw beauty. I left as the lake's best advertisement, and when it came time to write a book about traveling from Massachusetts to the Yukon, I found the perfect outlet for my affection. When I came to the part in my book where my protagonist reached the Canadian Rockies, I seized the opportunity to combine my love of hockey, the sheer joy of skating, and a mature, weathered appreciation of mountains and glaciers. Sitting at home one evening I remembered Jim Gormley and the joy I felt when I stood alone one cold, raw, wind-swept afternoon on Kluane Lake, in the Yukon. And I wrote the scene that Gormley later told me was his favorite in the book, the scene editor Laurel Boone at Goose Lane Editions later told me made her decide to accept *Dawson City Seven* for publication.

LAKE LOUISE SCENE,
from *Dawson City Seven*

When we had walked some way into the silent, snow-laden forest, our guide exhorting us to follow, the man finally broke and ran over a small knoll and appeared to jump for joy, and we hastened, probably twenty of us, to join him. And when I topped the hill I truly believe my heart fell from my body.

"Lake Louise!" our brakeman announced with a reverence bordering on love, and we strung ourselves out along the frozen edge of what must be the perfect lake of the world. On each side, falling to the ice were tree-covered slopes approaching angles of seventy degrees, and ahead, rising up beyond a point where the side slopes fall together, was the sheer mass of monstrous, sharp mountains, covered with a mantle of everlasting blue snow, all of it crowning this jewel of liquid, settled like a diamond flung down by the farthest star in this still remoteness.

I moved down the lakeshore a piece and ventured out onto the ice, windblown free of snow and black as night. Black ice was a special thing back home in Sudbury. Being able to see right through it, though it stood many inches thick, made walking or skating upon it seem delightfully dangerous when it was not. This we always knew, and yet it had its strange allure, so that whenever nature found itself creating black ice we would always oblige with our skates. I laced the skates as tight as I could and stood up, eager to skate for the folks but feeling the awkwardness of not using them for so long. But this feeling vanished after the first few long strides.

Out onto the lake I went, slowly at first and stretching my arms and legs, then grabbing my cap as it began to blow off my head. Encouraged, I built up speed and off I took across the ice, digging hard against the black, the wind whipping back my hair as my arms, one hand clutching my cap, swung back and forth before me. I fairly flew across that ice…and oh my goodness did I soar, as though my soul was lifted from my body and carried across the black ice of heaven, and only then, striding hard away toward the steep rockness of the sheer mountains did I hear the cheers of the others…and I turned hard and raced back at them at my highest speed, my legs pistons, my arms rods, firing away through the cold wind until I stopped in a sudden shower of ice chips that flew up and over their heads, their clapping hands. I took a deep bow and clomped up the slope and sat down, the men clapping me on my back, the women looking at me with admiration…

The whistle blew tinny over the trees. The others followed, each man patting my back one last time, each woman turning one last glance as they trudged slowly back over the small hill toward the train. They left me alone for a few minutes, alone with the terrible raw beauty. As I caught my breath I looked it over one last, good time. At that moment I loved where I was, wouldn't want to be anywhere else in the entire world, and though I knew nothing of what was to befall me I was certain then and there that only the sweetest winds would ever fill the sails of my lifetime.

ON THE TRAIN TOWARD EDMONTON

Sunday, March 16

The train personnel are overlooking certain rules and the card room, with money and beer on the tables, is active. As we play late into the evening, I evaluate my competition. Budd Docken is a very good card player, as is Chester Kelly. Wes Peterson and Dale Kulych are competent, but for various reasons the quality of the other players declines. Kevin Anderson, the requirements of his leadership minimal on the train, has relaxed to the extreme, and has trouble following the games. He invariably stays in each one to the bitter end, often asking, "What game are we playing?" as he pushes his money forward. Whatever fortune he had won in Diamond Tooth Gerties on the eve of our Dawson departure is quickly dwindling.

Earl Mackenzie does something I have never seen done at a card table. When he feels he's had enough, he merely pushes his remaining money into the pot saying, "You guys play for it," and walks away. Joe Mason hovers behind, jumping in when he can, but he doesn't know the games or how to play them. After losing yet again, I hear him mutter under his breath, "I never won a thing in my life."

I am not winning, and when I complain that too many games are ones of chance I get jeered and soon remove myself from the Cheshire grins of Docken and Kelly, my wallet substantially lighter. I go back into the drink car and join Willie Gordon. Anderson and McRae sit across from us. Willie has a full moon face that shines when he smiles. His voice is melodic, with a soft, native accent. A soothing, enthusiastic sound. His demeanor is generous, open, and almost naively honest. Our fiddler is universally embraced by the team, Margo Anderson describing him as "magical."

"I was one of twelve kids born at Aklavik, Northwest Territories," Willie tells me. "Same hometown as Chester Kelly. It's thirty-five miles due west of Inuvik in the Mackenzie River delta. Inuvik is eighty miles south of the Beaufort Sea–Arctic Ocean. My father is half Inupiat—Alaskan Eskimo—and half Scottish. My grandfather was from Scotland, married an Inupiat woman. In his early twenties my father moved to Canada and began working for the Distant Early Warning Line, radar bases scattered across the north. They were built by the U.S. military to protect North America from any possible Soviet invasion. I then had to travel to Inuvik for school for ten months of the year and return home for summer. After graduation, I made Inuvik my home.

"I began working for the Canadian Broadcasting Corporation during high school, and was hired full time after I graduated. For twelve years I had a CBC radio show called 'The Lovin', Hurtin', Ramblin', Travelin', Drinkin', Truck Drivin', and Mom Show.' I ended my show every night with, 'Be good to your mom.' They asked me to drop the 'Drinkin'' part of the name, because of the many suicides among the Eskimo and First Nation people.

"It was during my late teens that I got the notion to give a try at fiddle playing. I played the guitar and would accompany our old-time fiddle players. Fiddle music was and still is a huge part of entertainment for people in the Mackenzie River Delta. It was the time to entertain folks who spent a long winter in the bush upon returning to the larger communities. I then bought myself a new but good inexpensive fiddle and all by myself would begin to squeak away. I mean, squeak away! I worked for the Canadian Broadcasting Corporation where they had access to many a fiddle tune. I would record them, bring them home and tried my damnedest to learn. My poor wife's ears! Not to mention the neighbors! We also had a two-year-old who didn't mind the squawks as much and he would ask to be entertained during the evening baths. So, there we were, the two of us in the bathroom, he in the tub, and me sitting on the folded-down toilet seat, learning to play the ever popular *Red River Jig*. Thank goodness my son liked long baths. It was also during that time the children's television show called *He-Man* was his favorite program and he would say, 'Daddy, play me that *He-Man* song.'

"Over the years I would ask for help from our old-time fiddlers and they would gladly offer their expertise. After working for the CBC from 1974, I retired early in 1987. Business problems with CBC. I then moved to Whitehorse in 1990. Lived there for a year and half and then moved to Dawson City in 1992. I was hired by Duncan Spriggs to work at The Pit and have been there ever since. I now play with a band called the Pointer Brothers. We formed the group in 1994, and we play mostly country-rock.

"I really don't know exactly how I was asked to accompany the team. Kevin and Steve would listen in at The Pit, I think Pat was there also. They all liked the song, *Orange Blossom Special*, which we as the band would end the evening with. It's a well-known fiddle tune that gets your foot stomping. I think somewhere in there one of them said, why don't you think of playing music for the boys, either at the game or during the journey? I didn't know what to expect of it, but I was eager and keen about it.

"My motto is 'be good to your mom.' I'm going to meet my oldest brother in Toronto. I haven't seen him in many, many years."

"How many years?" I ask.

"Oh, twenty maybe."

"What will that be like? Will it be strange?"

"Oh no! I'll throw my arms around him and jump all over him! I met a friend in Vancouver whose two kids consider me a favorite uncle. It was so nice, they come up to me and just grab me and that feels so good, you know? Having little kids just hug me!" At this point McRae jumps up.

"Aklavik," he says to Willie, "is that spelt with a 'ck' or just a 'k?'"

"A 'ck,'" Willie responds. McRae rushes away, leaving Anderson with a perplexed look on his face.

"Hey Willie," he asks, "Aklavik's spelt with just a 'k,' isn't it?"

"Yeah," Willie smiles.

CHAPTER SEVENTEEN

"In the 'Peg they picked up
One extra player
Now they need one again
Some hack present day-er.

To fill out the squad
They need one more on the roster
Forget Bure or Fedorov
They need a Ciccarelli impostor.

To be picked as that player
Would be like a dream
To help us remember
It's about the game and the team.

Because I just love to play
And this may sound cocky
But the greatest game on this planet
Is the game we call HOCKEY!!!!"

— HARVEY DOWNES, *ODE TO A HACKER,* 1997

It is remarkable how accurately the original odyssey is being repli-
cated. Every member of the team has donned period costume, or
traditional Yukon wilderness garb. We had Brian Gudmundson
and Steve Craig among five dog teams as well as Dave Millar, Doc

170

Parsons, and Bob Sutherland on bicycles to recreate the original departure. Earl MacKenzie has come along as Joe Boyle, the original financial backer and coach of the team.

Even coincidences occur; Doctor Gerard Parsons is along, just as
Doctor Randy McLennan went originally. First Nation members of our
team mirror Hector Smith, of Indian and British blood. So much has
the team taken this aspect of the adventure to heart, that they have
decided to abide by yet another original requirement: they will not
put on skates until they reach Ottawa. Though delays made it a moot
point, the 1905 team had agreed to the Cup trustee's demand not to
play any hockey en route. The reason for this requirement is unknown,
but it is surmised that the Ottawas did not want the Yukon team to
play any games for fear a loss might affect the anticipated gate. To keep
in a modicum of shape, the Klondikers worked out by jumping rope
and lifting dumbbells. And so John Flynn and Chester Kelly lead several of the players on jogs whenever possible. But the most remarkable
adherence to our predecessors history is the acquiring of an additional
player in Manitoba.

By the turn of the century, hockey had woven itself tightly into
the fabric of Canadian plains culture. The Winnipeg Victorias were
the first team to bring the Stanley Cup west in 1896, and Manitoba
Hockey League teams would challenge for the trophy six times in the
next eight years, carrying the coveted chalice to the prairies again in
1901.

The *Brandon Daily News* of February 6, 1901 indicates the fervor
with which local fans participated in the matches: "The ambitious
hockeyists from the Sloughtown visited Brandon yesterday with the
avowed purpose of carrying home the scalps of the Brandon seven...
a large crowd of Sloughtownites accompanying the team. Over a
hundred of them came, decorated externally with blue ribbons and
badges, and doctored internally with rye and other inflammables,
they paraded the town in flocks, yelling and hazing...the streets
last night were made hideous by a howling mob from Portage. The
Portage contingent brought along with them a brass band, with
which to entertain the citizens of Brandon, after they put a finish on

our hockey team. The band was present at the rink with their instruments carefully concealed under their coats and were instructed to jump on the ice and give a concert...after which a procession was to be formed and the town was to be painted red. Unfortunately the services of the band were not required and Brandonites were deprived of hearing this aggregation of Sloughtown musicians blow themselves a few ragtime ditties..."

A hard brand of hockey was played in the west. The following description of a game played January 12, 1900 illustrates the direction Canadian hockey was taking at the time: "During the progress of the Brandon–Rat Portage hockey game at Rat Portage there occurred the first instance of rowdyism ever seen on western ice. The circumstances of the case were briefly as follows: Martin, of the home side, and Nicklin, of the visitors, had for the entire first half and a portion of the second been checking one another very closely, and the play of both men being at times rough. In the second half both went after the puck in one of the corners of the rink and in the scrimmage Nicklin hit Martin over the fingers with his stick. Martin retaliated, striking Nicklin across the body and the latter dropped his stick and struck Martin with his fist. In this he was of course in the wrong, but his action should have been dealt with by the referee and not in the way in which it was. The instant the blow was struck, one of the most prominent officers of the Rat Portage club jumped the railings and, grabbing the first Brandon man he saw, proceeded to choke him. The Brandon team interfered, but in less than a minute the ice was a mass of struggling humanity, nearly all the male spectators taking a hand in the melee..." Playing in this game was the Captain of the Brandon team, Lorne Hannay.

Hannay, despite teammates including future Hall of Famers Lester Patrick and Joe Hall, was considered the star of Brandon's early teams. The Rexton, New Brunswick native played cover-point, which in the era of seven-man hockey was a sort of rover whose primary job was defense. Newspaper accounts described Hannay as "invincible," "a stone wall," and "impregnable." They also repeatedly criticized the defenseman for being caught up-ice too often.

A Winnipeg newspaper interviewed Hannay in 1946. The article stated, "While Lester Patrick has been credited with being the first defense man to 'rush,' it was really Hannay who revolutionized the playing style of the rear guards. Hannay's great forte was in lifting the puck from one end of the rink to the other, and many of these great hoists were dead on the nets and scored. Later the defense man found that with a smaller blade on the stick, he could carry the puck the same as the forwards. So he tried the idea of 'rushing' up the ice. 'I have the clippings from *The Sun* in which I was severely criticized for leaving my post as defense man,' laughed Hannay, but the idea took hold. Two years afterwards when Lester Patrick joined the Brandon team he followed Hannay's example, and his zig-zagging style caught the fancy of the crowds thereafter."

Hannay was also prone to penalties early in his career, for which the local press castigated him to the extent that he remembered it sixty years later. In a 1960 letter to his grandson Dave Hannay of Cambridge, Ontario Hannay wrote, "I am sending you a few clippings of some hockey games of a few years passed. I think you will know some of the players. Our player you will notice the sporting editor roasted once in a while. But on other occasions he had to admit the truth. I don't think this player was so rough but where he hit an opponent they usually stayed hit. If you give them room to go between you and the fence, then Wham, they usually don't try it the second time!"

The 1946 article described Lorne Hannay as, "one of the all-time greats of the game in these parts," describes his place on the Brandon team that challenged the Ottawa Silver Seven for the Stanley Cup in 1904, but did not mention the fact that he joined the Dawson City Klondikers in January, 1905, on their way to Ottawa.

It is unclear under what authority Dawson presumed to add Hannay. The team's Stanley Cup challenge had been accepted under the condition that the all-star team be derived from Dawson's four teams. It has been assumed that Dawson had taken on Hannay because he had once been there, but there is no record of Hannay having been in the Yukon, nor does his family today believe he had gone there.[18] Shaken by the loss of Weldy Young and Lionel Bennett, perhaps Dawson panicked that they might not produce a worthy opponent for the Ottawas. Whatever the circumstances, Ottawa took a dim view of the news that Hannay, a man whose ability they well knew and who had scored twice in the Cup series against them the previous year, had been added to the Dawson City roster. They promptly protested the games on the premise of his ineligibility. But the deed was done. On January 9, 1905 Lorne Hannay stepped aboard the CPR at Brandon, Manitoba, and joined the legend.

TOWARD WINNIPEG

Monday, March 17
St. Patrick's Day

Riding the rails. My roommate is Steven Poncho Rudniski, who along with Richard Nagano form the team's goalie tandem. He and Dave Millar are the only two Yukon-born white men on the team. Poncho's an interesting guy about thirty-seven years old, and one of the players I had met in John Flynn's house five years ago. He's been a trapper for twenty-five years in the Yukon, born in Mayo, a hulking, round-shoul-dered, smiling brute of a guy, with a bizarre sense of humor. The first evening on the train, just as we both laid down in our beds, Poncho whispered from the top bunk.

"*Don.*"

"Poncho."

"*Don,* I think we have unusual trees outside our window."

"Why is that?"

"They're *moving...*"

---

18 The Yukon Archives in Whitehorse records a James S. Hannay of Brandon, Manitoba, as being in the Yukon. During the tour, the *St. John Daily Sun* of February 2, 1905, has a picture of all the Dawson team members, Hannay the only one in a suit. The caption: "Lorne Hannay,—Cover. Native of Brandon, he is a miner and went to Klondyke in 1900." Lorne Hannay's grandson Dave told me that the family has no knowledge of any members going to the Yukon. When I asked him, however, if he knew of any 'James S. Hannay,' he replied, "That was my great-grandfather's name..."

At breakfast in the dining car I sit with Joe Mason, Poncho, and Patty Dahlquist.

"You'll find hill rabbits in the Yukon," Poncho says to Patty and me, "and all they do is live on one hill. Always travel in the same direction, so one leg is longer than the other, eh?"

"It's hell when you try to stretch the hides," Mason adds, but their joke is too much for them, and they break up laughing. The Yukoners are relentless with people they consider green. Before our trip began, Pat Hogan had warned McRae and I of the "rope bridge" on the trail. "You guys won't have any problem…except maybe at the rope bridge," he told us. "It's strung out over this deep ravine, you have to come down on your skidoos just right, hit it just right, to make it over…" As McRae ranted in horror at the prospect, I acted cool—not sure if Hogan was kidding or not. Of course there was no rope bridge on the trail, nor do I believe it was ever truly considered to remove McRae and I from the trail, and now I want Mason and Rudniski to know, subtly, that they no longer can pull the wool over my eyes. I look outside our window at steel tracks, then back at the experienced trappers.

"What kind of tracks are those?" I ask, pointing down. Mason, who's next to the window, looks out, then back at me.

"What are those, railroad tracks?"

"Oh yes, certainly railroad tracks," Poncho replies.

"Are they fresh?" I ask, and they laugh nervously.

"I caught a big train in Vancouver once," I say.

I chat with Poncho in the dome car. When I ask him to sign my personal copy of *Dawson City Seven*, he writes, "To Don from your favorite roommate from the train love & Kissis Poncho #31".

"So you were born in the Yukon," I say.

"Yep."

"Second generation?"

"Yep. My father was a miner. Underground."

"Is he alive?"

"Nope." Poncho pauses, "Died at age fifty-six. The whiskey killed him."

"Alcohol seems to be quite a problem in the North, eh?"

"Yep."

The train breaks out of the Canadian Rockies onto the plains toward Edmonton. We are told the train here travels over ninety-miles an hour. Jim Nicol, the DCB assistant, walks the corridors tapping on doors, "Ten minutes to Edmonton, ten minutes!" Inside our room, Poncho and I try our best to get ready in our period outfits in the tiny compartment. Poncho, fiddling with his tie before the mirror, pauses.

"What's the matter?" I ask him. Poncho sheepishly glances at me through the mirror.

"I don't know how to tie a tie," he says. "Can you help me?"

We stop at the Edmonton station and parade through, Willie Gordon, rendering what has become our official team anthem, *Orange Blossom Special*, leading the way alongside Patty Dahlquist, resplendent in her extravagantly pink, flowery, feathered dress. We are met by a bank of blank stares, and a few media people and TV cameras. Dick Van Nostrand of the Downtown Hotel appears to join the journey, and we are shortly on our way once again.

There is excitement as the train surges toward Winnipeg, where we will pick up the winner of the "Be Lorne Hannay" contest that Deb Belinsky concocted with a Winnipeg radio station. We stop briefly at the tiny North Brandon station, the smokestacks of Brandon a few miles south clouding an otherwise clear, rolling Manitoba countryside.

There is drinking this morning, ostensibly because it is St. Patrick's Day. Even Pat Hogan, his gleaming eyes revealing that wild interior—who has been steadfastly sober in his duty as leader of this expedition—mentions to me a bottle of "Jack" in his stash which he intends to pull out after we leave Winnipeg. Soon we hear the familiar tapping and "Ten minutes, ten minutes!" and prepare for the events.

We parade into the high-ceiling expanse of the Winnipeg Via Rail Station to a bank of TV cameras, dignitaries, and milling crowds. The first order of business involves an application for Manitoba's two members of the original Dawson team, Hector Smith and George Kennedy, for induction into the Manitoba Hall of Fame. Lloyd Penwarden, fellow member of the Society for International Hockey Research, has coordinated the effort to involve our reenactment with the nomination papers, and is here for the ceremony. Selkirk Mayor Bud Oliver officiates, concluding with Pat Hogan, Mayor Oliver, and myself signing the application before a barrage of flashing light bulbs.[19] We then turn to the most important business at hand.

I watch as a stocky, medium-height guy is led through waves of onlookers, seemingly a bit intimidated by the intense media and fan attention. The entire team, half in period costume and half in game shirts, lines up behind him. He is introduced by a man representing the radio station which has run the Be Lorne Hannay contest, and is presented his #20 Dawson City Nuggets game jersey, which he dutifully holds up as Hogan plays to the cameras.

"In 1905 they picked up an extra guy from Winnipeg, his name was Lorne Hannay," Hogan announces. "He played some Stanley Cup challenge hockey before as I understand you have, so it shouldn't be a problem."

"No problem," Harvey Downes replies, "I'm looking forward to it. I'm now Lorne, Harvey's gone. All right!" Patty Dahlquist moves forward to officially welcome Downes to the team by giving him a long kiss. When Downes turns away from the kiss blushing, John Flynn leans forward.

"Wait 'till the rest of the team kisses you tonight!"

The addition of Lorne Hannay and the excuse that it is St. Patrick's Day draws everyone into the drink and card cars. Once again I parade my bottle of Dick Van Nostrand's Jack Daniels and my little Stanley Cup through the rooms and hallways. "Just a reminder of our goal," I say, and pour the shots. This completes the hat trick; we've had whiskey from the Stanley Cup on the banks of the Stewart River, on the ferry, and now on the train somewhere on the vast expanse of the Canadian shield. Van Nostrand himself gets to drink from the bottle he gave me

---

19 Despite their presence in the Yukon Hall of Fame and appearing in a prominent section of the Hockey Hall of Fame in Toronto, the application for George Kennedy and Hector Smith for induction into the Manitoba Hall of Fame will be denied.

the night before we left Dawson. He is a burly fifty-year-old with a finely manicured beard and controversial reputation. Some like him, and some concur with this assessment, from one of the First Nation members: "It seems to be a prerequisite in Dawson that in order to own a hotel, you have to be an asshole."

I find him engaging, thoughtful, and dubiously humorous. The first time I laid eyes on Van Nostrand he had on a joke-apron. When he lifted the apron to wipe his hands, a ten-inch-long red dildo rose up from underneath. He was chasing one of his waitresses around the Downtown Hotel's barroom with it. Van Nostrand tells me now of moving up to Dawson and buying the hotel; he tells me of a wild youth that saw him in Marrakesh during the hippie days. I tell him that some friends of mine back home try to fly out somewhere once a year to listen to country music. He tells me that once a year a group of his friends, including his sons, fly somewhere for Substance Abuse Weekend. This seems reasonable to me, coming from one who obviously had a wild youth, getting together with like companions, I thought, to support one another in their more mature, sober later years.

"Oh no," Van Nostrand says, when I said something to that effect. "It's a weekend when we *abuse substances...*"

It is a lively, gregarious evening on the train. I eventually catch up to Harvey Downes, who is finally able to relax from the attention and excitement.

"It was the 92 CITI-FM radio station," Downes tells me, "and they got involved through Deb Belinsky and DCB. They had an ad on the radio for it, and you had to write in and tell them why it was a neat idea for you to be on the team. I had seen—I think there was something about it on TSN, that's why when I heard on the radio I knew what it was about. That's all I knew, a one minute clip about the trip you guys were making that caught my interest.

"Normally I ride my bike to work, but this day I'm driving along with my wife, and the ad came on and I said that's pretty cool, and she said, 'Why not give it a shot? Send something in, you goof.' So I did some at coffee break and it was bad, so I did more at lunch. I wrote it by myself. I write songs and stuff, I call it my private hobby. And I sat

down at lunch and thought what the heck, why not try it. And I just
started writing, and it turned into a poem pretty quickly. I wanted to
involve the NHL players and my own hockey team, and then tie it all
together. DCB—I just found this out from Jim Nicol—thought it was
a skills contest! They thought I was gonna be some hot-shot player.

"A week and a half later the phone rings in the morning and
Trish and I are in bed, the phone rings on her side of the bed so she
answers it, some strange guy, and she says, 'It's for you.' She hands me
the phone and these guys are singing the theme to *Hockey Night in
Canada*. I realize it's on live radio, they say, 'Is this Harvey?' 'Yeah.' 'Is
this Harvey?' 'Yeah!' Now I'm getting ticked, and they tell me, 'This is
Tom and Joe In The Morning…'

"Now I'm awake. I'm on the radio, eh? And they read a couple of
paragraphs, they said they loved the poem and asked if they could call
me back at work and fill me in on the details. That was last Thursday
morning, and I have to leave today. I went into work and I said you
won't believe this…it was the worst timing. It's the worst week possible to be away, so I needed to have a meeting with my boss and
co-workers to cover me and they graciously did, and I can never thank
them enough for that.

"I came home and told Trish what the scoop was and said I'm leaving Monday morning, and she said I guess I can't complain because I
made you enter the darn thing. I don't really know what to expect."
Harvey Downes pauses, and stares at the Yukon color surrounding us.
"This is incredible…"

Toward the end of the evening I find myself with Earl MacKenzie
and Willie Gordon in the drink car, Willie holding his drink of preference, a screwdriver.

"I dreamt the Nuggets would win 4–3 in overtime," Willie says,
"the winning goal by Joe Mason at 4:23. Four-two-three…" We joke
that Downes is now called Lorne Hannay, and MacKenzie Joe Boyle.
Willie turns to me.

"When I leave the Yukon, I'm known as Itzhak."

"Itzhak?"

"Itzhak Perlman," Willie replies, with that smile.

CHAPTER EIGHTEEN

"The mystery story is two stories in one: the story of what happened and the story of what appeared to happen."

— MARY ROBERTS RINEHART,
MYSTERY AUTHOR, 1876–1958

What happened to Archie Martin? All good stories have a bit of mystery to them, and the original Dawson challenge contains a pretty good one. Martin appears in every account of the Dawson legend as the spare player who made the trip across Canada to play the Ottawa Silver Seven. But after researching this story, it is evident that he did not make the trip.

Archie Martin was a twenty-seven-year-old native of Aylmer, Quebec during the 1898 gold rush. The son of a County Monaghan, Irish immigrant and the youngest of four brothers—the others of whom all became dentists—he had applied for and been denied a place with an association of Aylmer men setting out for the Klondike gold fields. At 5' 6" tall and one hundred and thirty-five pounds, the group had deemed him too small to be useful. Undaunted, Martin traveled to the Yukon on his own.

Martin found work in Dawson print shops alongside Albert Forrest. Regarded as a talented lacrosse player, he joined the newly formed lacrosse league in the spring of 1903, playing with Randy McLennan and fellow Aylmer townie Norman Watt for the Maple Leafs. That winter Martin joined Paul and Albert Forrest on Joe Boyle's DAAA hockey team, playing forward. He soon began working at the Bear Creek headquarters of the Boyle Concession, as Boyle's seven-mile-long dredge-mining lease on the Klondike River was called. When Weldy Young and Lionel Bennett both resigned from the team, the Aylmer man was added as a combination spare player, trainer, and equipment manager.

Martin's departure with the team was documented in the *Dawson Dailey News*. The front page of their Monday, December 19, 1904 edition read:

"OFF FOR THE COAST
Klondike Hockey Team Start for Cup
Hitting the Trail"

"Randy McLennan, Norman Watt, Albert Forrest and R. N. Johnstone, leave today on wheels for the outside. They are members of the Klondike hockey team which goes to lift the Stanley Cup, and to play a subsequent series of games in the East. Archie Martin, Geo. Kennedy and Hec. Smith, who also will play with the team, left yesterday with a dog team."

Archie Martin did not play in either Stanley Cup game. Nor was he listed in the Ottawa newspapers as attending the after-series banquet. When Randy McLennan aggravated an old knee injury in the first match, Boyle immediately wired a man named Fred Fairbairn in Manitoba to take his place. He was on the train the next day. Martin is not in the famous photograph taken of the team against the outside wall of Dey's Arena. Though it seemed odd that a fellow who had traveled four thousand miles to be a spare on the team did not play when needed, nor appeared at any of the other functions, nor played in any of the following tour games, none of this was particularly vexing. It was reasonable to posit that Boyle and McLennan had decided the second game was too important not to play the best player available, and Fairbairn had played for years in the Manitoba Hockey League. Or that perhaps Martin, having been away from home seven years may have skipped the festivities to spend time across the Ottawa River in his

Aylmer home. The situation barely made an impression, until the day I went through the Joe Boyle file at the local library in Boyle's hometown of Woodstock, Ontario.

In that dusty old file, tucked among papers documenting the life and times of Joe Boyle, was a time-yellowed envelope. Inside was a newspaper article dated 1946, an interview with none other than Archie Martin. In the article Martin bares his gift of gab, bragging that he knew the man who shot Soapy Smith—though he confused Stewart, the man whose robbery triggered the final mayhem, with Frank Reid—and relates that he was Boyle's right-hand man for thirteen years. And then he unequivocally states that once he reached the Yukon, he did not come out for twenty-eight years!

It is inconceivable for him to have forgotten that he'd made a four thousand mile trek to play for the Stanley Cup, a legendary trophy even in 1946. It would have been the greatest story of his life. The fact is, Martin never made the trip. It explains why he did not replace Randy McLennan in the second game. It explains why he did not show up for the festivities. It explains why he did not play in any of the subsequent tour games. Which begs the question—what happened to Archie Martin?

It is possible that Martin was injured on the way out of the Yukon wilderness. It is possible that, after walking over three hundred miles in harsh winter conditions, he'd had enough. It is possible that with the delay due to the snowstorms in Whitehorse, he may have felt the team might never reach Ottawa in time for the games. And it is possible that the Dawson team was pulling a fast one.

One of the great controversies of the time in Canadian hockey was the use of "ringers." With teams traveling great distances and having none of today's visual media enabling fans or opponents to recognize players, teams often inserted players for those who were either hurt or less talented. Since no newspaper account of the time related the loss of Martin, nor the addition of Fairbairn, this remains a possibility. When the team landed in Seattle, the newspapers noted that seven players came off the boat. They did not name them. When the team arrived in Ottawa, the newspapers specifically mention Martin as one of them.

This was not a team of well-known individuals. The reporter would have asked someone who the men were, and that someone would have been Boyle, who was awaiting his team in Ottawa. Boyle and Martin were friends, and Boyle was in contact with the team as it made its way east, yet he did not alert any media to the fact Martin was no longer with the team. When Fairbairn was called upon to play in the second game, however, his circumstances became known, and there was no attempt to disguise who he was. An Ottawan named Fred Robinson was also added to the roster, though his circumstances were never divulged in print. Who these players were and why they were accepted on the roster has never been fully determined. Were they intended to be ringers but discovered, or were they simply new men added to the team? We don't know.

So what happened to Archie Martin? In historical research, often the people involved are all gone before an investigation is deemed worthy enough to pursue. And for this, we may never know.

TOWARD TORONTO

Tuesday, March 18

Claustrophobia. Again there is growing unrest from some who have been on the journey from day one. Today's rumor has Dick Van Nostrand dropping his pants last night, inspiring a hasty meeting of the leaders on the P.R. repercussions. Otherwise, there are few distractions, and many hours to kill. I stare out the window at the vast Canadian landscape, again marveling at the scope of this whole adventure. I wonder if it is the furthest a hockey team has ever traveled for a game. But then, those flights to the Japanese-hosted Olympics were longer. Perhaps the longest a team has traveled by land to play a game of hockey?

I laugh out loud thinking the word "Japan." Last August I worked in Mumbai, India with a Montreal native. We were working with three Japanese men employed by Mitsubishi. On the last day of the job, returning stuffed in the front seat of our car among the driver, the Canadian, and our Indian interpreter, and in the back the three Japanese, I began telling the Canadian about my upcoming adventure.

As I explained the Dawson Nuggets' agenda, describing the trip through the wilderness, down the inside passage, and then across the continent by train, the Indian woman interpreted my story into Japanese. When she was done, one of the Japanese men responded from the backseat, and I saw a grin form on my interpreter's face.

"What did he say?" I asked her.

"He say, 'Can I go?'"

"I was taught at a very young age to be a very good skater," Roy Johnson tells me as the train rattles east. "I just kept it up. At Yukon Hall in Whitehorse they had a skating rink and I kept it up there. I was a good athlete in basketball, baseball, and hockey. And when I couldn't go to school anymore, the government sent me home. I couldn't do school work that was required, so they sent me home in '68.

"I didn't get directly involved right away. I watched until David Farr and Chester Kelly asked if I could play hockey, and I got involved and I was a pretty good skater. At the time we could check each other, and it was fun.

"We played Clinton Creek every Sunday, or every weekend. It was fun. These guys were going after you, they couldn't skate that well. There was this doctor and he called for a breakaway, and I timed it right and he got the puck but I got him, I really got him. I think he moved to Whitehorse a few years later. I got pneumonia, and I went to Whitehorse and he said, 'Hey, you remember me? You knocked me on my ass!' I said 'Hey, I'm sick here. I got pneumonia.' But he remembered me.

"We played Elsa, John Flynn—did he say we played for beer? Every game we played for beer. In Clinton Creek it was ten cases, it was twenty cases in Elsa. It was a young line, it was Fred Farr, his brothers, Bobby Farr, John Flynn, Joe Mason, Chester Kelly, my brother Ben. And then there was this rival, Whitehorse bringing up a team, and they came up and beat us. They got a native hockey tournament going that year, Haines Junction, Whitehorse, Carmacks, Ross River. We won the first game. I set up John Flynn for the tying goal. Bobby Farr scored the winning goal in overtime, and we won the tournament."

Bruce Duffee recalls his experiences: "I was from Maple Creek, Saskatchewan. I left Moose Jaw for Ontario in 1959 when I was eleven years old, and I played lots of hockey before then. And when I moved to Ontario it cost money, like a fair amount of money to play hockey, so I think I played one season of organized hockey. But that was it. And the rest of that was just pond hockey. It was more money than my parents could afford. I never regretted it because I kind of liked the outdoor, unstructured play anyway. In university I played college hockey, but as a young man I ended up in the Yukon at Clinton Creek. I was there two years when a girlfriend bought me a good pair of Tacks, the first decent pair of skates I'd ever had. I had no idea how much that would improve my skating. It was unbelievable! I would have done it a lot sooner if I had realized it made me such a good skater.

"And so I played for Clinton Creek, and sometimes they had pretty good teams, and I couldn't make the team. Sometimes they were not so good and I could make the team. I played in the Clinton Creek games against Dawson. They were rough games, they were the rough guys as far as we were concerned. 'Cuz I think we had a little more, um, class players. But nobody worked harder than those guys. There was a fair amount of fights which was intimidating for me because these kids from Dawson had all learned how to box from this professional boxer, Art Fry. So it was kind of scary...you look at little guys like Roy Johnson and figure, piece of cake... There's tough guys that I'm not afraid of, and tough guys I'm afraid of. Freddy Farr is one of the guys I'm afraid of. He has the perfect NHL mentality, when you hit him he retaliates. He's ready to drop the gloves right now. I don't think he was one of the boxers, but he might have just sort of picked it up through association, but I think he was a little after the era of the guys who trained. Joe Mason, Chester Kelly, but Chester doesn't have that mentality where he'd start a fight. But if you gave him a shot, you could expect a fast one in the mouth.

"One thing I can remember was playing in Dawson in their old rink, and it was this siding without any inner wall, and when the knots fell out the sun shined right through. You'd get this ray of sunshine coming through that knothole, and I do remember skating through one of those things at one point and just being momentarily blinded just as some guy leveled me, just put me right on my back. Gawd, so from then on you were always watching for those shafts of light. I played right defense in that game, and I remember there was just one in my area by the goal, one I had to worry about. Couldn't keep my head down.

"I never played in their rink when it was really cold. It was some brutal in there! 'Cuz they had a big barrel stove there to keep warm, but that didn't help you out on the ice, that was just when you came off the ice. But it made fantastic ice.

"I guess it was the first winter I spent in Clinton Creek I spent every night in the bar for the first six months. At the end of six months I looked and saw I had no money in the bank. And I thought, I'm not gonna spend my life in a place like this for nothing, so I quit going to the bar. And I started writing for the newspaper and I ended up rec director in town. Honorary position. And so I ended up in charge of making the ice. I didn't know anything, but they had hot water heat. And we made a little zamboni out of a forty-five gallon drum and a rag. And at really cold temperatures, hot water makes the most incredible ice. We didn't hardly ever have to scrape that ice, and the speed you could carry on that ice was just incredible. The guys from Dawson really liked that. You didn't have to scrape between periods. It was just like glass. Grab a pair of skates and with young legs, holy cow, you could just fly! Which makes for pretty rough games. Charging was sorta, five strides. Which is pretty much the length of the ice!

"Actually, with those Dawson guys, the rather reason they came to Clinton Creek on Saturday night was because it was steak night. They were always part of the free buffet. And those guys would eat about two cows each. Yeah, they liked to come out to the mine.

"The Doctor was a really fine skater, good guy, but a little bit wimpy to the guys from Dawson. But he was just a so much better skater, he stayed away from them. His name was Dave Ruddock. Actually, his brother was a doctor there for a while as well, but Dave had this Swedish girlfriend, she came with another Swede and she switched partners. And his girlfriend was a hell of a hockey player, she played with us all the time and dressed in the same dressing room. She smoked a pipe. And she was an extremely attractive woman.

"So, this really tough Yugoslav guy came to the mine and he learned to skate, and he really tried hard to learn to play hockey. I spent a winter with him teaching him how to play hockey, and one point later in the winter—this guy was in his late twenties—he said, 'What do you think my chances of making the NHL are?' Ha! Fabulous! How do I break it to you Steve, what do you think my chances are of making World Cup soccer? This is what we're talking.

"Anyways, they had a game with the non-skating men versus the women of the town. Steve qualifies for this, he spent five years in Canada watching *Hockey Night in Canada*, and he's taken what I've taught him over the winter. His first shift on the ice, this Swedish woman wheels behind the net, picks up the puck and theoretically she goes all the way to the other end, but he did what he was told, he gave her the boards, she took 'em and he just pasted her! This guy was a Golden Gloves boxer himself, a really tremendous athlete with this psycho mentality, and he just leveled her and the whole place just…aahhh…it's supposed to be a fun thing, a spectator event, and the whole place is aghast! Mortified! He gets a penalty and he's in the penalty box and everyone's yelling at him, and he stands up, finds me in the crowd and starts screaming at me, 'Vat you teach me? Vat you teach me?'" Duffee rears his head back and laughs.

"I always liked that story, now that I'm away from there."

After dinner I visit the drink car. Several of the boys play poker; Willie Gordon sits smiling, screwdriver in hand. Duffee waves me over.

"You just missed Titanium Dick," he says.

"Titanium Dick?"

"Dick Van Nostrand," Duffee says. "This older couple's sitting here, and Dick is quite a talker, eh? Telling everyone in this loud voice why he's called The Dick. He's swearing and going on about The Dick, and we're all feeling a bit self-conscious about this, wishing someone would get up and tell him to shut up. Anyways, Dick's going on and on about The Dick, and this little woman got up, walked over to Dick, extends her hand and says in this quiet little voice, 'I'm sorry, we haven't met. My name is Lorena Bobbitt.' Blows us away! We *love* this woman! Dick's taken aback, stumbling for words and we're all laughing at him, our way of putting him down, and he stammers, 'well...well...it's a *Titanium Dick*.' It was his best comeback, but we just *love* this woman now!"

McRae holds court in the drink car: "First time I ever met Gretzky in person was in the dressing room after a Canada Cup game in '87. Had a towel around his waist. Surrounded by reporters. All I did was stand there thinking, I don't get it. He's small, he's skinny, he's pale, he's frail-looking, he has no muscle tone. He looks like every wimp you ever saw on the beach. How is it this nothing-looking guy standing before me is the greatest effin hockey player who ever lived? I don't get it!"[20]

I chime in with a story I know they'll like: "A local Massachusetts newspaper sent a reporter to my house to get the story on the upcoming Dawson adventure," I tell them. "They sent this kid who seemed to know little about hockey, and less about geography. So I'm telling him the story, Yukon this and Yukon that, four hundred miles through the Yukon bush on snowmobiles, the ferry down the inside passage, and a train ride all the way across Canada, to Ottawa. The whole time the kid's looking at me kinda funny, jotting notes, until finally he says, with this perplexed look on his face, 'Isn't UConn in Connecticut?' Everytime I said 'Yukon,' he thought I meant *'UConn,'* the University of Connecticut!"

In Edmonton McRae received copies of his articles appearing in the *Ottawa Sun*. The team is excited to see the coverage we are receiving in Ottawa, and eagerly pass the columns around. He's written one about Freddy Farr being out of cash and too proud to mention it, and of Freddy's guilt over his brother's death. McRae sees the article making the rounds.

"Oh Jesus," he says, "Not that one! Don't show Freddy that one!

---

20 Hockey stars through the years have made similar impressions. An unknown contemporary describes in the *Dominion Journal* his first impression of Frank McGee: "I heard of McGee as a marvel and was ready for a savage looking player. I was fooled. McGee pushed open the little side door of Dey's famous rink in Ottawa and stepped on the ice—a regular dude. His golden hair was parted exactly in the center, his hockey pants were snow white and actually creased. His boots, I believe, were actually polished. I was never more surprised in my life. I asked Bob Shillington if that was really the famous McGee and he only nodded..."

He's gonna kill me, I know it. He's gonna take a tomahawk and cut my fucken head off. He's gonna kill me. I don't want to be around when he reads it."

McRae sees Farr walking toward us and promptly departs for safer havens. Surreptitiously I watch Farr for his reaction when he picks up the newspaper. He reads it, then nonchalantly turns the page. Poncho Rudniski, sitting next to me and also watching for Freddy's reaction, is less discreet.

"Hey Fred, what do you think of that article, eh?"

"It's OK," Freddy says in his high voice.

The first eight days through the wilderness were nothing less than arduous; the days on the ferry nothing but a quasi-catatonic state of weariness, and rejuvenation. Now refreshed, if somewhat cramped, there is time to reflect.

I try to determine the essence of the Yukoners as a whole, to interpret the common threads of their existence which led them north to the harshest corner of the continent. The bush defines the Yukon. It is its primal lure, it is how the Yukoners view themselves, and how they judge one another. Duffee tells great stories of his friend Jack Smith who, while traveling in the bush, would not warn newcomer Bruce of any mistake he was about to make, but let him suffer the consequence as the way to learn. And they were serious mistakes, causing pain or misfortune, but silence, and then a wearied cast of an eye, the only teacher. There is a no-holds-barred, no-sympathy-extended mentality when old meets new, and I realize that this, more than any personal conflict, may be behind some of the treatment I have received.

Great respect is accorded those who have learned their way in the bush, and particularly those who have lived there. It is the primary reason Cowboy Smith is held in such high regard. Bush stories dominate conversation; Anderson tells of Parsons' and his yearly moose hunt up the Stewart River. Anderson grows animated when retelling the harshness with which they dealt with newcomers who were unfortunate enough to be asked along. There is a palpable satisfaction in their humiliation, or any revelation of their ignorance. There is an old fashioned, well-ingrained tradition of harassing newcomers, or cheechakos as they are called, and of proving oneself.

I have been told that Millar was surprised to learn that I was angry with him, that he had forgotten the whole thing. To him it was nothing unusual, nothing extraordinary on which to dwell upon. The rookies get harassed, that's all.[21] And it comes in so many ways, not only confrontations in barrooms, but more subtly with rope bridges and hill rabbits. It seems somewhat sophomoric, but when taken in context of a throw-back wilderness, it makes more sense. Many of the people I've met appear to be ones that would be swallowed up in larger cities. Dawson, like any small town, allows people to establish an identity, and many flourish in the wide-open spaces as well as in their notoriety as inhabitants of the Yukon.

As a word dink, I have found the slight nuances of Canadian speech interesting. The letter "Z" is pronounced "Zed." Schedule becomes "*shed*ule," process "*pro*-cess," and the Yukon is, well, "the" Yukon. It's never *the* Alaska, or *the* Manitoba, but it is always *the* Yukon. I notice the predilection of Canadians to pronounce statements like questions? And I notice differences in vernacular. Street hockey back home is here called road hockey. They use what I call the singular plural; in Boston you'd drink "two beers," while here is consumed "two beer." One time in the bush, my group of wilderness snowmobilers awaiting Hogan, I watched as he mounted his hog and declared, "Let's fuck off!" I turned the key to my machine off and leaned back, while everyone around me roared off with the leader. And quickly, of course, I find even myself using the ubiquitous and much maligned, "Eh?" I tell my Canadian friends that they can't help this, that they are taught

---

21 The timelessness of this aspect of interaction among men was discussed by R. H. Dana almost 170 years ago in his *Two Years Before the Mast*: "Crossed the equator…I now for the first time, felt at liberty, according to the old usage, to call myself a son of Neptune, and was very glad to be able to claim the title without the disagreeable initiation which so many have to go through. After once crossing the lion you can never be subjected to the process, but are considered as a son of Neptune, with full powers to play tricks on others. This ancient custom is now seldom allowed, unless there are passengers on board, in which case there is always a good deal of sport."

it early in life. I receive, always, a blank stare.

"They teach you as kids to spell Canada," I explain. "C–eh?–n–eh?–d–eh?..."

I think of toughness. Back home, growing up on the harsher east coast of the United States, I had certainly come to equate toughness with meanness. I once saw the toughest guy I ever knew kill a squirrel stuck in a chain link fence with his bare hands. Now I think of Cowboy Smith's words, how tough isn't mean, but patience, and perseverance, and I see that these guys are a throwback to earlier times. Tough isn't mean here; here a tough man is likely to be a quiet man, a small man, as Thoreau once said, "a man who doesn't drill well." I see Millar proudly declare that he runs his own gold mine because "no one else would hire me." Hogan openly discusses past marijuana use, because he simply doesn't care what anyone thinks. Cowboy Smith doesn't care what anyone thinks about anything. There is enough room in the Yukon for all to spread out, and live together peacefully despite the atmosphere of bad moods, idiosyncrasies, and sometimes downright strangeness that extends from so many living there. It all makes more sense to me now.

"The Yukon," Gudmundson had said, "seems to attract those out of the mainstream." I can say now from experience: it most certainly does.

CHAPTER NINETEEN

"Man with the heart of a Viking, and the simple faith of a child."

— Inscription on Joe Boyle's gravestone, donated by Queen Marie of Rumania, inscribed with words from Robert Service's poem, *The Law of the Yukon*

oday one can piece together the events of 1905 with relative clarity. Discovering the nature of the men involved is more difficult. Researching individuals who, with the exception of three months one hundred years ago, led normal, insignificant lives is daunting. Death certificates are an excellent source of information, but in order to obtain a death certificate, one must know where the person died. Because of the transient nature of gold rushes, I knew where none of the original Dawson hockeyists lay buried, with the exception of Joe Boyle.

Boyle was accessible because of heroic efforts during the First World War, as well as his notable business acumen. He was one who viewed the primitive Yukon gold fields and imagined the process on a more sophisticated level. The Canadian government awarded Boyle a large timber and mining concession eight miles up the Klondike River. Onto the "Boyle Concession" were imported huge, steam-powered gold dredges. The entrepreneur made his fortune, and when war came in 1914, the man who considered himself a problem solver turned his efforts to larger game. Essentially he forced himself upon the conflict at his own expense, earning medals from Russia,

England, and Rumania, as well as Canada.

In 1938 his daughter Flora Boyle Fisch had published in *MacLean's Magazine* an article entitled, *Who Was Joe Boyle?* In it she stated, "I can speak intimately of my father, as I came to know him. He was a man who always walked hand-in-hand with success. Daring and courageous, he was a brilliant business man, and although his enterprises had their ups and downs and he met with inevitable reverses, he always came back, fighting to ever greater triumphs...the picture of Joe Boyle at that time remains firmly in my memory. He was almost six feet tall, and he weighed about 189 pounds. He carried his broad shoulders and deep chest gracefully. All his movements and gestures were light and graceful, belying his age. His eyes were the most arresting feature of his face, gazing out coolly, appraisingly, from beneath black, bushy eyebrows. His nose was straight and rather big, his mouth strong and firm, bespeaking the determination that was in him, and his chin square and out-thrust.

"His personality was that of a fighter. A bold and strong man, he combined bodily brawn with the rapier weapons of a shrewd mind, a keen wit, and a wealth of psychological insight, some of it instinctive, much of it natural development of his adventurous life, being among all sorts and conditions of men. While his normal manner, when things were going right, was that of a purring kitten, he could become a roaring lion when opposed, was in fact at his best at such moments. He was a fine musician, and an after dinner speaker of some fame, his native Irish wit responding at once to any opportunity; and he was very much accustomed to getting his own way."

The trail led to Ed Bennett in Boyle's hometown. Bennett was president of the Joe Boyle Repatriation Committee which orchestrated the return of the man's remains from England to Woodstock in 1983.[22] When I visited him in his home, Bennett proved fascinating. He told

---

22 Bennett told me during the course of our discussion, "We decided to look in on ol' Joe once we had the casket out. We peeked in and he was nothing but a few black bones..." The Joe Boyle Repatriation Committee also had the 1000-year-old carved cross of stone that Queen Marie had placed on Boyle's grave moved to Woodstock. I visited Boyle's grave the day I visited Bennett, and found that vandals had tipped over and broken the famous stone.

of being a tank commander captured during the Canadian debacle at Dieppe during World War II, and his subsequent imprisonment and exchange. As our talk turned to Boyle, Bennett provided a remarkable glimpse into the man in the form of a letter written by Queen Marie of Rumania to one Colonel Zvegintzov shortly after Boyle's death in 1923. In its entirety the letter is moving testament to heart-felt affection, and has provoked speculation of an affair between Boyle and Queen Marie. She wrote, in part, "For me he is not dead. He was so big, he belonged absolutely to nature. For me he is in the trees, in the sky, in the sea, in the sun and in the wind that sweeps around my house. He is in the freshness of the early morning and the silence of the night—and the stars seem to watch me with his eyes and the clouds seem to bring me messages from that great heart that was mine.

"Never has woman had a more magnificent friend and his loss is a grief which cuts right into my life like a great wound that nothing will ever quite heal...he was all strength and honour...A man so straight, so simple, so without ruse or guile cannot succeed in our false, grasping, commercial world, his big ideals and vast visions were doomed to fail...You rightly compare him to Don Quixote and Cyrano, he was an idealist, but did not know that he was, he had the mightiest brain man ever had, but at the same time was like a child and like a child others used to deceive him...In spite of having that colossal brain, he was generally deceived and finally denied—he did not believe in dreams— he was furious at the dreamy, mystical, what he called the 'Russian' side in me, what he also called 'the vanquished, fatalistic side' and yet when one comes to examine his life, he was always led by dreams—by impossible dreams..."

The only book about the Dawson challenge was Brian McFarlane's *The Youngest Goalie*. I had called the Yukon archives looking for information, when, almost as an afterthought, the assistant on the other end of the line said, "By the way, there's a novel already about the Dawson series." Nothing deflates a project more than discovering that it has already been covered. I ordered the book through the archives and anxiously awaited its arrival. The novel focuses on Albert Forrest's role on the team. I was relieved to see that it was essentially for adolescents and not a serious work of historical fiction. In the Acknowledgements the author thanked members of the Forrest family, mentioning that one lived in the Seattle area.

Working in Seattle shortly thereafter, I began calling every Forrest listed in the phone book. After a few awkward failures, I reached a woman who said she was the ex-wife of Ken Forrest, Albert Forrest's grandson. She graciously gave me Forrest's phone number; Ken, in turn, gave me McFarlane's. I was nervous when I called the well-known Canadian celebrity. McFarlane is known not only for his own considerable accomplishments, but also those of his father, who had written some of the books in the Hardy Boys series.

McFarlane was proud of his father's work, open and cooperative about his own. He was gregarious, and generous with his research and writing on the Dawson story. Toward the end of our conversation I made a rookie writer's mistake which would haunt me later.

"The nickname 'Gloomy' that you have in your book for Johnstone, is that a real nickname, or did you make it up?" I asked McFarlane.

"I made it up."

"Well, I like it. Would you mind if I used it in my own book?"

"Not at all."

I made McFarlane laugh when I ended our conversation with, "You know, *While the Clock Ticked* was my favorite."

Four years later, shortly after *Dawson City Seven* was released, I received an anxious call from my publisher. I was told that McFarlane had contacted them and accused me of plagiarism, and threatened a lawsuit for "stealing" his story. "He says you used his story, the same names, plot, everything," the managing editor told me. She then asked where she could get a copy of his book to assess the allegations. After assuring her that his accusations were groundless, I sought out my notes of the interview and a chill ran down my spine when I remembered that I had, indeed, used his nickname for Johnstone. Concerned that this alone might be a problem, I called my publisher. By this time the managing editor had read McFarlane's book.

"There is no problem," she said. "We spoke with Mr. McFarlane, and everything has been taken care of."

Coincidence then played a role in my research. Out of the blue came a letter from a woman named Lydia Watt from Ottawa, who explained that she had been visiting her daughter in Whitehorse and had gone to the library to research her father Norman Watt. Inquiring at the reference desk for information on the man, Lydia was overheard by another assistant who told of a phone call the previous day from a writer in Massachusetts interested in the same man.

Lydia Watt was proud of her father, who had fought in the First World War and been severely wounded a month before it ended. Her father had died of a heart attack before she was a year old, and she carried his obituary in her wallet. She did not know that her father had played for the Stanley Cup, and was astonished and thrilled to learn of Norman Watt's participation in the Dawson legend.

Lydia and I soon faced a problem never resolved to her satisfaction. One of the lessons I would learn in writing historical fiction is that real dead people have real live descendants, who care deeply about them. When I started writing *Dawson City Seven* I knew little of the men involved. I had envisioned gold-seeking wild men, bearded recluses, hard-drinking and harboring eccentricities enabling them not only to chase their rainbows, but remain there years after the rush had subsided. Generalities are generally true, and in conversation one evening with Lydia Watt I explained that I had arbitrarily chosen her father to be the craziest of them all, a hard-drinking, wild hockeyists to whom I also attributed the unwise remarks that allegedly infuriated Frank McGee before the second game. I had even nicknamed him "Crazy" Norman.

There is some historical record on which to base such assumptions. Norman Watt spend almost half of the first game in the penalty box. After fighting Alf Smith during the first half, he was involved in an ugly affair with Ottawa defenseman Art Moore in the second. "Watt was ruled off for a piece of work that recalled nothing so bad since the time that Murray knocked Harry Ketchum in Shamrock–Capital lacrosse match," the *Ottawa Evening Journal* reported at the time. "What led up to the act was a piece of rough work between Watt and Moore at the side. Watt tripped Moore, who retaliated with a slap of the stick. The blow smarted evidently, for Watt, who had gone down, picked himself up and skating deliberately over to Moore, struck him a wicked blow on the back of the head, cutting him deep." The cut took four stitches to close, and earned Watt a fifteen minute penalty. But this was all lost on, or unknown to, Lydia Watt.

My description of Norman Watt's portrayal in my novel was received with an ominous silence on the other end of the line. Then, "My father never drank at all," in a voice clearly expressing not only disappointment, but abhorrence. Stumbling, I promised to temper Norman Watt's behavior in my novel, but in truth it would be difficult to change it completely.

After working on the problem, I received a letter from Lydia which read in part, "Thanks again for giving me a copy of your manuscript. It was quite a thrill reading about my father in print, and you did a good job of portraying him as a fun-loving individual. Again, let me say that I was not offended by any of it. I agree with Ken Forrest that, for all we know, my father and his grandfather might very well have been drinkers back in those days…"

After the novel was released, however, Lydia's tone changed. To what extent I did not realize until I came to the Yukon for the reenactment and found myself confronted with clippings of her letter campaign to Yukon newspapers. Her letter read in part, "Don had already made Dad out to be a boozer, so it seemed a logical choice that he would also be the loud-mouthed heckler. Since Dad did not drink, he did not frequent bars. He would not have been in Cassady's and so could not have been the player who shouted insults at the Ottawa team…I will always regret that when I had the chance to do so before Don's book was published, I didn't insist that he rewrite the parts that defamed my father. It never occurred to me that his book would later be used as a source document since it was classified as fiction…"

Lydia's criticism stung. I visited Ken Forrest in his Marysville, Washington home. After a pork chop dinner with his companion Graeta, we enjoyed a far-ranging conversation. The grandson of Dawson's goalie was enthusiastic about the original Dawson story.

"This is one great story," he said to me. "It's like the Everett What-The-Fucks against the Oakland Raiders!" Ken pulled out a box that held his grandfather's gold medals won at the Dawson City winter carnivals. I told him about Lydia Watt, and Ken shocked me.

"My grandfather never drank either."

There is evidence that someone on the team drank. One of the only instructions Joe Boyle—himself a reformed alcoholic—had for his hockeyists on their journey was, "I know many of the boys need no admonition but I insist that on leaving Dawson all players cut out liquor…" In retrospect, this statement indicated a division on the team with respect to alcohol, but during my initial research I missed it. It was also stated in the Ottawa papers that the team "did not sleep for the last thirty-six hours." When Weldy Young finally reached Ottawa behind his teammates, the *Citizen* reported, "Weldy Young has arrived in town, and is surrounded by his arm-bending friends…" On my book tour in Whitehorse, I had occasion to share breakfast with Yukon historian and writer Dick North.

North is a gentle, sixty-ish-year-old man with a disarming, self-deprecating nature. He told me that he never knew any of the Dawson players, but knew some oldtimers who had. Turning my book in his hand, he casually commented, "You know they partied their asses off in Ottawa. In fact, did you know that one of them puked on the ice before one of the games?"

I knew now it was not Forrest or Watt. Nor was it Captain McLennan, who I discovered was secretary of Dawson's Temperance Society. Nor was it Archie Martin, had he even been there at all, who stated in his 1946 interview that he'd never had a drink in his life. In my discussion with North we filtered the suspects to Manitoba's Hector Smith and George Kennedy, and Ottawans Jim Johnstone and Weldy Young. Ken Forrest and I also agreed that perhaps at a young age, off on a journey across Canada to wrest the Stanley Cup from the Ottawa Silver Seven, maybe some of the others also had a nip or two.

"Jesus," Forrest said, "I don't even want to think about what I did when I was nineteen. I'm sure we've all done things when we were young that our grandchildren will never know about…"

The suspicion that Hector Smith was one of the drinkers was verified several years later in correspondence with Lloyd Penwarden, who had arranged the Manitoba Hall of Fame application for Smith and Kennedy in Winnipeg. Lloyd wrote me, "I made a phone call to an old lady that lives north of Selkirk and has lived around there all her life. And knows most of the people in that part of the country. My conversation to her was like this:

'Vera did you ever happen to know a man by the name of Hector Smith?'

'Well you know, Lloyd, I really never knew Hector Smith, but I often heard the men talking about him.'

'What men were they, Vera?'

'They were men that came in from working on the lake.' (Lake Winnipeg)

'What were their names, Vera?'

'Oh Lloyd, that was so long ago them guys would be all dead now...'

'Thank you, Vera.'

'You're welcome, Lloyd.'

"This conversation left me thinking about whether or not I could remember any old timers that worked on the lake. I came up with one that lives in an old-folks home in Winnipeg now. Bill spent all his life working on the lake. My conversation after greeting him was like this:

'Bill, did you ever know a man by the name of Hector Smith?'

'Oh sure Lloyd, I knew Hector Smith, but that was a hell of a long time ago.'

'How come that you knew him, Bill?'

'Well Lloyd, I was a young man at the time and I was working in a lumber camp along the lake, and Hector Smith lived across the bay from us. He looked after a fishing station there.'

'What bay was that, Bill?'

'That was Sturgeon Bay. During the fishing seasons the fishermen were there, but between fishing seasons Hector lived there alone and looked after the fishing station. We used to go over and visit him. He was quite a lot older than I was, but he was a friendly guy and he liked to drink beer, but sometimes he had stuff that he made himself. You know, one time in the winter Hector went over to Gypsumville with his dogs to get some stuff and he got some beer, too. He stopped at our place on the way back and he brought his beer into our bunk house so it wouldn't freeze while he was visiting.

'But you know Lloyd, Hector was a very friendly guy, but sometimes I thought he was kind of a loner, too. He spent quite a bit of time at that camp by himself. He used to raise huskies there also. He used to raise them then sell them to the fishermen to pull their sleighs for winter fishing.'

'Bill, what did Hector look like?'

'Well, he wasn't a big man. I guess you would call him medium size. He was either a Metis or an Indian. He looked more like an Indian to me.'

'Hector would have to be dead now, wouldn't he?'

'Oh hell yes, he would have to have died a long while ago.'

'Have you any idea where he might be buried?'

'Well, there was no cemeteries around out there. I imagine he ended up coming back to Selkirk and is probably buried there somewhere.'

'Did Hector ever mention the Klondike or Dawson City to you?'

'He could of Lloyd, but I don't remember of it. We used to just drink together and have a good time. Hector liked to drink, you know..."'

Gravestones themselves are invaluable in research. From Archie Martin's family plot in Aylmer, Quebec I learned that his father was from Ireland, and that his three brothers were all dentists. Perhaps the greatest coincidence occurred in locating Johnstone's grave. I had learned that he was the only member of the team buried in Dawson City, but when Terry and I walked up to that historic graveyard on the hillside above Dawson in November of '93, we found that a light snow had obscured most of the stones. Making matters worse, when we located the section that held his, we saw that most were flat and faced upward. Walking in a circle and throwing my hands up in frustration, I bent over and swept the snow from the grave on which I stood. It was Johnstone's.

Lloyd Penwarden would later write that he enlisted the aid of family members in his quest to provide me with the location of Hector Smith's grave. He wrote, "My sister and brother-in-law took quite an interest in this. So they done a little more investigating. One day they were talking to an old time resident of Selkirk and they mentioned this. This man said Hector Smith's father was British. Just about five miles south of Selkirk there is a place called 'Little Britain.' It is a place where the early British immigrants settled. He said there is a cemetery there, so go and try there. So after checking the cemetery books, and doing some searching they found Hector Smith's grave, along with the other members of his family.[23] Hector was named Hector Morrison Smith. He was born in 1882 and died in 1964. That would make him about twenty-two years old at the time of the Klondike game. His father Roderick was born in 1850 and died in 1925. Hector's three sisters were also in the family plot. Christie, Jean and Catherine. Jean worked in the Selkirk Post office for many years, I knew her through that..."

Forrest and I discussed McFarlane. The premise of *The Youngest Goalie* is that at age seventeen Albert Forrest was the youngest goalie ever to play for the Stanley Cup. To my knowledge, he may very well be the youngest goalie ever to play for the Cup, but it soon became apparent that he was not seventeen years old. Ottawa newspapers heralded Forrest as a seventeen-year-old. Emil Forrest, in his memoir, states he was eighteen. From the dates Ken Forrest gave me from Albert's gravestone, not only was he nineteen when he played against the Silver Seven, but had turned nineteen the day the Dawson team arrived in Ottawa.

And then Ken Forrest gave the most personal insight into one of the original Dawson players, when he told me about his grandfather Albert: "I was a wild kid, always saying 'I betcha this' and 'I betcha that,' and my grandfather would always take me literally. 'I don't bet, Kenneth,' he would say to me, as though I really meant I wanted to bet.

"He was a very quiet man. I hesitate to say it, he was probably very boring. He was proud to be a pretty good swimmer, did the side stroke. Growing up in the far North, the other members of the family didn't swim at all, and Albert was proud of this. He was a very proper

23 Dawson Klondiker burial sites: Hector Smith, Little Britain, Manitoba. Joe Boyle, Woodstock, Ontario. Norman Watt, Victoria, British Columbia. Albert Forrest, Everett, Washington. Lorne Hannay, Vancouver, British Columbia. Archie Martin, Aylmer, Quebec. Randy McLennan, Mayo, Yukon. Jim Johnstone, Dawson City, Yukon.

human being; every day that I knew him he wore a dress shirt and garters. Very religious—he probably wasn't a ladies man. A serious, serious guy—they were French Canadian, you know. And you know the old French Canadians, very narrow, very cautious. No flexibility. He did not have a sense of humor. He took everything you said literally, he was incapable of understanding humor. He was very, very frugal. I remember as a little kid going to church with him, and when the plate was passed I remember him pulling out some change from his pocket, hesitating, and then carefully placing a nickel in it.

"He never drank, not once did I ever see him drink. He wouldn't have participated in any drunkenness. His only vice was he enjoyed cigars and a pipe. Spoke Chinese from the years he spent in Grass Valley. He never mentioned the Stanley Cup trip to me. The only hockey story I remember is, later in his life he moved down to Juneau, and one day the family went out on a winter picnic at Auk Lake. Well, Grandpa apparently had a reputation as a hockey player still—this is when he was in his fifties—and some fellows started goading him into pulling on some skates, and skating. Grandpa refused but they wouldn't give up, and he finally borrowed some skates, put them on—and this is the story—he astounded them all with how well he skated, just made their jaws drop, this fifty-year-old guy who hadn't skated in ages…

"He was supposed to be on the *Princess Sophie*, you know. Do you know about the Princess *Sophie*? [24] The most famous wreck in Alaskan maritime history, everyone on board died, and my grandparents and their whole family were supposed to be on it, but weren't. They missed the boat. I wouldn't be sitting with you today, if they hadn't. We were all thrilled when McFarlane came out and talked to us, told us about the book he was writing. I'll give you his number, I don't know exactly what's true in his book and what's not, you can call him and ask. He won't mind, he's a pretty good guy, sent us out a copy

---

24 The *Princess Sophie* left Skagway and ran onto a reef during a snowstorm on October 23, 1918. Two nights later the ship sank, taking all 268 Yukoners aboard with it. The loss was a full ten percent of the white population of the Yukon, mostly from Dawson City, devastating the town and the Territory.

and everything. We didn't realize what the whole hockey thing really meant. You won't believe this, but we just threw Albert's skates out about five years ago. They'd been hanging down cellar forever, and we just threw them out...

"His last years were not good. After his wife died, he moved down here with us, and I think he suffered from Alzheimers. He used to go down cellar and just walk in circles around the boiler, just walk in circles talking to himself. And even though he was sick, this seems to me to reflect also how very, very quiet and reflective he was.

"I never knew Uncle Emil. After Albert died, Emil came down and took back all the family stuff to the Yukon. All the papers, letters, the sports trophies, and they were on the Keno when he died. All the stuff was in the Keno. No one knows what happened to it all. Do you know how Emil died? He was the Captain of the Keno, and on its maiden voyage from Whitehorse to Dawson he had a heart attack at the wheel. Can you imagine that? That's great! That's exactly how he'd want to go, right at the wheel. What a great way to die!

"You know, if you ever get up there to do any research, there's something you might do for me. Albert's father, my great-grandfather left them all, you know, just disappeared. He'd worked in the Grass Valley gold fields down in California, went up to the Yukon in the rush, then came out and went home to Three Rivers, Quebec, and brought up the boys. Then one day he just up and left...no one's heard from him since. It's kind of like the family mystery. But I think I know where he went, I think he went to Nome. Went to the new gold rush in Nome, but god knows whatever became of him. So if you ever get up there..."

TORONTO

Wednesday, March 19

We arrive in Toronto to the arm-spread of Dawson fans and families. Unfamiliar with many, Dawson City Mayor Glen Everitt is pointed out to me, as is notorious Duncan Spriggs, owner of the Westminster Hotel. The station is a cacophony of arm-draped wives and friends laughing, cheering, hooting and hollering, a large Dawson contingent here to experience our final leg into Ottawa.

I meet four new teammates: goalie Richard Nagano, defenseman Bob Sutherland (he with the quintessential flowing Yukon beard), winger Chuck Barber, and trainer Rod Dewell.

Wives appear: Margo Anderson, Jayne Fraser, May Gudmundson, Monica Kulych, and Bonnie Barber. Aedes Scheer, who has met the team in all its Yukon stops, at Pelly Crossing, Carmacks, and Whitehorse, is here. All churning into a wild reunion, Willie Gordon's fiddle scratching above it all in Toronto's wide, high Union Station. We make our way to the regal Royal York Hotel where our fur-covered, period-dressed mob, accentuated by Anderson entering with the bashed-up camp stove tied to his back, draws awkward, amused, and sometimes indignant glances.

The stress of our long trip manifests itself in other ways. Margo Anderson corners John Flynn in the gift shop, "John! What's this about Kevin going into a queer bar in Vancouver? *I worked too long and too hard to be known as the wife of the only homosexual on the Dawson City Nuggets! John, Kevin's not homosexual!*" Flynn is taken aback by Margo's onslaught, but emits his signature cackle.

"It's all just a joke!" he assures Margo.

In the lobby I go to a small stand and order some water. I have my team jersey on, and the young woman manning the booth asks me about the wild and woolly procession of furs and period costume loitering about the grand foyer.

"What are they like?"

"You wanna know what they're like?" I ask. The girl nods eagerly. "You know that show *Northern Exposure?*"

"Sure!"

"Well, these guys would make those characters look *mundane*." My wit has never been confused with that of Oscar Wilde's.

We make our way down Yonge Street to the Hockey Hall of Fame, our jerseys attracting stares from the parting crowds. Once inside, we are escorted by former NHL star Ron Ellis on a personal tour. When the team enters The Vault where the Stanley Cup lies, Steve Craig falls to his knees and does an "I'm not worthy" salute. The guys gather around the Cup, taking turns posing for photographs.

"I'm speechless," Kevin Anderson says to documentary voice Ken McGilvray as Brendan McEwen continues filming for CBC. He points to Dawson's inscription on the famous trophy. "Probably the first time in my life that I'm speechless. I can't explain the feeling that's in my head…I really can't. It's a lot of hard work and it's coming true, and just, just love to see that Cup. Dawson City, 1905."

"It's real now," McGilvray says.

"Yup. It doesn't get any realer than this," Anderson agrees.

While the team loiters around the Cup, I head downstairs to utilize the time for research on the book I am currently writing on Frank McGee. I know several Hall of Fame employees from previous inquiries and from meetings of the Society for International Hockey Research. Jeff Davis is here, as well as Phil Pritchard.

Though his Hockey Hall of Fame business card states, "Manager, Resource Centre & Acquisitions," Pritchard primarily performs what must be considered one of the greatest jobs known to mankind: he is one of four official Keepers of the Cup. He has the lean, chiseled, and scarred face of a hockey player; indeed, one of his favorite stories recounts a 1994 parade commemorating the 20th anniversary of the Philadelphia Flyers first Cup win, and his filling in during the parade when not enough old Flyers showed up. "Just get on the float and wave and pretend you are Gary Dornhoefer," were Joe Watson's only instructions… Pritchard allows me into the reading area, and retrieves the documents I have requested. I give a brief run down on our journey, and The Keeper tells me that he is bringing the Stanley Cup to Ottawa for the Yukon Gala on Saturday night, as well as to the game on Sunday. He leaves me to my reading. An hour later I see a white haired, middle-aged man approach, attracted to the Dawson City Nugget game jersey I wear. It is Brian McFarlane, I realize, and rise as he approaches with an entourage of Hall attendants.

"Brian McFarlane," he announces. He has a bandage on his right hand, and extends his left for me to hold.

"Nice to meet you Mr. McFarlane," I reply, "Don Reddick." The man recoils at the name.

"You…you're that *writer!*" he stammers, withdrawing his graciously extended hand as I nod and smile. "You're traveling with the team?"

"All the way!"

McFarlane whirls on his heels, and strides away without uttering another word.

We hold a press conference at Gretzky's Restaurant. A local dog team has been rounded up by Deb Belinsky and Jim Nicol, and Dave Millar, resplendent in his ancient, colorful skin jacket lined with beads and fur, sits in the sled as Toronto photographers snap away. Fake snow is driven through the air as the doors to a conference room are opened and our Yukon contingent strides in. My impression of the group of photographers, writers, and other interested parties is a sense of bemusement. They listen as Hogan, Flynn, and Anderson again explain the history, progress, and aspirations of the Dawson Nuggets. I sense uneasiness at the lukewarm reception, as if the embarrassing moment entering Carmacks resurges into our collective consciousness. *What if nobody in Ottawa cares?*

This evening many are going to Maple Leaf Gardens to see the Maple Leafs play the Philadelphia Flyers, and others, surrounded by old as well as Dawson friends, plan to hit the town. McRae and I bow out; the columnist suggests we visit his favorite Toronto restaurant for dinner. We walk a few blocks from the Royal York, until McRae scratches his head.

"I know it's here somewhere…"

We circle the same block three times before finally locating his restaurant. McRae is beside himself, ecstatic to be on the verge of arriving home. He is wild inside the restaurant, bug-eyed with caustic, cock-eyed imitations of various Dawson teammates. The man mimics perfectly. When the waitress approaches, the Ottawa columnist looks at her, picks up the salt shaker, and tells her there is a microphone inside.

"We work for the CIA," he tells the young woman. She looks tired, never cracks a smile. McRae points to a chandelier. "They're everywhere! Listening devices everywhere!"

"It's almost over, Dangerous Don," he says, looking back to me. "Can you believe it? It seems like a fucken lifetime. I can't wait. We never should have given in to Suzuki. We should never have succumbed. He was trying to get back at us for Japan losing the war! If I'd been using my head at the time, I would have gone out in the dead of night and spread rumors that he was going around saying Cowboy Larry's a homo…"

McRae suddenly slumps in his chair and silences, as if shin-kicking drains his energy. In a soft voice he says, "You know, of all the places we've been, everywhere we've gone, you know where I'd like to go back to? You know what I'd like to do? Remember that cabin in the middle of nowhere where those bastids left us out in the hundred-below-zero cold while they laughed at us with their feet up on the wood stove? I'd like to go back there and spend some time, a vacation." His eyes go distant, his hands start working. "The quintessential image of the Yukon, smoke swirling up from the chimney, utter isolation…" And then his eyes narrow, his mind turns and the shin-kicking regains its momentum, "…and those *bastids* left us outside while they *laughed* at us with their feet up on the wood stove…"

I mention my encounter with McFarlane.

"He showed up while the guys were in the Vault with the Cup," McRae says. "Said he'd been listening to the radio and heard the interview with Flynn, tried to call in but couldn't get through. He came down to the Hall when he heard we'd be there. Passed out his card to everyone, told them he was the expert on the original story, and that he'd be happy to come up to Dawson—expenses only—to give a talk on it."

We revel like little kids in the fact that we've both assumed Yukon nicknames. We discuss other nicknames we've bestowed upon the team. Rockin-Budd-Docken, Chester the Molester Kelly, Mumbles Peterson. McRae laughs when I refer to Harvey Downes as "Harvey Wallbanger."

"He's lucky he didn't make the whole trip," McRae says. "Those guys would eat him alive. Did you hear Chester Kelly made him take off his earring his first night on the train? I'm so sick and tired of the bullshit. It's good to get back on my own turf. I felt so silly in the woods, Hogan tying up my sled each morning. Like I'm some little kid that can't tie his skates! I can't wait to meet them on my own turf! Home field advantage!" The writer dons his half-crazed look, and imitates various members of our entourage.

"MacKenzie was starting to look at me funny in the bush..." he intones. "Gawd, I wish I saw you threaten to boot-stomp the brains out of Millar in that bar in Whitehorse. I'd pay more than Pay-Per-View asks for a Tyson fight for that one... It's almost over. Can you believe it, Dangerous Don? Like a fucken lifetime. The hell with the Yukon. It's the Human Holding Pen. Bunch of inbred, idiot-savant, moose-fucking imbeciles..."

I order pork chops and McRae haddock. He is on a roll and regales me with tales from his sports reporting days, salacious stories not found in newspapers and magazines. He tells of an NHL star arrested in a dress in an Edmonton gay bar; he tells of a Hall of Famer who was the go-to guy for cocaine in the '80's. He tells of the player who had to be traded because his entire team had become too, ah, friendly with his wife. The infamous columnist manages to denigrate, insult, disparage, and offend all he touches upon in voices and looks that leave me crying with laughter.

He was the four-eyed, lippy little shin-kicker to the end.

CHAPTER TWENTY

"Frank McGee was the most marvelous hockey player who ever laced on a skate."

— ALF SMITH, TO THE *OTTAWA CITIZEN*, 1916

The Honorable Frank Charles McGee is a retired immigration judge in Toronto. He is an engaging personality, thoroughly comfortable with sharing one of the most famous names in hockey history. I visited him and his wife Moira the summer before our trip. Frank warily eyed his wife until she shuffled out of the kitchen, leaving us alone. As soon as she disappeared Frank jumped up and said, "Good. Now we can drink." He pulled a bottle of Chivas Regal from a shelf, and poured a single glass when I held up my palm.

The man was lovably arrogant. The son of Walter "Dick" McGee exuded delight and interest in many topics, and seemed incongruously as pretentious as he was affable. Capable of swearing like a pirate, he interrupted me whenever I call him "Mr." McGee. "The *Honorable* Frank McGee," he corrected, "The *Honorable*." He bemoaned a dearth of grandchildren with an unprintable quote, and was anxious to show me his father's First World War battalion's yearbook.

The judge did not know how his famous uncle was killed, or where he was buried. He did not know who has the medals awarded to the family; he had never seen them. All the family knows is what can be found on Frank McGee's Hall of Fame plaque: he was killed on September 16, 1916 on the Somme battlefield in France.

I told him of the coming Dawson City Nuggets adventure. I mentioned that I had been in touch with Lydia Watt, and asked if he would be interested in shaking hands before the game at center ice with Lydia, representing the original participants. Frank McGee readily agreed.

"But can I ask one favor?" he added. "Can my ten-year-old grandson go out on the ice with me?" I shrugged. My relationship with Pat Hogan was one in which I made suggestions and passed along messages, but could guarantee nothing myself. I doubted Hogan would assent to the grandson, but promised to relay the request, and to get back to Frank when I had concluded my investigation into his uncle's demise.[25]

Frank McGee was the sixth of eight children born to Elizabeth and John McGee, an Irish Roman Catholic family well known at the turn of the century not only because John was Clerk of the Privy Council, but also half-brother of famous orator and assassinated father of Confederation, Thomas D'Arcy McGee.

Military Service was an accepted part of McGee life. Uncle James McGee of New York City fought with Thomas Francis Meagher's Irish Brigade during the American Civil War. Older brother Charles served with the Canadian Expeditionary Force in the South African Boer War, returning a hero to the McGee compound on Daley Avenue in the prestigious Sandy Hill section of Ottawa.

As members of the Non-Permanent Active Militia of Canada, two of the McGee brothers were mobilized for active service when Canada entered the Great War in 1914. Charles was appointed Captain at Valcartier on September 25, sailing shortly thereafter with the first Canadian contingent. In November Frank was transferred to the

---

25 I mailed the following article—almost exactly as it appears here—to Frank McGee later. Anxious for his appraisal, I called him soon after and was aghast at his response: "It's too much, too much...I couldn't even show it to Moira. She lost a brother in the Second World War, you know, it's just too much..." Once again, the historical novelist's lesson that real dead people have real live descendants, who care deeply about them.

Canadian Overseas Expeditionary Force and appointed Temporary Lieutenant, 21st Battalion.

On May 5, 1915 the 21st Battalion embarked for Europe. Soon after their arrival in England, the war's cruel reality was visited upon the McGee family with word that Captain Charles Edward McGee had been killed in action at Festubert. On September 14, after a tedious summer in rainy England and undoubtedly harboring the burden of his brother's death, Frank and the 21st proceeded to France where Canadian units were slowly being integrated into the trenches.

The all-too-common experience of the Great War soldier is illustrated with excerpts from letters written by Frank Charles Slavin, the son of Joe Boyle's old barnstorming partner Frank Slavin, to his mother in Dawson City:

"Sept. 21—We are out for a few days rest now but I have been training for the Core Sports until yesterday when I was sent back to the battalion. I won the Divisional Championship without any trouble. But owing to there being no other Heavyweight entries in the core, I won't have to box so it's back to the line again.

"Nov. 5—I think that good sprite you speak of must have surely been looking after me, as my chums were pretty well cleaned out in this last do, and I never got a scratch. I am not allowed to give any names or numbers but by this time you will have read of the Canadians advance and the way the Fritz's ran before us was some treat believe me. It seemed a shame to kill them as they are mostly kids and won't show any fight at all and if it wasn't for their artillery we wouldn't have many casualties. They have a great trick of staying with their machine guns until you are right up on them and then throwing up their hands with "Mercy Commerad" but it wouldn't work with this O'Slavin. It was just like slamming a bunch of caribou only a caribou wouldn't run away as quickly.

"June 7—I was over to see Norman Watt and the rest of the boys the other day, and also had a talk with George Black. He seems to be tickled to death with the idea of me going back to them and wrote in regards to my transferring.

"June 28—Last night I took a little walk and to my surprise I met

Norman Watt, he is attached to a reinforcing company and is worrying about not being in real active service yet.[26]

"Sept. 10–We are out again, enjoying a few days breathing spell after a very hard time, but as my usual luck was following me, I never got a scratch. A lot of the old Dawson Boys got theirs this time and most of them got nice little "Blighties" only to get it on the way out.[27]

"Sept. 22–Captain Pottaulo informed me today that he had just heard of Joe Boyle being killed in Rumania. What do you think of that?"[28]

And then the all-too-common final letter: "Oct. 11, 1918. Dear Madam, I am writing on behalf of my platoon and myself to convey to you our heartfelt sympathies in the loss of your son, Corporal Frank Charles Slavin. His loss to the platoon can never be filled and I can safely say he was the best soldier we had. On September 29th our Company was standing in a sunken road when a shell struck close by instantly killing him and also his Company Commander Captain Grey. I cannot speak highly enough of your son's work in these recent actions. He was a great favourite amongst his platoon and his absolute fearlessness commanded their greatest respect."

There can be no understating the mental and physical rigor of trench warfare. The experience ranged from mere discomfort in rain-soaked, rat-infested ditches lining areas where a "gentleman's agreement" had been reached with the enemy, to a virtual hell on earth like Ypres where body parts were "embedded in the walls of trenches,

---

26 Norman Watt was severely wounded on October 11, 1918 outside of Cambrai. Hospitalized in England, he was nursed back to health by his fiancee Dorothea Acheson, a nurse with the Canadian Red Cross. They married after their return to Canada, in April, 1919.

27 The word "blighty" is British slang for "home." A "blighty wound" was a non-mortal wound serious enough to remove the victim from the war. Considering the brutality of trench warfare, it was considered good fortune to receive one.

28 The rumor was false. Boyle survived the war a hero, and died of heart failure on April 14, 1923 in Hampton Hill, England. He was reinterred at Woodstock, Ontario on June 29, 1983.

NOTE: Robert Service, poet of the Yukon, dedicated his book, *The Rhymes of a Red Cross Man* to his brother Lt. Albert Service, a Canadian infantryman killed in action in France, August 1916.

heads, legs, and half bodies, just as they had been shoveled out of the way by work crews," amidst the stench of putrefaction "so disgusting that it almost gives a certain charm to gas shells."

On December 17th Frank McGee was wounded at Dickebusch. A medical report stated, "This Officer, whilst in action and handling a gun in an armored car, which was blown up by the bursting of a H. E. (high explosive) shell into a ditch six feet deep, and into this he fell striking his right knee against some part of the car and received a small puncture wound of superficial tissues just inside the patella. Synovitis was caused by the blow, and the knee became much swollen."

After six months of medical evaluations, McGee's sabbatical ended on July 7, 1916, when it was determined he was "Fit for General Service (Without Marching)." It was the very same day that younger brother Walter, who had enlisted after Charles' death, was transferred to the 77th Battalion, which was then preparing to cross the English Channel into France.

This was six days after Sir Douglas Haig, leader of the British Expeditionary Force, had ordered 170,000 soldiers of Lord Kitchener's volunteer army over the top across a ten mile stretch bordering the river Somme. It was days before this folly was fully realized, but it did not stop the sanguine summer of '16, the horrors of High Wood, Delville Wood, Bazentin Ridge, Contalmaison, Bernafay Wood, and particularly Pozieres consuming hundreds of thousands of soldiers both of the Allied and Central Powers.

McGee was returned to his 21st Battalion on August 29, 1916. Two days later he was "Taken on strength," rejoining his comrades on September 5th, just in time to participate in Canada's first involvement at the battle of the Somme. In a letter dated September 4, 1916 and received by his oldest brother D'Arcy in Ottawa, Frank claimed that he had been offered a post behind the lines in Le Havre, but had refused so that he could rejoin his mates at the front. It was a decision that would cost him his life.

The battle of the Somme was the Allied response to Germany's onslaught at Verdun. In order to relieve that pressure, Kitchener's thirteen divisions went over the top on July 1, 1916. On that day, and it is suspected mostly within the first ten minutes, 60,000 casualties were inflicted upon Lord Kitchener's army, including 21,000 deaths. For the next two and a half months, with an average "wastage" of almost 7,000 casualties a day, the attack stalled into yet another war of attrition within the trenches. Frustrated with a lack of progress and facing winter, the Allies decided on one last "Big Push," scheduling it for September 15th.

The Canadians relieved the Australians in early September from their trenches crisscrossing the long, sloping ridge at Pozieres. The area, particularly around a windmill atop the ridge, was the scene of some of the worst carnage in the war. The English had failed to gain the ridge during July and had given way to Anzac Divisions, who were anxious to restore their pride and honor after their humiliation at Gallipoli. The Australians accomplished what the English could not, but not before suffering 20,000 casualties, forever linking their name with that place in the annals of warfare. "Pozieres was the last word in frightfulness," recounted Philip Gibbs in his book, *Now it Can Be Told*. "Many of their (Australian) wounded told me that it had broken their nerve. They would never fight again without a sense of horror." It was into this web of earthworks that the 4th Canadian Infantry Brigade, including the 21st Battalion, entered on the night of September 14, 1916. At dawn they would go over the top and enter what is now known as the Battle of Flers-Courcelette.

I walked the Courcelette battlefield in August, 1996. Standing at the Courcelette British Cemetery, resting at what was approximately the Canadian jumping-off trenches, the most striking feature of the long, rolling landscape is its utter openness. Attacking entrenched machine gun positions from here was nothing short of suicidal. But the Canadians did so, attaining all their objectives for the battle, particularly the capturing of the ruined structure of a former beet processing plant, referred to as the Sugar Factory.

I try to imagine what occurred here, my research uncovering accounts such as this from survivor Thomas Trembley of the 22nd Quebec Regiment, "If hell is as bad as what I have seen at Courcelette, I would not wish my worst enemy to go there." An Englishman related, "We went up to relieve the Canadians. We'd never seen anything like it. Going up through this area it was just as if an earthquake had been there. It was all mud and I was frightened to death. Sign board in the rubble, 'Pozieres,' that's all there was to tell us where we were."

Future Hockey Hall of Famer Conn Smythe wrote of his time on the Somme: "In front of Courcelette were three places, sort of redoubts, gun emplacements in the chalk that were supported by trenches. Being Canadian, we had named them Regina Trench, Kenora Trench, and Desire Trench...that's when I knew I could be as scared as anyone living. I was shaking so much I could hardly put a cartridge in a gun at all..." A German account indicates their own confusion. "The men we relieved had no idea where the enemy was, how far away, or if our own troops were in front of us. No idea where our support trench is. We found the English, 400 yards away, by a windmill." Another Austrian youngster, destined to be wounded at the Somme in October, would later describe his impression of the battlefield in his book *Mein Kampf*, "...A whirlwind of drumfire that lasted for weeks...it was more like hell than war." A soldier of the 17th Bavarian Regiment wrote, "We are now fighting on the Somme with the English. You can no longer call it war. It is mere murder. All my previous experiences in this war, the slaughter at Ypres and the battle in the gravel-pit at Hulluch, are the purest child's play compared with this massacre, and that is much too mild a description...we are in a very bad way."

These images, combined with the fastidiously kept British Cemeteries dotting the landscape, provoke great emotion. There are guest registers here that record messages from returning survivors. "Came back for one last good-bye, fellas," one read. Others, such as "I never knew you, Uncle John, but I've come to pay my respects today," create a surreal comprehension of what actually occurred on the ground before me.

I am disappointed that Frank McGee is not among the register of names of those interred at the Courcelette British Cemetery. I learn that fallen officers were removed and interred at the Bapaume Post Military Cemetery outside of Albert, but find that McGee does not lie there either. I search the registers of other cemeteries in the area, the Regina Trench Cemetery at Courcelette, the 2nd Canadian Cemetery, and the Pozieres British Cemetery, all to no avail. I return from France unable to say exactly how or where Frank McGee fell.

Once home, however, there is a break. Paul Kitchen, hockey historian and former President of The Society for International Hockey Research, has been kind enough to assist me in scanning microfilm at the Ottawa Archives. Asking him to look into The War Diaries of 1916, he has uncovered a stunning find. The War Diaries are the day-to-day hand-written accounts for each Battalion. In the 21st's diary the course of the battle is recorded, how tanks were used for the first time, how the boys "jumped the bags" and engaged in a horrific hand-to-hand struggle in attaining their objectives, and then repulsing wave after wave of German counterattacks before enduring the worst of all Great War experiences, intense shelling. The discovery is a specific mention of Frank McGee on the day he died.

On the 16th the diary states, "At 11:00 16th Lieut. McGee reported to Battalion H.Q. with 50 O.R. (other ranks) who had been engaged on various other duties and proceeded from there to Sugar Factory line." This is an amazing discovery, considering we are searching for the fate of one of eleven million souls lost in that war. To have him mentioned in dispatches on the day he died is nothing short of miraculous. It locates him at the Sugar Factory about noontime, and suggests other details of his last hours. Almost certainly he did not participate in the assault on the previous day, his knee discouraging that. Once the 21st had lost most of its officers in the advance, however, bad knee or not he was needed up front. That he "reported to Battalion H.Q. with 50 O.R." confirms he was behind the attacking lines. The War Diaries also state that during the afternoon of the 16th, "The position was held all day and under heavy shell fire from guns of all calibre. Casualties about twenty-five killed." But as important as this discovery is, it merely locates him at his time of death, it does not explain it. It would take one last trip to Ottawa to determine how Frank McGee died.

In October I returned to Bytown, staying at McGee's Inn at 185 Daley Avenue. The original house on Sandy Hill that John McGee built in 1886 now entertains guests. At breakfast I sat in the same room that received the heart-wrenching news of the McGee casualties, so long ago. At the Archives I received the three fighting McGee's military records, and returned to Sandy Hill to study them. When I opened Frank McGee's file I immediately saw the words that ended my quest: "Body unrecovered for burial."

After the Great War ended, it took years to locate and bury the dead on the Somme battlefield. Over 700 bodies were discovered in 1935 alone, nineteen years later. On memorials in France are listed over 220,000 men with no known grave; in the cemeteries are buried only 110,000 unknown soldiers. Considering the pains with which officers were located and removed from the field of battle, it appears that Frank McGee has died in the most feared manner possible to a Great War participant—he has died by shell-fire. Probably the best insight into his last moments on earth can be gained from this Frenchman's description of shell-fire: "…when one heard the whistle in the distance, one's whole body contracted to resist the vibrations of explosion, even the most solid nerves cannot resist for long, the moment arrives when blood mounts to the head and where nerves, exhausted, become incapable of reacting. Finally one gives in to it, has no longer strength to even cover oneself and scarcely strength to pray to God—to be killed by bullet is nothing, to be dismembered, torn to pieces, reduced to pulp is fear flesh cannot support—it is the greatest possible suffering."

Several years later Bill Fitsell, like Paul Kitchen a former president of the Society for International Hockey Research, uncovered the letter that we all knew must exist somewhere, but had yet to find. It is a letter from McGee's commanding officer Lieutenant-Colonel Elmer Jones, reprinted in Loyola College Review No. 3, 1917. The letter is dated October 18th, 1916, and states, "I have intended writing to you ever since Frank left us, but I have a great deal to do. That is my only excuse.

"Frank only came back to me two days before we went over on the morning of the 15th of Sept. I left him with the reserve during the first attack, but, during that day, I lost every officer save one, and in the early morning of the 16th, Frank brought up 50 men to hold the line and push on past Courcelette. He reported to me, and I put him in command of my first line. He knew what it meant, and he laughed as he went into it. He took most of his men through and reached the front trench. I had a message from him there, telling me his disposition, and that he would gather up more men and push on. He had to go up under extraordinary shell-fire. He then came back to the Sugar Factory, and was gathering men there for another attack, when he was killed. I need not tell you what he was like under shell-fire, because you know better than I can write; but his bravery always inspired the men under him.

"When he was with me first, I had learned to rely on him, but in the Somme, during his few hours there, he was wonderful. I can't tell you more. He was buried where he fell, and where so many of my battalion lie. If I come home, I will be able to tell you more, but it is harder writing than you can know."

The front page of the *Ottawa Citizen* exploded with casualty lists following the advance of the 15th. On Friday a rumor of Frank's death was answered by brother D'Arcy, who referred to his letter of the 4th. "As far as we know," he told the *Citizen*, "Frank is alive and well." The next day, however, saw the rumor confirmed when a member of the Militia Department paid yet another visit to 185 Daley Avenue. Newspapers conveyed the ensuing shock, "...once again there has been brought home with gripping grief and pain the grim reality of the present conflict of nations. It is doubtful if the loss of any one of the splendid young Ottawans who have fallen at the front since the outbreak of war has occasioned such keen regret as that of the late Lt. Frank McGee...Frank McGee dead? Thousands of Ottawans knew him. Few seemed able to believe that he too had given up his life in the struggle for freedom..."

Frank's death did not end the McGee family's suffering. On November 18, barely a thousand yards from the Sugar Factory and the body of his famous older brother, Walter McGee received a gunshot wound through his left shoulder when the 87th Battalion went over the top assaulting Desire Trench.[29] Walter was awarded the Military Cross for his conduct that day, the citation stating, "For conspicuous gallantry in action. Although wounded he continued to lead his men

---

29 Walter McGee's military record in the Ottawa archives states that he was shot through his right shoulder. His son the Honorable Frank McGee insisted to me, "He was shot through the left shoulder, I vividly remember the scar on his left shoulder." A lesson that "official" documents are not necessarily accurate.

with great courage, and remained in the front line until his battalion was relieved some thirty hours later." The youngest McGee brother survived the war and was returned to Ottawa on compassionate grounds in 1919, to walk the forever changed streets of Sandy Hill.

After the war most trench veterans could not even articulate what they had experienced. Perhaps the most accurate assessment of these men's souls is expressed by the words of Henry James in a letter to a friend shortly after the beginning of the war, "They had been taught to believe the whole object of mankind was to reach out to beauty and love, that mankind, in its progress to perfection, had killed the beast instinct, cruelty, blood-lust, the primitive, savage law of survival by truth and claw and club and axe. All poetry, all art, all religion had preached this gospel and this promise. Now that ideal was broken like a china vase dashed to the ground." Eighty years later, sitting with Walter McGee's son in Toronto, I asked what his father told him of the war. Frank McGee's nephew and namesake shrugged and said, "He would never talk of the war."[30]

There are respected hockey historians who claim other early stars such as Tom Phillips or Russell Bowie were as good as McGee. But Frank McGee will always remain the legend for two reasons. First, he is the only legitimate Hall of Fame athlete of any sport to be killed in action fighting for his country, and second, for what he did to the Dawson City Klondikers on January 16, 1905.

TORONTO TO OTTAWA

Thursday, March 20

The train is alive, the air thick with myriad sentiments, expectations, concerns, and one overwhelming fact—our traveling is coming to an end. Troy Suzuki, camera to eye, records the scene, capturing emotion from normally staid Wes Peterson.

---

30 The inability of trench veterans to speak of their experiences was widespread. Paul Kitchen's father Percy served in the trenches and it was only after he passed away and his papers gone through that Paul learned that his father had been wounded in action. His father had spent a lifetime with his family, never once mentioning what must have been the most traumatic experience of his life.

"Feeling kinda sad," our coach explains. "Spent all this time getting here, and ah, now ah, there's no more traveling. It's a fast three weeks. The first two days were long, but three weeks goes fast. Amazing. Totally confused."

Everyone bedecked in period costume or game jerseys, Patty Dahlquist flowing in her pink flowered dress, Dawson City Mayor Glen Everitt resplendent in an $85,000 gold "Chain of Office" necklace, Aedes Scheer in 1890's hat and dress, as Willie Gordon strolls the aisle, fiddle-to-chin scraping and smiling that smile, breaking into our *Orange Blossom Special.* Hogan restless, moving up and down the aisle grabbing the backs of the chairs with each hand as he goes, speaking with all. The entourage of family and friends eagerly participate, one an imposing, round-shouldered hulk with a Smith Brothers' beard showing photographs of the road hockey game in Whitehorse, and handing out his card, "Jaime Smith, SHRINK." The presence of the Yukon's lone psychiatrist elicits great jokes: "He's got the biggest waiting room of any doctor in the world: 480,000 square kilometers." McRae is an empty bag of exasperated exhaustion and relief, his eye missing nothing, muttering "Finally...finally..." as we sit at a table, jotting notes.

There is silent concern, born of disappointing experiences in Carmacks and Whitehorse, that our reception in Ottawa will be modest, embarrassing. We are encouraged by a Bruce Duffee story circulating the train.

"When we stopped in northern Ontario," Duffee relates, "I was running to a store and I had my sweater on, and as I was racing down the street some guy hollered as I went past, 'Hey, are you one of the Nuggets going to Ottawa?' Yeah!"

For myself, there is tremendous eagerness to see a row of friendly faces flown north to greet me, my wife Terry and three daughters Becky, Sarah, and Allie, as well as my father and my sister Connie and her son, Sam. I know how McRae feels; for so long a fish out of water, for so long not truly understanding exactly my role, for so long on a trip with strangers, and yet the trip I couldn't wait to end, now I wish wouldn't.

Onward through lightly snow-dusted Ontario countryside we rumble, the trip a mere two hours but seemingly endless in our gut-queasy anticipation. The Yukon Territory flag is unfurled by Dave Millar. Nervously exchanged glances and acknowledging nods. Smiles conveying the unified experience, the bond, that we have done this trip, that we have arrived. *It's happening!* Jim Nicol bounces along the thin aisle shouting "Ten minutes! Ten minutes!" As we approach Ottawa's Union Station, we rise to stare from windows, hang from poles, responding in shouted unison to Flynn's call, "One, Two, Three—*NUGGETS!*" As we slow to a stop, I search through the window for familiar faces, and find them outside and to the right. We pile up in line to exit the train and when I step out I am engulfed by family, hugs and kisses, a shaken hand and patted back—we are in Ottawa!

I look about at the frenzy of news cameras and reporters, the stride of nine or ten Ottawa Senator alumni in their black, red, and white striped game jerseys crossing the station grabbing every extended hand, a big white sign held by two women, "Welcome Home Wrong Way McRae." It is joyous, exciting, full; all doubts of our arrival smashed in the energy of the large crowd gathering about us, sports writers and beat writers cornering every odd looking figure they can, scribbling madly the thoughts and feelings of this Yukon contingent. Ottawa Mayor Jacquelin Holzman and Kanata Mayor Merle Nicholds are on hand to officially greet, as well as alumni Captain Brad Marsh and his Senator players. The two troupes collide and mill about, coalescing into an impromptu news conference.

A multitude of images: McRae animated, surrounded, waving his hands in mock horror at his near-death experiences in the bush, pointing to the fading scab on his frost bitten nose; several of the Nuggets without family standing self-consciously aside, taking it all in; a woman in outrageous white shorts getting it autographed by all involved; the faces of the media, not exactly understanding the whole business but appreciating its news-worthiness, clicking away, jotting away; cameras and microphones stuck in your face, questions on all that we have done—*Ottawa!*

The word war accelerates as individuals lean into microphones, stare into cameras. John Flynn: "It's the Ottawa Senators behind the eight ball. I mean, we're here, we did this trip, I don't think we've anything to lose. We've already made our point, we're here. I think they're a little worried right now, because they really can't lose this game I don't think."

Brad Marsh, laughing in response: "Well, I'll tell ya, I don't think it'll be the same as playing the Broad Street Bullies in the 70's and Moose Dupont and the boys, but I think it's gonna be a great hockey game on Sunday afternoon. It think it's gonna be highly competitive right to the end."

Pat Hogan: "We're back to avenge it. Let me put it this way. Bally's in Las Vegas has the Senators as favorites by two and a half goals. I think the Senators will be fortunate to get within two and a half goals of us."

Laurie Boschman: "We want to get going early, and see if we can jump on them quickly."

Brad Marsh: "This is not going to be a Harlem Globetrotter's game. There is nothing going to be staged in this game at all. Both teams play hockey. Once the puck is dropped, we'll both be playing to win."

Yukon M.P. and former NDP leader Audrey McLaughlin: "My policy has always been to abolish the Senate. It will be the Dawson City Nuggets who will abolish the Senators."

There is so much commotion on the platform; only by following the turn of TV cameras can one follow the action. The crowd concentrates around Hogan and Marsh, who are now introduced by Mayor Everitt. Hogan takes the microphone, "It took us a few years, but we throw down the challenge." Hogan dashes his huge fur mittens to the floor of the podium. "You beat us bad last time, we're back to avenge it. I dare you to take up the gauntlet of challenge."

Marsh, a bemused grin across his broad face, bends over and picks them up. Taking the microphone, he elicits a laugh by pausing to smell the mittens, one by one. He accepts the challenge of the Dawson City Nuggets!

In Ottawa there is little time and much to do. Our first stop is the dedication of the Dey's Arena plaque at the corner of Bay and Gladstone. The team busses over to a nearby Community Center for pizza and soft drinks. Paul Kitchen, who spear-headed the drive to get the monument placed at this historic site, is on hand, as well as descendants of original Ottawa Silver Seven players. I am introduced to Robin Westwick, the granddaughter of Rat Westwick. I am introduced to Don Finnie, great-nephew of goalie Day Finnie. My father, unfamiliar with Ottawa hockey history, is fully informed by Paul Kitchen.

"When the Senators returned to Ottawa a lot of newspaper coverage was given to the early history of the original club," Kitchen explains. "I noticed that there were confusing and contradictory references to the rinks the team played in. I thought it would be a good idea to do some research on early Ottawa rinks. This led to a pamphlet identifying three successive rinks built by the Dey family. Joseph Dey built the first one in 1884, and his sons Edwin Peter, William, and Frank put up the next two in 1896 and 1907. Few people, in 1992 when the Senators began playing again in the NHL, were aware of any of these rinks, and no one knew there had been three.

"The second rink, at the corner of Bay Street and Gladstone Avenue—then Ann Street—was the site of Ottawa's first Stanley Cup victory in 1903 and where the original Ottawa–Dawson games were played. The rink burned down in 1922 and on the site today is a corner coin laundry and some duplexes. Thousands of cars travel by that intersection every day. I thought what a pity that people had no opportunity to know of the significance of that site. A plaque or other commemoration would be a good thing, I thought. I enlisted the help of Ottawa sports historian Jim McAuley and sports aficionado Mike Bolton as a committee to mark the spot. My first step was to write a proposal to City Hall, asking for official assistance in putting up a plaque. Meetings with the ward representative and letters to all city councilors followed. I appeared before a meeting of the Council of Heritage Organizations and obtained their endorsement.

"Aldo Chiappa at City Hall was designated as the city's representative to get the plaque put up. We soon realized that there was nowhere to put the plaque and that an insertion in the sidewalk would not be very visible. We began to think of a more substantial marking and agreed a bronze plate with a suitable inscription and mounted on a granite pedestal would be the best thing. The city supervisor in charge of roads and sidewalks had the designated place on the sidewalk surveyed to be sure we were not infringing on private property. We found a supplier who manufactured the monument, and up it went. The cost was $4,000, privately funded by someone.[31] Jim McAuley personally delivered invitations to every household and business in the neighborhood. Aldo Chiappa, a good Italian boy, got this free pizza from the Prescott Hotel, a good Italian watering hole known as the 'Last Chance' because in earlier days if you were heading to the west end, the Prescott was the last chance to get a beer..."

At 4:30 the hall empties and a crowd strolls to the corner of Bay and Gladstone. Paul Kitchen speaks a few words and the Dey's Arena monument is unveiled by the Mayor of Ottawa. I watch Paul Kitchen, pondering the demeanor in which he spoke to my father and I in the hall. Through our research efforts I have come to know the man, and he seems somewhat reserved, somewhat less gregarious than normal. I edge my way over to him through the crowd and congratulate him on his accomplishment. I then mention that he does not seem himself today. The gentlemanly hockey scholar shrugs.

"Well, I just came directly from the cemetery," he apologizes. "I buried my mother this morning. She was one hundred years old."

As the team checks into the Westin Hotel, I pick out my bags and accompany my family to McGee's Inn. We drive up through Sandy Hill and its brick-lined elegance, pulling in front of the house that John McGee had built over a century ago. Inside I lay down and fall fast asleep, but am awakened soon after for yet another event. The Ottawa Senators NHL team has provided the entire Dawson team with tickets to their game at the Corel Center this evening against the Florida Panthers.

It is sobering to enter the arena in which our team will be playing on Sunday. The grand balconies, the crowd, the polished image of the height of hockey aspirations as encompassed in a National Hockey League venue provides a jarring juxtaposition, the Dawson hockeyists,

---

31 After failing to acquire corporate sponsorship, Paul Kitchen paid for the monument out of his own pocket. The monument was smashed and the plaque stolen by vandals in June, 2008.

no doubt, comparing it to Moccasin Square Gardens, as they call their aging, permafrost shifting, unheated shack of a rink back in Dawson City.

The team makes its way up to the Molson box and its free drinks and snacks, reveling in the attention. We are thrilled to see the team appear on the jumbo-tron, waving to the crowd. My daughter Sarah sneaks into the box, compliments of Roy Johnson. The game ends a 2–2 tie, and the team quietly makes its way back to Ottawa. I decline invitations to hit the town, and retire to McGee's Inn, exhausted. The others, led by the Wild Bunch and perhaps subliminally adhering to yet another thread of the original story's replication, may not sleep these last thirty-six hours.

Hope no one pukes on the ice, I silently muse, before falling asleep.

CHAPTER
TWENTY-ONE

*"Where, may I ask, can be found a more enthusiastic
audience than at a championship hockey match? The
very roof-timbers seem to creak with excitement; yells and
shrieks that would silence a band of Sioux warriors are
heard from every nook and corner of the building. The
clashing of sticks, the stamping of feet, the yah-yahs of
the admirers when a long and well-aimed shot for goal
is fired, or perhaps when one player more cunning for
the time than the rest, by his superior judgment, and
surprising ability, darts with the puck, gently coaxing it
from one side to the other while traveling at lightning
speed through an entire line of adversaries until finally,
like a pistol shot, it cracks through the goals, when a
thousand, yes, five thousand throats shout and scream
until the pandemonium reminds one of a dynamite
factory cutting loose!"*

— GEORGE A. MEAGHER, *LESSONS IN SKATING*, 1900

At 4:45 P.M. on January 11, 1905 the Dawson City
Klondikers stumbled off the train into a frenzied Ottawan
embrace. Executive members of the Ottawa Hockey Club
were on hand to welcome the weary travelers, who had spent twenty-
four days en route. They immediately repaired to the Russell House,

where "they registered, became a centre of unusual bustle, crowds thronging the rotunda and vicinity in the hope of catching a glimpse of the famous travelers." The *Ottawa Citizen* listed nine men in the party, including "Fred Robinson and Archie Martin, spare men, both from Ottawa."

The newspaper noted that, "Two days rest should put them on their feet again after the railway journey and it is probable that despite the fact that dispatches say the team desires a postponement of the first game, they will be in shape to go ahead on Friday night. With the advertising done, tickets printed…it is rather curious that the challengers should leave it until the last moment to propose postponement."

The Dawson contingent considered Ottawa's unwillingness to postpone the games a jaded decision, but in truth Ottawa had already delayed the games once at Dawson's request, and were a week into their Federal Amateur Hockey League schedule. The *Dawson Daily News* had its own interpretation: "The Ottawas evidently are afraid of the Yukoners, because they are allowing the visitors only one day in which to practice for the match." The paper noted the atmosphere in Ottawa, "Albert wires that great interest is taken in the matches. Now that Parliament has just assembled and the capitol city is full of visitors from all parts of Canada, the hockey matches will be attended by thousands and the Yukon will receive one of the best advertisements ever given it in a popular way…Everywhere in Dawson today the hope is expressed that the Yukoners land the cup and bring it to Klondike and keep it here forever."

The ramifications of the rule requiring all Stanley Cup games to be played on the defending champion's ice was not lost on eastern Canadians. The *Ottawa Evening Journal* noted that if Dawson won the series, "1000–1 it would stay there, as Winnipeg is considered far enough west to travel." Dawson was even planning ahead. "It is likely that when the Klondike hockey team returns to Dawson with the Stanley Cup that it will have something to do to defend the battered trophy against the ambitions of rival Dawson teams," the *Dawson Daily News* reported. "Already Brother Paul (Forrest) is out with a scheme to capture the mug. The brother thinks he can pick up an aggregation today that will put Brother Albert and the other six worthies now in Ottawa under the frost line…"

Dawson's confidence was countered by a more sober Ottawan view. "As they said all the way East, their trip is no joke, and they mean to show that they can play hockey tomorrow night. That they will is the earnest hope of all, though their chances of victory are none too great," the *Citizen* opined.

The first game was played in a sold-out Dey's Arena. "It was the largest crowd on record and the enthusiasm was most marked," Joe Boyle reported. Governor General Earl Grey was escorted to the game by Denis Murphy, President of the Ottawa Hockey Club, and Cup trustee P. D. Ross. The Governor General spoke at center ice to the two teams, then shook hands with respective captains Alf Smith and Randy McLennan. After the players gave him three cheers, he placed the puck on center ice between opposing centers Harry Westwick and Hector Smith, walked to his box, and blew a whistle to start the game.

Frank McGee opened the scoring ten minutes into the contest, Alf Smith and Harry Westwick also tallying for Ottawa before Randy McLennan scored for the Klondikers. The first half ended with a ten minute-long scoring drought and the score merely 3–1. The Klondikers must have entered their dressing room much encouraged, but the travel-weary northerners fared poorly after returning to the ice.

"The second half opened very slow," the *Citizen* reported. "Off-sides occurred rather frequent…" Ottawa began to score, Smith, Smith, Westwick and then White twice and Smith again, before Sureshot Kennedy notched Dawson's last goal. "The Strain Tells," headlined one of the last paragraphs of game description in the following day's newspaper. "Things were getting slower still, and it was apparent that the Yukon team was not equal to the strain…" The game ended 9–2, Ottawa.

"It was only when the Yukonites tired and showed the effect of their long journey that Ottawa began to pile on the score," one scribe wrote. "At the end of the game Yukon were so tired they could hardly stand on their skates and they went to their hotel as limp as wet rags."

Ottawan newspapers were generous. "9–2 sounds pretty bad, but wait a bit. It represents the play, but it does not represent the relative merits of the two teams…how does the story of the match read when put this way: Up to the time the Ottawas were leading 2–1 it was anybody's game, and the Yukon men had had most of the play. Indeed at half time there was also some doubt…two goals were got when the Yukon's clever young goalkeeper was off the ice, and three others might without evil have been given offside. There was a good yard on two of them and a foot in the other…how does that read? Take these five goals away, and the score doesn't look so terrible. Add also that for the major portion of the game Yukon were playing a man short, and sometimes two, and it looks a good bit better. This is all from the point of view of the Dawson players, and a good many people in Ottawa, too. There is more than a grain of truth in it. Some go so far as to say that given equal conditions this is the best team that has come after the Stanley Cup for two or three years…"

The Dawson players and coach, for their part, complained bitterly. "It was a great game, and the score is no criterion of it nor of the relative merits of the two teams," Joe Boyle wrote in his dispatch to the *Dawson Daily News*. "It was a fast, rough game, and Ottawa in the first half made four goals from offside plays which Referee Stiles of Cornwall was not fast enough on his skates nor with his eyes to follow…Ottawa was continually offside, thus putting our boys to the disadvantage which always belongs to the side playing a clean game when large liberties are allowed the other side…" Albert Forrest, in his own dispatch, claimed there were six offside goals.

"Nearly everyone agrees," the Dawson newspaper rationalized, "that the Klondikers ran into an unfair shake in having to go on the ice immediately after completing a trip of 4,000 miles over ice, seas, and across the continent. The general consensus of opinion is that the Dawsonites would have done much better had they had time to work off their muscle and wind, and to develop a little team work. Hannay who joined in Manitoba, never played with the team."

All agreed that Hannay was Dawson's best player, ostensibly because he did not endure the same trip as the others. Alf Smith was said to have played best for the defending champions, Day Finnie also excelling in goal. Boyle promised a better showing for the second game, scheduled three nights later. There was reason for optimism. Weldy Young, encouraged when the team was delayed in Whitehorse, had fudged his election return duties and promptly fled the Yukon, trying to catch up. With a report that Young was in Vancouver awaiting the next CPR car east, Boyle announced that when Dawson won the second game, Weldy would arrive in time for the third, ensuring Dawson's victory. The team would also have time to rest. But there were also problems. Randy McLennan aggravated an old knee injury, and was unable to continue. Boyle immediately wired Fred Fairbairn to hustle on to Ottawa from Portage la Prairie. But something else happened during the next night or two that indeed posed a problem for Dawson City's Stanley Cup ambition.

It is unverifiable oral history handed down through generations. It is unmentioned in contemporary newspapers. But considering the sequence of remarkable events, it is probably a story with some truth to it. Legend has it that an unnamed Dawson player disparaged Frank McGee in Sam Cassidy's barroom. Despite scoring the first goal of the game, the *Citizen* had observed, "McGee did not exert himself much," and related an embarrassing episode: "An amusing scene occurred at the north side of the rink, when McGee and Smith both tried to take the puck from Johnstone. The former Ottawan was on the alert and used his body to advantage with the result that both the Ottawa men went down and the crowd roared..." McGee scored only once in the match, suggesting Ottawa's star did not play his best game. Legend holds that one of McGee's teammates overheard the insults in Cassidy's barroom, and relayed them to the twenty-four-year-old star, setting up the astonishing events that followed.

On Monday night a sellout crowd again jammed little Dey's Arena. The ensuing onslaught by Canada's greatest hockey team came quickly, and steadily. "If any hankering doubt lurked in anyone's mind as to whether Dawson really had any license to challenge for the Stanley Cup, much less travel 4,000 miles for it, they were removed. About as speedily as the Ottawa Hockey team has ever done anything, and that's somewhat lightening-like to say the least, from the first motion of the elusive puck on its erratic journey the champions went at the men..." the *Citizen* reported. "Friday night's exhibition was bad but there were the excuses of long and withering travel and a generous public made allowance hoping for better things to come. But come they did not, instead a farce just as bad as can be imagined from a score of 23–2. Ordinarily when one team is making a gold brick exhibition of the other the people go home early and leave the teams to sit it out, but last night they remained to see how high the score would go and for their patience they were rewarded to the extent of witnessing the piling-on of what, if there are any records bearing on the subject, will probably be found to be a world's record score."

Frank McGee's first goal of the game was called back for being offside. With Ottawa leading 3–1, McGee scored again. He would add three more before the half, when the Ottawas tromped off the ice with a commanding 10–1 lead. But what occurred in the second half defies comprehension.

McGee scored the first goal, followed by a White goal. McGee then scored eight consecutive goals before he set up Alf Smith for a tally, and finally scored his fourteenth goal of the evening, putting Ottawa up 22–1. Both teams scored once more before the embarrassment was complete, the game being called early with a few minutes remaining.

How possessed was Frank McGee? At one point in the second half he scored four goals in a minute and forty seconds. Seven times he scored less than thirty seconds after a previous goal. The enormity of his fourteen-goal accomplishment is put into perspective when it is remembered that the previous record for goals in a Stanley Cup match was *five*.

With the results in, hockey scribes showed no mercy. "Go back a few years," *The Toronto Telegram* published, "and try and imagine the feelings of Napoleon as he wearily retraced his steps from Moscow, mentally cursing the author of 'Beautiful Snow,' and you have the inner reflections of the Dawson City team as they left the ice at Dey's rink and slid into their store clothes. For though it is said in all kindness, never has such a consignment of hockey junk come over the metals of the CPR as the latest claimants for world's championship honors...the visitors couldn't shoot, couldn't skate, in fact they had about as much chance to lift the cup as the liberals had of beating Ed Dunlop in North Renfrew...taking candies from a baby or robbing a child's bank couldn't have been easier."

Dawson's view, not surprisingly, was defiant. "It was a good game," Boyle wrote, "and there was at one stage of it fifteen minutes of the fastest and fiercest play without a score. Then Friday's game told on the Klondikers, and they were 'all in' and Ottawa scored at will...in short, our team was broken up and in no condition to play in such a game as was put up against them. While our men have been traveling the Ottawas have been put through a course of training, and the players are, of course, in the condition of race horses." Dawson City seemed oddly unaware of the enormity of their hometown heroes' defeat. "Had it not been for young Albert's fine stick work at goal," the local newspaper declared, "hundreds of shots would have rained into the goal in the Stanley Cup series, and Dawson would have gone down to the most ignominious defeat ever recorded in a championship contest."

The records set that evening will stand forever. The fourteen goals by McGee and the twenty-three Ottawa goals prompted the description of the Dawson City Klondikers as the team that traveled furthest to lose by the most in all of Stanley Cup history. There were no hard feelings between the players, however. At the Ottawa Hockey Club banquet thrown for the Dawson men, "From the many pleasant speeches exchanged it was quite evident that the players of the two teams have fraternized considerably during the past week, and will part with the warmest regard for each other. The Stanley Cup, coveted trophy of the World's Hockey Championship, was filled with sparkling Champagne and circled the restive board repeatedly..."[32]

The irrepressible Boyle vowed to challenge again for the Stanley Cup. Norman Watt was quoted on his return to Dawson, "Our team can be strengthened next winter by putting in some stronger men and by getting in better shape before leaving here." Boyle also invited the

---

32 Hannay told grandson Dave Hannay that he "scratched my name on the Stanley Cup with a penknife."

Ottawas to visit Dawson for an exhibition series. It is said he declared he would make a cup of solid Yukon gold to be awarded the winner of the series. But there is no evidence such a trophy was ever crafted. The Ottawas never traveled north, nor did the Klondikers return for a rematch. It would be ninety-two years before another Dawson team skated on Ottawan ice.

OTTAWA

Friday, March 21

For the first morning in three weeks I lay in bed with nothing to do. I am passing up the 6:00 A.M. interview in front of the Parliament buildings. After a leisurely breakfast with my family in McGee's dining room, I make my way over the Rideau Canal to join the team for the morning Parliament session. Despite great excitement at being in Ottawa, the festering resentment of some surfaces.

"Jesus Christ," Joe Mason complains, "we get up at five in the morning just to freeze our asses off while those three get to talk again." He is referring, of course, to Flynn, Hogan, and Anderson, who have handled the morning's TV interview in front of the West Block while the rest of the team stood dutifully behind. The complaint is only valid to a point. While it is true the three have handled most of the media interviews, they are, in fact, not only the leaders of this expedition, but also the most eloquent. Deb Belinsky could not have dreamed of three more engaging, colorful, or intelligent messengers. With Hogan's gleaming-eyed intelligence, Flynn's signature cackle, and Anderson's blue-collar earnestness, the Dawson City Nuggets are well on their way to capturing Ottawa's heart.

The Honorable Audrey McLaughlin, last seen brandishing a hockey stick on the frozen streets of Whitehorse, organizes the group for our House of Commons session. We check our coats, file through a metal detector, and are ushered up stairs to the balcony. The guys fiddle with headsets, some listening to the debates in French. Below lies the ornate hall, seats facing one another, half filled. We observe the rancor and one-upmanship between House members, a cacophony of interruptions, accusations, and demands. The ruckus is so loud and disheveled one of the Nuggets leans close and apologizes for the spectacle. But when The Honorable Audrey McLaughlin gains the floor, we hush and lean forward.

"Mr. Speaker," she begins, "in 1905 the Dawson City Nuggets hockey team traveled by dog sled, by train, by boat and by foot to challenge the Ottawa Silver Seven for the Stanley Cup. The team lost those games and today a shameful banner commemorating that Senators' victory flies high in the Corel Center.

"As part of the centennial celebrations marking the discovery of gold in the Klondike the Nuggets are back. They are back to avenge those losses. A new team of Nuggets has retraced the steps of that first team of trekkers. They have traveled by dog sled, train and boat, and on Sunday the Nuggets take on the Ottawa Senators alumni at two P.M. at the Corel Center. They have been accompanied on the trip by Dangerous Don Reddick, author of the *Dawson City Seven* book on the original games, Diamond Tooth Gertie, and Earl Wrong Way McRae.

"This team not only has true grit, it has true heart. The profits of the trip will go to the Heart Institute and Special Olympics. I congratulate the Ottawa Senators for all of their assistance but say that we will show no mercy on Sunday."

The smiling Deputy Speaker, ensconced high up on his ornate chair, waves an arm toward the balcony. "And the Nuggets are with us in the gallery," he says. We rise as a team and wave to all below as House members chant, "Hear, hear."

The afternoon schedule includes practice sessions for both teams and a media scrimmage for the Nuggets at Sandy Hill Arena. As the zamboni sweeps the ice I chat with Rick Smith, he of the quintessential hockey mug, and receive a colorful glimpse of the opposite end of the hockey spectrum.

"I'm from Kingston, Ontario," the former Boston Bruins defenseman tells me. "Minor hockey sort of thing, all your friends play hockey and one day someone says Hamilton drafted you to play hockey. You hear some kids dream, to me it was more of a surprise. I had some success there and Boston drafted me, but I didn't expect to go to Boston, but to Oklahoma City. And all of a sudden I'm staying at the Madison

Hotel and going over to the Boston Garden to play hockey. It happened so fast, I wasn't prepared for all the excitement. I understand it better now, you have a chance to understand and appreciate as opposed to being twenty-one years old and you win the Stanley Cup. It happened so fast, you don't appreciate it.

"Some injuries, good fortune, and I had a pretty good camp. Player by the name of Barry Gibbs told them that he'd rather play regularly in Oklahoma City than sit on the bench in Boston. It wasn't extreme what he said, they would have called up Barry Gibbs, but he said let me stay. So they put me on the bench. Occasionally they threw me out and I'd make a fool of myself. The Stanley Cup is just so exciting, but it happens so quick. You're so completely focused on the game. It was the Cup when Bobby scored the goal against Glen Hall, the diving picture, and suddenly you're in a parade...

"The Ottawa Senators started in 1990 and didn't have a lot of history, and even the guys that retired didn't stay in the area. Boston has so many guys that some can't get into the alumni games. They have three teams and kind of rotate. So I'm an adopted kid, Brad Marsh and Laurie Boschman are the only two real Senators. We have a combination of guys who play for the Senators. Fred Barrett had a great career in Minnesota, he was the guy that got it going. He and his brother Johnny got the alumni going, Boschman and Brad Marsh got active, and we play for local charities. We go around, and whatever we can do for the community, we do. Hopefully by doing that we build the Senators' reputation. It's kind of desirable for the NHL for alumnis to be goodwill ambassadors. Gary Bettman made that point to me. It's the history of the game we want to get out there. Alumnis should do whatever we can do for the good of hockey. The Senators treat us well. Molson pays for a box at the Corel Center, gives us free beer. Free tickets and free beer—can it get any better than that?"

The Senators alumni first take the ice. As they skate around and form lines to do drills, three on twos, two on ones, the Dawson City Nuggets quietly observe from the stands. The sight is not only impressive, but sobering. These guys are huge, many six feet tall and over two hundred pounds. Brad Marsh is perhaps most intimidating at

6' 3" and well over 220 pounds, but Mitch Babin is also 6' 2", and Moe Robinson a good 6' 4". It is not only their size that draws attention, but that essence of sheer talent that so gracefully fills the rink. The fine turning, the strong, driving strides, the sharp cut of skates on ice and their crisp, accurate, and flawlessly accepted passes all demonstrate ability far above the norm. The Dawson City Nuggets silently face for the first time the well-known but heretofore under-appreciated fact: we will be playing former NHL players.

Laurie Boschman, who has been vocal in responding to the taunts of Anderson and Hogan, scored 69 goals for the Brandon Wheat Kings of the WHL before being drafted in the first round, 9th overall, by Toronto in 1979. After a junior career that saw him selected WHL and Memorial Cup All-Star, he scored 229 goals in his NHL career before retiring only four years ago. Center Murray Kuntz scored 51 goals for the New Haven Blades of the Eastern Hockey League before netting a league-leading 51 goals for the Rochester Americans of the American Hockey League, earning him AHL first team All-Star status and a seven-game—and one goal—cup of coffee with the St. Louis Blues in 1975.

Frank St. Marseille flows on the ice. He scored over 40 goals twice for Port Huron of the International Hockey League before beginning an NHL career that saw him score 140 goals for St. Louis and Los Angeles. He was elected an IHL All-Star in 1967, and played in the 1970 NHL All-Star game. The Ottawa Senators Team and Business Development Director and alumni captain Brad Marsh was a first team Ontario Major Junior League All-Star before being selected in the first round by the Atlanta Flames in 1978. He played in the 1993 NHL All-Star game, and is a veteran of 97 Stanley Cup playoff games. Rick Smith was twice elected All-Star in the Ontario Hockey Association before becoming Boston's 1966 second round selection.

These are the guys we're playing, I think to myself. I glance at the silent ones sitting around me. And these are the guys the stars are up against, guys whose resumes include, "...and so I played for Clinton Creek, and sometimes they had pretty good teams and I couldn't make the team, and sometimes they were not so good and I could make the team..."

The dressing room is a gold dredge of commotion.

"We're gonna kick their *ass!*" Anderson shouts, half-naked and looking for some tape.

"Remember," Hogan yells, "I've wagered my beard on this game, and my wife hasn't seen my face in twenty years!"

When Hogan first invited me to join the team, I asked if I could play in the big game. Hogan explained that just as in 1905, only Yukon veterans were eligible. But I am skating in today's scrimmage on the media side. I have not laced on skates in eight years. I am concerned when the bag of hockey equipment my wife has brought up from home does not include a cup. I am careful not to mention this delicate fact to anyone.

Out on the ice there is confusion. Impressed with the organization of the Senators' practice and keenly aware of their presence now in the stands, our leaders attempt to duplicate their success. But no one has done any drills in years, as is readily apparent. The team is disorganized; passes go astray, guys over-skate the puck. The drills are a dismal failure.

Troy Suzuki as well as Brendan McEwen and Ken McGilvray of the CBC documentary crew are at work. McGilvray calls me over for an interview.

"This is real hockey," I say into the camera, motioning behind me. "For every guy that plays on a Stanley Cup winner there are thousands and thousands of guys like this who have gone through midgets and atom games and intercollegiate games and senior teams like this, in a tavern on Wednesday nights, and I think by coming to Ottawa we're playing guys who are better, but we're bringing real hockey to them." McGilvray is happy with the piece, but hesitates.

"Hey Don, that was just great, but I think we ran out of film. Can you do it again?"

We quickly start the scrimmage. I center Troy Suzuki and Yukon newspaper correspondent Adam Killick, and after two shifts I am spent. Hockey is a sport that one cannot just step into; one must prepare, and be in shape. Visions of cardiac arrest as I sit bent-over on the bench, gasping for breath. At one point on the ice I turn to receive a pass from behind only to be broken up by John Flynn, who gives me that eye as he skates past that says, "I coulda *nailed* you..."

It's curious how the pride of an old hockey player kicks in. I am unable to keep up in this game, out of breath, using a stick that is new to me and not the right lie, yet I want to show these guys that I know how to play this game. But it's futile trying to persuade my arms and legs that they are twenty-two again, and I flub my only chance at scoring. Flynn pops in a pair of goals and the scrimmage ends, 4–2 Nuggets. We discover that coach Wes Peterson is nowhere to be found. We later hear that he had gone to the Prescott Hotel with Fred and John Barrett, Larry Skinner, and Gerry Armstrong of the Senators alumni. "Hey, they invited me," Peterson would argue. "Do you think I'm gonna pass up the opportunity to have a few social pints with those guys?"

Duffee has something else on his mind. He is rushing out to a local sporting goods store. He later explains, "I'll tell ya, after practice, after seeing Brad Marsh shoot, I went down to Houle's Sporting Goods Store and bought the most expensive shin pads they had..."

After showering we loiter in the rink. I am once again cornered by Ottawa sports reporters. The inevitable question arises.

"How do you think Dawson will do against the alumni on Sunday?"

Now, I know how well these guys play hockey after sitting in Dawson the night before we left and watching the final Dawson league game. I know the level of hockey I played at in high school and college, where I played against future NHL players Mike Milbury, Robbie Ftorek, Tommy Songin, Mike Fidler, and Cap Raeder. I know the level of NHL skills after sharing season tickets for five years in Section 28 of Boston Garden in the mid '80's with old traveling companion Mike Lydon. I know the answer to this question.

"You never know..." I told them.

This evening the *Ottawa Sun* is hosting a Welcome Home Earl "Wrong Way" McRae dinner at Moe's World Famous Newport Restaurant in Westboro. My family and I meet the team at the restaurant, and are greeted just inside the door with a huge sign, three lines one under the other:

THE ELVIS SIGHTING SOCIETY
Welcomes To Ottawa
Earl Of The Yukon

It is the first time the entire team and supporting cast is together in one place. Keith MacNeill, CBC boss of McEwen and McGilvray, has flown in from Yellowknife to oversee the final filming of their documentary. Zoran Rajcic, the team's marketing man from Winnipeg, has arrived. Winnipeg Blue Bombers new head football coach Jeff Reinebold is here, joining Deb Belinsky and Jim Nicol of DCB Productions. Adam Killick is here, as is another hockey writer, Brian McFarlane. Patty Dahlquist has been joined by several of the can-can girls that compliment her show. An entourage of over fifty Dawsonites, led by Dick Van Nostrand and Margo Anderson, noisily join in. Even Bob Charlebois and McRae's brother-in-law Larry Skinner of the Senators alumni appear, drawn by the magnetic north.

The gargoyle of concern appears at my elbow as I sit watching my daughters work the crowd for pictures and autographs.

"Is she all right?" McRae asks. "Which one is she—is she all right?"

The highlite is the team introduction by Earl McRae. He stands on a chair in one corner of the noisy establishment and introduces, one by one, every member of our team, giving a brief, always humorous and sometimes sentimental synopsis of each. With the mention of each name, the team member stands and waves, and is acknowledged by an enthusiastic, highly partisan crowd. I buy a round for my family's table, I buy a round for a nearby table of Dawson City Nuggets.

After dinner Willie Gordon takes center stage among some local musicians, and rocks Moe's World Famous Newport Restaurant like it's never been rocked before. Willie is in his element, smiling broadly, the foot-stomping, beer-bellowing crowd loving every minute of this Dawson City Nuggets reunion. The fiddler from above the Arctic

Circle brings down the house with a triple-length rendition of *Orange Blossom Special*. McRae comes up to me, excited.

"I got them good, did you hear? I got them back good!" He is referring to some inside slights extended to a couple of our less favorite teammates during his chair-standing oration. I smile at the man's loyalty to my dubious conflicts, and nod. McRae is off before I can reply. He also is in his element, surrounded as though he is not just President of the Elvis Sighting Society and the Mayor of Moe's, but Mayor of all Ottawa. The evening is the highlite of the entire trip for me, a chance to have some fun with my family by my side, relax a bit, and enjoy the frenzied, excited scene the team has created in Ottawa. At closing there is an announcement that the team bus will carry those willing to party-on to a yacht club for further festivities. After serious consultation with Terry, we pass. As we are leaving, I look in my wallet, and casually remark to McRae how much I must have spent on rounds for the boys. McRae laughs.

"Well, I hate to tell you this, Strangler," he replies, "but my newspaper picked up the tab. The beer was on the house!"

CHAPTER
TWENTY-TWO

"Perhaps I am stark crazy, but there's none of you too sane,
it's just a little matter of degree...
I've a vision, I've a prompting, I've a call;
I hear the hoarse stampeding of an army on my trail,
to the last, the greatest gold camp of them all."

— ROBERT SERVICE, *THE PROSPECTOR*

The place described in statute as "the town of the City of Dawson" and designated on the Yukon map as "Dawson City," began with the great gold discovery on nearby Rabbit Creek. The ensuing rush poured over 50,000 adventurers into one of the harshest, most unforgiving wildernesses imaginable. By the time this horde arrived in Dawson, virtually every creek was already claimed. The fact that gold-bearing ground was as dramatically small as it was enormously rich, combined with subsequent gold discoveries in Nome and Fairbanks, caused the population of Dawson to evaporate quickly. Advances meant to aid Dawson actually conspired in its decline. In 1900 the White Pass & Yukon Railway was completed from Skagway to its northern terminus of Whitehorse, spurring development of that town. Gold dredges imported to more fully and methodically glean the land of its treasure made obsolete vast numbers of men required to manually operate placer operations. By 1911 Whitehorse was larger than Dawson, and the former Paris of the North was well into its downward spiral.

Gold production in the Dawson Mining District reached a peak of $22,000,000 in 1900, and steadily declined thereafter. By 1921 production was barely $1,000,000, and the population dipped to 975. By '23, only one steamer worked the Dawson–Fairbanks Yukon River route. The great depression of 1929 further eroded the town. Unable to attract investment money to operate costly dredge operations, Dawson entered a quiet, lost time. Despite a spike of interest when the price of gold jumped from $21 to $35 an ounce in the early '30's, Dawson's population shrank to 72 in 1939.

Whitehorse surged in importance during the Second World War, when the Alaska Highway was begun on March 1, 1942. The railway terminus thrived with increased traffic, and the Territorial Government was moved there from Dawson in 1951. In '53 the capital was officially changed from Dawson to Whitehorse. With completion of the Stewart Crossing–Dawson Road in 1955, steamship service ended, isolating the struggling town from all other Yukon River communities save Whitehorse.

During the late 1960's and early 70's Dawson saw a small but steady influx of those out of the mainstream, as well as a rising tide of tourists. When the gold standard was abandoned in 1980, skyrocketing the price of an ounce of gold to over $800 before settling around $300, new money flowed into the old gold diggings. Today Dawson supports a year-round population of about 2,500. Tourism now drives the local economy, with over 60,000 souls visiting each year. There are approximately two hundred working gold claims in the Dawson area. Though hardly immune from small-town friction—offenses real and imagined drive the oldtimer hockey teams to frequently change the venue of their post mortem arguments, settled over a wee Dock an Doris—it is a vibrant and exciting town, proud of its history and quality of life. For every individual out of the mainstream, there are twenty hardworking, family-oriented individuals, the kind of people who form the core of any viable community. Despite recent strides, First Nation people are still in the process of assimilating, all of which has morphed into the essence of the unique, idiosyncratic, colorful dot on the map that is today's Dawson City.

But what of the town's original surveyor Ogilvie's assessment of George Dawson as, "The greatest man I know"? At first glance, it seems ironic that a man once described as a "deformed dwarf" would have his name applied to an historic town synonymous with health, wealth, and testosterone. But a steadier gaze turns this misconception on its end.

George Mercer Dawson was born in Robert Henderson's home-town of Pictou, Nova Scotia on August 1, 1849. Of Scottish heritage, he was the son of Sir John William Dawson, a distinguished paleobota-nist and principal of McGill College in Montreal. At age nine Dawson began experiencing the ill affects of a rare and devastating form of spinal tuberculosis called Pott's Disease. Principle symptoms include leg weakness, gibbus, pain, and "palpable mass," caused by compression and deformity of the spine. If left untreated—treatment today means decompression surgery and anti-TB chemotherapy—it can result in severe spinal deformity and even paraplegia. Those afflicted endure a cessation of growth in the back and upper body, often creating what we call a hunchback. If an unfortunate contracted this debilitating disease during the mid-nineteenth century, it usually ensured a painful, as well as severely restricted physical and psychological life.

The upper half of Dawson's body never matured further than that of a ten-year-old. For several years the boy was bedridden and suffered recurring headaches, and in testament to his family's determination to overcome his misfortune, he was provided bedside tutors as well as a specially designed chair in which to study. At age nineteen Dawson entered McGill. A year later he attended London's Royal School of Mines where he studied under some of England's finest scholars, gradu-ating first in his class three years later. He returned to Canada bril-liant, determined, and very much possessing characteristics of Victorian gentlemen, exemplified by "A desire to exert oneself against formidable odds; to cast one's character in the light of ennobling ideals; to sojourn among exotic things; to make collections and erect monuments..."

In 1873 Dawson began a quest to utterly destroy any consequences of his physical disability. Accepting work with both the British North America Boundary Commission and the Geological Survey of Canada, he began a twenty-year odyssey of exploration of the newly opened

Canadian west, enduring all the hardships a roadless, mapless wilderness provides. His most remarkable achievement was a 1,332 mile investigation into the Yukon Territory, resulting in the *1887 Report* so often quoted within.

Photographs of Dawson on this journey are jarring. Standing among men hardened by wilderness travel, he looks like a boy half their size. Yet reading the words of his weathered companions, you understand how thoroughly the Little Giant, as he was called, had overcome his childhood misfortune: "...his readiness to share all work, and laugh at every hardship, was the reason for his extraordinary popularity with the Indians, who are not generally eloquent in their praise of white men. I have it from the lips of Indians, that the Doctor was not only 'Skookum', but had a 'Skookum Tumtum'; to translate, 'Was not only a strong enduring man, but a cheery, brave man, ready to endure all things and suffer all things, saying nothing, or making a merry jest of what some travelers might call dangerous hardships.'"

Dawson became one of the finest field scientists in Canadian history, the length, breadth, and precision of his voluminous writing earning honorary doctorate degrees from Princeton, Queen's, McGill, and Toronto, as well as recognition with his election to the Royal Society of London. Honors included the Bigsby Medal of the Geological Society of London, as well as the Companion of the Order of St. Michael and St. George, from Queen Victoria. In 1893 he was elected President of the Royal Society of Canada; in '94 elected a member of the Zoological Society of London; in '95 elected a Fellow of the American Association for the Advancement of Science; in '96 appointed President of the Geological Society for the Toronto meeting of that organization; and in 1897, the year his name was bestowed upon the greatest gold camp ever known, Dawson was awarded the annual gold medal of the Royal Geographical Society, for lifetime achievement.

Such is a first glance irony utterly shattered. George Mercer Dawson, maligned with an affliction that ruined most, essentially willed himself into one of the toughest, most determined, and accomplished explorers in North American history. A hero to emulate for one such as Joe Boyle with his impossible dreams, or Pat Hogan, the man who took a team of aging players from the Yukon to win a hockey game in Ottawa.

OTTAWA

Saturday, March 22

A palpable buzz permeates Ottawan air today, the entire city focused on the rag-tag group of hockey players from Dawson City, Yukon. Everywhere we go, dressed in game jerseys, people honk from cars, people stop on sidewalks to chat, all excited to see in the flesh these souls they have followed in McRae's columns for the past month.

McRae's newspaper *The Ottawa Sun* has blared in bold print the news on its front page since our arrival on Thursday. The rival *Ottawa Citizen*, scooped by the *Sun's* maneuver of embedding its controversial columnist with the team for the entire trip, seems grudgingly to keep the story off its front page. I catch up with three days of newspapers, and follow the printed narrative:

"I was just in Beaver Lumber yesterday," Brad Marsh tells a reporter, "and a couple of customers wished me good luck in the game. It was kind of neat. I haven't heard that since I was in the NHL."

"We've never felt better," Pat Hogan tells one reporter, while at the same time Dave Millar tells another, "Most of the guys are just whipped. It's been a long haul so they're pretty tired. We were out on the ice for a practice yesterday and it was a little scary..."

Quotes from the Senators vacillate from generous to determined.

"If they have shown that kind of determination just to get here," Bill Kitchen tells the *Sun*, "you can imagine what they'll do Sunday afternoon."

"We're shooting for the same score that happened to Dawson City in 1905," Laurie Boschman says. "We want to get going early, get our goals early, and see if we can jump on them quickly."

But when they get to Kevin Anderson, the blunt, earnest heart and soul of the Dawson Nuggets, The Kevin Factor emerges: "We don't go into any hockey game to lose."

"We're here and we're ready to play," John Flynn says, taking up the banner, "especially after all that we've done to get here. I don't think we have anything to lose, but I think they're a little bit worried right now because they can't lose..."

"We have a chance at this because we're determined," Pat Hogan offers. "We showed our determination getting here."

"On any given day," Budd Docken concludes, "a game can go either way. We're just going to try and tire them out with our four lines and dazzle them with what we can come up with..."

Today's major event is the Yukon Gala at the Westin Hotel. I am directed to a side room where tables of Ottawa Senator alumni and Dawson Nuggets are seated, signing souvenir posters of the match. One after another we sign, passing them along to the next guy, until hundreds are completed. An official Dawson Nugget game jersey is passed around and signed; for whom I do not know, and don't think to ask. As I sit signing, Terry interrupts me.

"Don, these people would like to meet you," she says.

"Hello, my name is Dave Hannay," the man says to me, "and this is my wife Margaret. I'm the grandson of Lorne Hannay." Hannay hands me a package.

"It's something I want you to have," he explains. "It's my grandfather's scrapbook." I thank Dave profusely, and accept the volume.

"You know," Dave says, "I wish I had known about you guys picking up Harvey Downes as my grandfather earlier. I would have jumped on the train at my own expense in Winnipeg, just to come along..."

Five hundred tickets have been sold for the Yukon Gala. The hall has a stage where Patty Dahlquist and her can-can girls, bedecked in turn-of-the-century vaudeville costume, will perform. Willie Gordon, the incessant smile pasted across his face, stands waiting, fiddle and bow at his sides. Bruce Duffee, in bowler hat and 1890's suit and tie, stands behind a trough of water, giving gold panning lessons. The crowd is punctuated throughout with gold and blue Dawson Nugget game jerseys, each surrounded by admirers.

I meet Lydia Watt for the first time in person. I am apprehensive, but Lydia and her family are gracious and friendly, Lydia enjoying her notoriety as the daughter of original Dawson Klondiker Norman Watt. When Millar walks by I grab him, and introduce him to Lydia and her family as one of the true gold miners from the Yukon.

"Just don't tell 'em about the barroom," he whispers, and smiles.

Word spreads, as it has for the past three weeks, of the previous day's stories. I am told that Dick Van Nostrand, after leaving Moe's World Famous Newport Restaurant, tried to hijack the team bus, and either ran it into a snowbank, or was thrown into a snowbank. Rumor has Brad Marsh irritated with the Dawson Nugget war of words, and bent on beating us badly. Harvey Downes, err, Lorne Hannay ran into Hall of Fame defenseman Denis Potvin in the foyer of the Westin Hotel, sat down with him and explained who we were and what we were doing. But our favorite story is about Mike Fraser. A group of Nuggets and their wives were relaxing earlier in the Westin Hotel's foyer lounge, and Mike had gone to the men's room. When he returned he said, "Hey, do you know there's no urinals in that men's room?"

The biggest attraction, as usual, is the Stanley Cup. It sits on a table framed with Hockey Hall of Fame and Ottawa Senator banners. Phil Pritchard has it set up outside the doorways to the main hall, where for five dollars you can have your picture taken with it. Despite the photo-fest enjoyed in the Hall of Fame in Toronto, we again line up for the opportunity. I sidle up to The Keeper and whisper, "What's the deal, Phil, when do we drink out of this thing?"

He whispers back, "That's what we do when everyone else goes to bed."

The Yukon Gala is a smashing success. An overflow crowd crams the room, Willie Gordon gets everyone up and moving with his foot-stomping fiddle. The event is yet another reunion with people from across the continent. Bill Fitsell, hockey scholar and founding President of the Society for International Hockey Research, is here along with fellow SIHR members Lloyd Penwarden, Paul Kitchen, and Ed Grenda. Fitsell is the moving force behind the team's reenactment next Tuesday in Kingston of a game played there during the 1905 tour. Joining the Hannay's from Cambridge, Ontario and Lydia Watt from Ottawa are descendants of Ottawa Silver Seven players including Robin Westwick and her father Dr. William Westwick, Don Finnie, nephew of goalie Day Finnie, as well as the Honorable Frank McGee, tall, beaming, and spreading a charming self around the hall.

CBC team McEwen, McGilvray, and MacNeill are here. McGilvray's is the voice of the CBC documentary, heard the room over with what must be one of the world's greatest laughs. If John Flynn's is a signature laugh, McGilvray's is a certifiable John Hancock, a laugh so loud and raucous it forces all within earshot to pause and listen, then join. Brendan McEwen stuns the audience as he dances with Terry, exposing a formidable talent on the floor.

Many of the Ottawa alumni are present, but I know only two by face, Rick Smith of my old Boston Bruins, and towering Brad Marsh. The Honorable Audrey McLaughlin, last seen brandishing the Dawson Nuggets during a Parliament session, is here. And there is one more celebrity, I discover, also present. As we sit for dinner, Pat Hogan takes center stage and performs his Dawson Nuggets spiel, and concludes by introducing one of Canada's foremost hockey scholars and writers, the former announcer "who has written a book about the original Dawson team," Brian McFarlane. As McFarlane steps to the microphone, Hogan presents him with the autographed team sweater.

This is a stunning blow. Gail Caldwell, when drawing the now famous poster for The Challenge of the Century, used page 297 of *Dawson City Seven*, the frenzied scene as the Klondikers took to the ice in '05, as a model. I had been the conduit for Bill Fitsell in Kingston for the upcoming reenactment there of the Queen's game. I had been the conduit for Lydia Watt and The Honorable Frank McGee, suggesting they shake hands at center ice before the game. I had been the conduit for Lloyd Penwarden and the induction papers for Smith and Kennedy at Winnipeg. I had been the conduit for Paul Kitchen and the Dey's Rink plaque dedication. I have spent over four thousand U.S. dollars to complete the trip, and bring my family up for the Ottawa game. I have used two year's vacation time to get the month off. And I sit slumped in a chair at the Yukon Gala, watching a man who once accused me of plagiarism accept an

autographed Dawson City Nugget game jersey as I sit in one borrowed, and told must be returned.

The consensus is you're a bit sensitive...

The Canadian hockey icon begins by espousing his great novel on
the Dawson story, claiming it is being reissued in the fall, and that
Hollywood is currently considering optioning it for a movie. Then
McFarlane drops the hair that breaks the camel's back.

"Americans don't know anything about hockey, and they don't
know anything about this story," he begins. I move up in my seat and
listen as the Canadian icon not once, not twice, but three times insults
Americans. He's talking to *me*...

"Hey," I say to my father sitting next to me, "he's talking about
me!" My father casts me one of those *get over yourself* looks, and I
silence. But when McFarlane finishes, an Ottawan writer, familiar with
my history with the man, comes from behind and leans close.

"He's a sonnafabitch!" he whispers. "He's a sonnafabitch!"

A moment later John Flynn pauses at our table and says to me, "I
told the guy next to me that if Reddick's here, he's gonna be *bullshit!*"

I order another Budweiser, and bide my time. Later, by a doorway,
my time arrives. As I stand with Terry, Brian McFarlane strolls by.

"Hey *Brian*," I say, stopping him, "I want you to know something.
I want you to know that Americans know quite a bit about this story,
and that one of them wrote a pretty damn good book about it."

"Oh yeah?" McFarlane fires back. "How many copies did it sell
in the United States?" The fury with which the reply was delivered
surprises me. "And don't tell me about Americans," he adds, "my *wife's*
American!" And then, indelicately as possible lest my message be lost,
I essentially tell McFarlane he can shove his attitude up a place not
mentioned on any map of Ontario. He shoots back in no uncertain
terms that I can shove my attitude up a place not mentioned on any
map of Massachusetts. To which Terry blurts, "I can't stand *looking* at
that man!" and storms away, I shortly behind.

The night winds down, the crowd slowly filtering out, good-byes
and good-lucks. I'm concerned to see that the Stanley Cup has been

removed from the lobby. Not seeing The Keeper anywhere, I find the house telephone and dial Pritchard up.

"Are we on?" I ask.

"C'mon up," he replies. "Remember, no cameras and no media."

Terry and I gather my closest friends on the team, from those remaining in the hall. I see Bruce Duffee and nod—he understands. I catch Budd Docken by the elbow and nod. It's time! I make eye contact with Earl MacKenzie and curl my finger at him.

"What's up?" he asks.

"Trust me…"

"No cameras, no media were his only rules," I explain as we walk toward the exit. I ask my father if he'd like to join us and he declines. He will later explain, to his regret, that he thought we were going up to party all night long. My three girls beg for a chance to accompany us, but I decline, much to my later lament. Concerned with not imposing too much on Pritchard, I want to keep the numbers down. We enter the elevator, but while waiting for the door to close, Joe Mason rushes inside.

This is uncomfortable; no one knows what to do or say. For a moment I thought Mason must have gotten wind of our secret and decided to join, but Joe pushes the fourth floor button and when the elevator stops there, he walks out. Vague feelings of remorse, but rationalization that he does not drink anyway.

Pritchard holds the door open as we file past. At the foot of one of the two beds is a large, black trunk. Phil unbuckles the sides and opens it, and there it is! The Cup lies on foam padding neatly cut to perfectly hug the contours of the beveled bowl. Phil lifts it gingerly and places it on top of the bed. Docken and I, each with two bottles of Budweiser, move forward and pour them into the silver chalice.

"I'm first!" I declare, and as Docken and MacKenzie gently tilt the Cup forward, I kneel on the edge of the bed and *drink out of the Stanley Cup!* When I step back and up, the others take turns, each of us rotating to help tilt the unwieldy Cup, Duffee, Docken, MacKenzie, Terry and then once more through the line so that we each drink from the mug twice. Concerned that we are imposing on Pritchard, we hastily conclude our visit. We help Phil replace the Cup in its carrying case, emphatically thank him, and make our way to the elevator. Once inside, we stare dumbly at one another, until I raise a fist in the air and shout, *"Yes!"*

"We're not to tell anyone," Duffee reminds.

"It was all a dream," Docken replies to Cheshire grins.

We say good-nights, and as Terry and I head for the escalator, we run into an Ottawa alumni. I don't know who he is, but we chat for a moment.

"What's going to happen tomorrow?" I ask.

"Well," he replies, "it's going to be a hockey game. Those things that they've been saying, well, we're all pretty proud, eh? We didn't get to where we got by not being proud of our abilities. And all we've heard, all we've read in McRae's articles...no one wants to be embarrassed out there. And some of the guys are...

"It's going to be a real hockey game."

CHAPTER
TWENTY-THREE

"History repeats itself. That's one of the things wrong with history."

— CLARENCE DARROW

"They're smart. They've got the skill. That's not our style of hockey."

— KEVIN ANDERSON

GAME DAY

Sunday, March 23, 1997

There is great excitement as the troupe gathers in the Westin Hotel's lobby, awaiting the departure of the team bus. Several Dawson City Nuggets appear somewhat less than at their best and brightest. Docken spies me standing with Terry. He sidles up, a wry grin on his face.

"Dangerous Don," he nods in greeting. Then, closer and in a whisper, "You won't believe the dream I had last night..."

I board the bus and find a seat in the rear next to Jeff Reinebold. Reinebold peers about, assessing the wild chatter of the dance hall girls, players, and writers that form this rainbow Yukon entourage.

"You know," the professional football coach says, "team busses are the same no matter what the situation, whether it's high school or college or professional football or the Dawson Nuggets, the feeling of being alive, anxious, excited…they're all the same."

I am holding my personal copy of *Dawson City Seven* and ask him to sign it. When he finishes, I take the book back and read, "Don, thanks for the honor of signing this copy. In the words of Freddie and the Fisters, 'Bop till you drop' Jeff Reinebold W."

We take the long ride to suburban Kanata, where the Corel Center squats, visible from a distance. The bus, much to the players' delight, pulls around back and directly into the basement of Ottawa's NHL venue. It is an hour and a half prior to game time, and the players shuffle into the dressing room, picking out their spots on the benches. I wander outside into the arena and stand by the bench, staring up at the cavernous, empty Corel Center. Willie Gordon stands nearby, taking it all in.

"It's not so big a place from here," he says, surprisingly, for I sense the opposite.

"Are you ready?" I ask the man from the silent spaces of Aklavik, Northwest Territories, about to play the national anthem in front of thousands in his nation's capital. He turns to me, eyes gleaming, fists clenched by his sides.

"Oh I'm ready! I'm ready!"

I spot the Honorable Frank McGee near the dressing room, an arm slung around the shoulders of Brian McFarlane. He calls to me, "Don, c'mon over! I want you to meet someone!" I feign hearing loss and wave, and enter the dressing room. The guys are bent-over putting pads in stockings, taping up sticks, checking skate blades for sharpness, the sights and sounds familiar in any hockey dressing room. Suzuki continues to rove, filming, as do McEwen and McGilvray. Friends and fans appear at the door, guarded by Rod Dewell and Earl MacKenzie. Cat-calls, nervous laughter, a surreal disbelief that game day has finally arrived, that years of planning, frantic months of preparation, and now the past three weeks of travel has come to an end.

There are chores I must attend to. I have kept five copies of *Dawson* that I wish both teams to sign. My teammates had signed these copies during our signing session at the Yukon Gala last night, the only complaint from Kulych, "He's making money off of us." Now I head toward the Ottawa dressing room, my #34 game shirt my pass. Brad Marsh stops me at the door, takes the books and tells me to come back in twenty minutes when they will be done. I return and enter the alumni dressing room, and find myself standing in front of a line of twenty ex-NHL and WHA players, busy pulling on shoulder pads, taping sticks, and tying up skates.

"All right," I say, trying to think of a joke. "Everyone listen up! Don't tell anyone I told you guys this, but our goalie's biggest weakness is right *here.*" I point to the center of my chest. I get a modest laugh, and find myself dreaming. I direct my story to Rick Smith.

"You won't believe what we did last night," I begin, and relate how Docken, MacKenzie, Duffee, Terry, and I made our way up into a hotel room to drink out of the Stanley Cup. As I conclude my tale, I realize that the room has silenced, all eyes focused on me. Suddenly I feel foolish; here I am, a forty-three-year-old American high-school caliber hockey player in front of a room full of men who have skated in the Montreal Forum and Madison Square Garden in pursuit of sport's most legendary trophy. Vaguely aware of a tradition among NHL players never to even touch the Cup until they have won it, I shrug my shoulders.

"Well," I stammer, "it was important to *me...*"

"Don," Rick Smith replies, "it's important to *all* of us."

Back in our dressing room, I follow the CBC filmmakers as they interview individual Dawson City Nuggets:

"We didn't come here to lose," Hogan says. "We'll give it one hundred and ten percent, that's all you can do. We'll see what happens."

"Have you got any message for the Ottawa Senators?" McGilvray asks. Hogan thinks a moment, shrugs his shoulders.

"Keep your head up."

"Both teams are out there to win, the best team will win," Anderson declares. "We're giving it a hundred and ten. All the way. Short shifts, we'll do our best, we'll leave it to history."

"Any message?" Flynn responds to McGilvray, the lesson of Frank McGee and the Dawson taunts well known to him. "I think after the game they'll get their message. Not before." He emits his signature cackle.

Suzuki moves about the room, capturing the scene on tape. The gut-churning realization that it is game time is evident in all eyes. Nervous laughter, attempts at jokes. Suzuki follows up on the obvious, asking each player if he is nervous. To a man they acknowledge the same emotion, which Duffee sums up best.

"Aw fuck," he says, "I don't think I've ever been more nervous in my life."

These are men used to wide open spaces, empty vistas, and silence. Hockey games in the old Dawson rink drew few fans, the occasional wife or girlfriend, a townie or two, and when it went cold, nobody attended. Today we listen as the crowd increases, we hear stomping feet, and notice the doorway grow crowded with well-wishers and the curious, seeking a glimpse of the Dawson Nuggets. Word arrives that former Prime Minister Joe Clark is here.

The players line up and exit the dressing room for the pregame warmup. I wander out to the bench with Roy Johnson's camera. When I step on the bench, Millar turns to me.

"You're not allowed on the bench during the game, you know."

"Jesus Christ," I say to him, "*relax.*" I had no intention of being there anyway, but I'm disappointed that the underlying tension remains. After warmups less disheveled than before our media scrimmage, but still in dubious contrast to that on the other side of the ice, we return to the dressing room. The atmosphere, as game time approaches, intensifies.

Hogan stands and delivers a pep talk. Anderson, The Kevin Factor in full bloom, rages. Eyes are glassy, vacant, even those of normally staid Gudmundson. There is a palpable paralysis born of anxiety and excitement. *It's happening...*

MacKenzie enters the room and nods toward Hogan. It's time. The players yell it up and rise to their skates, making last moment adjustments to their equipment, pulling a suspender here, moving a chinstrap there, the awkward shuffle of skates on rubber as they line up by the door. The noise ratchets up as the time clock on the jumbo-tron winds down. The players crane their necks to get a peek at the filling house, to see thousands who have accumulated in the stands. We hear chants, clapping, and roars. All eyes keen, all ears open, every nuance captured by enervated, adrenalined bodies tense with anticipation.

We hear the pregame ceremonies begin, Mark Smith of Yukon Anniversaries the master of ceremonies. He recites lines from Robert Service's *The Cremation of Sam McGee,* followed by the ignition of two pyrotechnic devices set up on the ice. The lights dim, a spot light focuses on the bench door where the teams will step onto the ice. Two Royal Canadian Mounted Policemen, resplendent in bright red uniforms, shiny black belts, brown boots and Stetsons, stand at attention, one on each side of the bench door. The Dawson City Nuggets are announced.

"All right, let's go!" someone yells, and the slow shuffle becomes awkward jogging as the team jerks out into the corridor, through the parting crowd up into the arena, and onto the ice. The nervousness is immediately apparent: the announcer is introducing the team individually, but all the players skate onto the darkened ice at once. They are unaware that twenty feet from the doorway, lying unsuspecting in the dark, is a carpet to center ice for the dignitaries, and the Dawson Nuggets receive their own unique red carpet treatment. Duffee catches a skate on the rug and staggers but does not go down, but Downes, Parsons, and Craig sprawl head-long onto the ice.

Our disorganization is accentuated when the Ottawa Senators alumni are introduced. One by one they confidently, professionally pause at the bench doorway, wait to be individually introduced, and then glide onto the ice. The Nuggets now realize they are lined up on the wrong blue line and casually, as if no one will notice, skate slowly around to the other side.

The lights go on to a massive cheer. The crowd fills the entire lower tier of the stadium, as well as parts of the upper. Walking to center ice are Lydia Watt and the Honorable Frank McGee, McGee accompanied by his ten-year-old grandson. They are introduced to the crowd, and shake hands. Willie Gordon and Patricia Dahlquist, both dressed to the period-costume nines, are escorted onto the red carpet by the can-can girls, and perform the Canadian National Anthem. As they approach the end, as in all great hockey matches, the crowd begins a crescendo of noise, breaking into a spirited roar with the final chords.

The players do a final skate around, the Dawson boys gathering in front of their net and emerging from their huddle with a shout. Starting lines glide to their positions on the ice, the other players enter their benches and doors are closed. The noise increases as the referee raises his hand toward each goaltender, who respond in kind with raised gloves, *we're ready!* The ref crouches a bit, speaks to Laurie Boschman and John Flynn as they prepare to face off—and drops the puck!

It is happening!

Sticks crack together, blades cut the ice, players shout to each other as the crowd enthusiastically remains on its feet. It is overwhelmingly a Dawson crowd, the underdog aspect of the team, or perhaps the travel so well reported by McRae, winning them over. But it is the bigger, stronger men in striped red, white, and black that dominate from the beginning.

Mitch Babin takes a pass from Laurie Boschman a minute and a half into the game, and fires the puck past Rudniski. For the next seven minutes the skating flows, tending more back than forth for Dawson's defense. Fraser has two good chances, but comes up empty. When Duffee comes off the ice he bends over gasping. The game plan of quick changes is being tested; as more and more time is spent in the Dawson end, the players cannot come off. When Gudmundson finally makes the bench after a double shift, he too bends over, convulsed with dry heaves. Just under eight minutes Babin again receives a pass from Boschman, and scores on Rudniski.

The constant pressure begins to wear on defensemen Craig and Sutherland, and Kuntz scores, Hodges scores a minute later, Charlebois scores. The bench quiets, the crowd quiets, only to rise to their feet with every Dawson chance. Anderson breaks down the right side in on Gerry Armstrong, but misfires a clear shot. Farr has a chance, doesn't connect. Johnson sets up Docken for a clear shot, but the puck jumps his stick. Though the game is being played under oldtimer rules, which forbid slap shots or body checking, an angry Freddy Farr knocks Eddie Hatoum into the boards. Hatoum responds by immediately scoring, and the players tromp off at the end of the first period, 6–0 Ottawa.

The dressing room is abuzz.

"They're so quick," Gudmundson says. "You know the usual 'get the puck, take three strides and pass,' well forget it. Get to the puck, and *move* it."

"I went up against Marsh," Duffee gasps out, "absolutely no good... like a rock...good balance...I just went after his stick."

"I'm having trouble skating," Downes says, between pants. Downes, it is now clear, can skate. But he complains about the ice, and also the Ottawa Senators. "They say OK when you guys come out, go out to your right and go behind the net and line up on the other blue line. I come out, go right, go full tilt and I hit the carpet and do a complete face plant right into the ice! The Senators are sitting on their bench, they're in tears. I got up and said, 'You bastards knew that!' and they said, 'Sure we did!'"

It is apparent that the Ottawa Senators have shown up to play. The ex-pros are shooting hard. None appears to be trying harder than Marsh.

"I know they're trying to win," Duffee tells me. "They're not dipsy-doodling, they're passing. If they wanted to put on a show, they'd just dipsy-doodle right past us. They're passing to get the best chances."

O'Donnell scores three and a half minutes into the second period, Boschman and Babin assisting. Despite the six first period goals, there was still a sense that we were in the game, but this first goal is deflating. Frank St. Marseille sets up Mark Paterson five minutes later, and then Boschman scores two in a row, prompting the replacement of Rudniski with Richard Nagano in the Dawson nets. Boschman is dominating the ice; every time the Ottawa center nears Hogan he cuffs his chin and yells, "It's coming off Hogan! It's coming off!" Heinbigner, Kelly, and Johnson skate their hearts out. Boschman promptly sets up Babin for his third goal of the game, and Jerry Skinner adds Ottawa's last goal of the period two minutes later.

The dressing room is quiet. There is now no doubt of the game's outcome. Duffee talks of the small nuances which delineate professional hockey players from lesser mortals: "St. Marseilles comes down on me, I'm watching his eyes. His eyes are telegraphing what he's going to do; I see him following the guy to his left, and just as he's about to pass it, I step in that hole between them. At that instant he floats a soft pass right through where I was to the guy on his right, a guy he never even looked at. Made me look like a dummy."

I make my way toward my family's seats for the last period. I run into the Honorable Audrey McLaughlin in the corridor under the stands. As we chat a young boy approaches, his open program in one outstretched hand, a pen in the other. Everyone in a Dawson game jersey has been signing autographs all day long. I turn, but when I reach for the pen, the boy pulls it back.

"Not you," he says to me, *"her."*

The crowd, the Senators, the Nuggets, all understand as the third period begins that the game is over. The Senators still come at us, though, Boschman scoring unassisted twenty-two seconds after the puck is dropped. Dale Kulych has the best chance of the game for Dawson when he pulls the puck to his backhand, Armstrong sprawls on the ice, but Kulych fails to lift it over his flailing pads. Farr has another chance, but misses. Parsons, Barber, and Mason stick to it. Flynn is playing a strong game, but Payette scores, Babin, in his Frank McGee impersonation, scores two more, Hedges scores. Finally, in one last replication of the original blow-out game in which time had been called early, the timekeeper, with about five minutes to go, lets the clock go to running time. The game ends 18–0, Ottawa. As the teams crowd their goalies, tapping sticks on pads, the announcer blares, "The scoring summary of the game: by the Ottawa Senators alumni *a whole lot*; by the Nuggets *none at all...*"

The teams line up at center ice and slowly glide down the line, shaking hands. John Flynn officially presents the fifty ounces of gold to Brad Marsh, who triumphantly raises it above his head. Photos are taken of both teams together, everyone smiling, everyone, despite the loss, on the Dawson side satisfied. No one in the stands is leaving. The crowd remains transfixed, as though savoring every last lingering moment with these guys they have followed across a continent. Suddenly Flynn begins a lap around the rink and his teammates follow, waving to the crowd. The crowd, already afoot, raises a mighty cheer as the team slowly wends its way along the boards, pointing, blowing kisses, waving to all who came to watch.

"We went through the presentation," Flynn later explained to Suzuki's camera, "of giving gifts out and stuff, and the line-up shaking hands, and we had our pictures taken, and some of us were starting to leave and I remember saying hey, let's skate around. And someone said, ah, no, no, no, and I said we're never gonna be here again. You know… and so I took off and started skating around and waving to the audience, 'cuz the audience stayed there, and they were clapping and cheering… And I found out later that people cried at that, when we did that. 'Cuz I remember talking to a guy that I knew, and he said that he was fine up until we did that skate around, and then he started to cry. And he started to feel embarrassed until he looked around and he said everyone standing around him was crying also, and they were Ottawa people. We found this out later. That was pretty special…yuh…and why not, I mean, we're never gonna go back there and play…"

The dressing room is jubilant. There is a feeling, despite the great loss, of tired accomplishment. Reporters and photographers mass inside, every player, in his turn, accosted by halogen lights and questions. CBC's McGilvray and McEwen corner me.

"It's hard to even imagine what we've done at this point," I say into their camera. "We've gone through so much, we've come so far…it's been the experience of a lifetime for all of us. I'm sure with the passing of the years it'll become bigger and bigger in my mind—it's probably the greatest thing I've ever done in my life."

Steve Craig, still in full uniform except for his skates, gives his assessment.

"It was the experience of a lifetime," he says. "Nothing else in my life compares to this."

"Their talent was phenomenal," Dale Kulych tells another reporter. "But to us, it was a four-year plan come true. I'll never forget it. This game was the highlite of my life."

"We're used to one or two fans at our games back home," Chester Kelly says. "I never had butterflies like this before. This will be the biggest highlite of my life, for sure."

"We knew what was going to happen," Hogan says. "But I didn't think it'd be eighteen to nothing. But at this rate, look at it this way. We've got the people in the Yukon, in seven hundred years we'll have caught up. At a challenge, you know—we're two, three goals better this time—a challenge every ninety years, in seven hundred years we're right there in the money!"

"I know you're gonna ask me if I'm disappointed, and I'm not," Anderson tells another reporter. "We would have liked to have scored a goal obviously, we had a few chances…those guys, I mean, they're professional hockey players, you know."

Quotes out of the Ottawa dressing room were telling as to how seriously they took the game.

"I had four as a junior in North Bay once, in a playoff game," Mitch Babin told a reporter, discussing his five-goal game. "But never five. You get a chance to play with Laurie Boschman, well it's like I won the lottery out there. It seems like every time I turned around he was making that same move and laying a pass right on the tape of my stick…"

But Brad Marsh provided all the summing up necessary.

"We talked about it beforehand and we agreed we didn't want a Harlem Globetrotter kind of game," the former NHL all-star explained. "They came here to play a real hockey game. We could have given them a breakaway or something, but that doesn't happen in the NHL. I was saying to the guys before the game, don't feel sorry for them if we start to get ahead. There was some question about giving them some penalty shots, or something like that. It doesn't happen in a real game, and it shouldn't happen in this game. They wanted a game…

"We gave them a game."

Marshy's Bar-B-Q and Grill, Brad Marsh's pub located on the mezzanine level of the Corel Center, is where the players of both teams are to meet after the game. As I reach the doors to Marshy's, I am inundated by dozens of kids reaching at me with their souvenir programs, looking for autographs. I take the time to put my signature to every one. When the last is signed, I am confronted by a young woman.

"Are you Kevin Anderson?" she asks me. A closer look finds the woman teary-eyed, and anxious.

"No, I'm Don Reddick."

"Do you know where I can find Kevin Anderson?"

"He's in the dressing room right now," I tell the woman. "But he should be coming up here when he's dressed." When she nods, my curiosity gets the better of me.

"Why are you looking for Kevin?"

"I'm Ronnie McPhee's sister," the woman says. "I want Kevin Anderson to know that my family read Earl McRae's article about him putting Ronnie's picture on his snowmobile for the trip, and I want to thank him. You have no idea what that meant to me and my family."

Marsh's bar is packed. One by one the Nuggets arrive, surrounded as I had been by autograph seekers. One by one the Ottawa Senators alumni arrive, Bob Charlebois, Frank St. Marseille, Rick Smith. Marsh enters, beaming. They are as happy and excited as we are, eager to talk of the game, eager to hear details of our journey. Bob Charlebois is particularly eloquent in his admiration of the Nuggets and our journey. Rick Smith describes the Senator alumni experience: "We were at an event against somebody in a small community, and Brad Marsh said we have an event at the Corel Center coming up. First of all, to have a game at the Corel Center...we knew the first time we heard Corel Center and Dawson City, we said 'Wow, that's gonna be neat.' So from that point we were excited to be a part of it. I was aware there was a lot of talk with the guys and talk about McRae's articles, and the excitement grew as it came closer. It was important to us, we were barnstorming in little towns, we'd have maybe two hundred people turn out and you make a couple hundred bucks for charity, and all of a sudden, you're playing the Big Apple. What do they call it in baseball, The Show. This Dawson City thing skyrocketed, there was so much more enthusiasm not only with the players, but the community.

"It is surprising; when you go into those games in these small communities, you don't know what to expect. We were more caught up in the event and all of a sudden Brad, he's like Knute Rockne, he's standing up and giving this speech and we're like, Whoa! 'You're professional hockey players, and the building's full.' When we came in here we were part of an event, and then Brad gave his speech. 'It's a hockey game, we're professional athletes and we want to go out and play like professionals.' It was a side of Brad I've never seen before. You go into these little towns and play these guys, let's be nice and let's have a few beers after, but this was like the Stanley Cup finals!

"I've seen it on different occasions. There's the old competitive spirit that comes out. It's part of our ingredients. It's the way we learned the game. It's oldtimer hockey, let's have a beer and have fun, but once in a while… We didn't know. We didn't know what we were gonna face. We go into these little towns, and sometimes they throw Junior A players at us, great young legs, and sometimes it's a bunch of old guys. We'd heard a lot about the hype, but we didn't know about the individuals. We had a couple of goals before we knew what we were up against. We played our 'A' game.

"Our guys jumped on 'em, peppered a few in. Remember Don Cherry? He had a rule of thumb, if you're ahead by enough, back off a step. So I was backing off, enjoying the game. I started cheering for them in a way, for them to have a positive experience. I kinda got into that mode, while other guys on the team kept on barreling. It reminds me of John Ferguson, remember him? He couldn't play it any other way. We'd hear he was playing in an alumni game and we'd say, 'Oh no!'

"Bosch is our leading offensively skilled player. Brad and Freddy Barrett are more defensive—I see this as humorous—Brad and I were stay at home defensemen, but now we think we're Bobby Orr! Brad Marsh and Freddy Barrett were so good defensively, Dawson City couldn't do anything. Jerry Armstrong is outstanding, even if they got by our defense they had a rock in goal. Another guy indicative of what we're talking about is Jean Payette. He played center for the Tulsa Oilers in the Central Hockey League, and they won the championship and he was the star, he was a real skilled player—played with Quebec

Nordiques of the WHA—he's older, but this guy played like a horse. He played all out, he was going for the gusto! He in particular reminds me of that thinking, 'Wait a minute, we're professional hockey players, there's a crowd, let's do what we do, we're not figure skaters...'"

Marshy's ebullient atmosphere is the perfect post-game venue for the players of both teams, and no one wants to leave. But the Dawson team bus leaves the Corel Center at 5:30, and we reluctantly break it up. The party resumes later in The Elephant, next to the Westin Hotel. It is odd to see Hogan, Farr, Duffee, Craig, and Anderson without beards. True to their word, they have been shaved off because of the loss. Hogan, who has a clean-shaven identical twin, had threatened to have his brother stand in for him if we lost. But here he stands, looking like a stranger. We have a few drinks, and I see that there is no plan now, no itinerary anymore. The team will travel to Kingston to reenact the Queen's game Tuesday, but I will be leaving with my family for Massachusetts in the morning. Few on the team know this; it is disquieting to sit and watch them all, see their joy in accomplishing their great goal, knowing I will be leaving.

People head in every direction; I hear some are going to the Lafayette for drinks, and I decide to go. My family, with the exception of my sixteen-year-old daughter Sarah, decide to retire to McGee's, spent with four busy days in Ottawa.

Sarah and I locate the Lafayette on a small, cobblestone street. We enter to find several of our entourage well into their celebration. Steve Craig is on the dance floor, dancing away. My sister Connie plays pool and dances with Bruce Duffee. Harvey Downes is here, already glassy-eyed and mute, absolutely enthralled with his week with the Dawson City Nuggets. Kevin and Margo Anderson are here sitting with Jayne and Mike Fraser, but Margo pulls Kevin out early. The two come to me and say goodbye.

The bar is loving the presence of the famous visitors from the far North. At closing time the bartenders unfold newspapers and tape them over the windows so that we can continue partying. A chair collapses under Harvey Downes, and everyone laughs. The bartenders love Sarah, the big joke—though of course she is not drinking—"I can't *believe* you're old enough to drink." Wes Peterson shows up, Craig still dances, Duffee keeps shooting pool. I sit and stare at them all, disbelieving that it is over. That for Downes and myself it ends abruptly; we will not be returning to Dawson to any hero's welcome. At three in the morning Sarah and I say our goodbyes.

When I lay down in McGee's Inn, my personal copy of *Dawson City Seven* lies on the bed stand. I turn my head and stare at it for a moment, then pick it up and open to an arbitrary page. It is the page on which Adam Killick, reporter for the *Yukon News*, has penned his name. His inscription reads, "Don, I have absolute respect for a man who follows a dream, and, as a writer, I hope you write something about this trip." I lay the book down.

I lay my head back on my pillow, and turn out the light.

AFTER

"I dream my painting, and then I paint my dream."

— Vincent Van Gogh

I saw Margot Anderson in Calgary a few months later, who told of the team's reception back home in Dawson City.

"This is terrible and will bring tears to my eyes. I have bitter feelings. When it first started, I called other wives and everyone turned me down. They felt it was the guy's thing, let them do it. You know what I did, I was a volunteer. People didn't realize how big this would be, it became fucking huge. I came back and miners came to me and asked where their thank-you letters were, everyone now wanted to be part of it. Suddenly lots of anger toward the team, because they hadn't been involved. Most of the miners wanted thanks. They were thanked in the newspapers, before the trip even began. Pat Hogan finally did thank you notes.

"Dave Millar came to my house and yelled at me because we hadn't sent notes or acknowledgements, and I showed him and he stormed out. We're talking about a man who once told me if I were any woman at all I'd quit my job and stay home with my kids. He told me he could prove through history that there were no problems in the world until women got to vote. I grabbed him by the scruff of the neck and pants and threw him out and never allowed him back.

"Dick Van Nostrand came back three days ahead of everyone else and told everyone how bad everyone was, that the Nuggets did nothing but yell at him. It was hard to come back and face so much anger.

When the boys spoke to Dick about his behavior on the train, he thought it wasn't a big deal. Couple months later he went to Watson Lake with them and pulled his pants down and stuck his ass in the trophy case.

"My favorite part was the Yukon Gala. I had my dress on and I had dinner, nothing left to do as far as the trip goes, and Brian McFarlane is my hero. When he acknowledged me in his speech, that was just huge for me. I grew up watching him on TV. McFarlane had been invited to Ottawa but didn't get the message. He was offended that he wasn't invited. McFarlane was on the bus to the game with us, and he told me these things. 'This was my story, I felt a personal attachment to this story,' he told me. He wanted to have more to do with it.

"One piece of total anger I have, I am very offended—we sent Don Cherry a Dawson City Nuggets tie, but on his the puck was a real gold nugget. He never acknowledged the thing at all. Nothing.

"When you guys left on March first, the Corel Center wasn't even booked. Brad Marsh thought we'd never show up. They thought we were a bunch of bar boys. After the game in his bar Marsh said to me, 'I don't get it, I don't get what the big deal is.' He was watching everyone lined up to get the Nuggets' autographs. Fred Barrett came up to me and took my hand and held it right in front of Marsh. He had tears in his eyes. He said, 'I want to thank you because we play in all these dirty little arenas and playing in the Corel Center you've made all our dreams come true. None of us had played here before.' I turned to Marsh and said, '*That's* the big deal.'

"Some of the Ottawas suggested they let up and let Dawson score, but Brad Marsh refused. He wanted to teach Dawson a lesson. When Kevin and Hogan went to Ottawa in January for the interview, no media had been called. Deb Belinsky made all the calls. Marsh was shocked—he wanted to keep them out.

"Another thing for me that was huge, I was having lunch with you, and I tell people how many people write a story and then live it? It was huge. I am absolutely in awe of you. You read books, believe in your dreams, and they'll come true. I was in the kitchen one day and got a sponsorship, and I realized this is a dream that's happening to us. And when you realize a dream you worked so hard for, it's the greatest feeling in the world."

I lost touch with most everyone, except Bruce Duffee, Steve Craig, and Earl McRae. A typical narrative email from McRae:

"Earl I-ain't-doin-no-fucken-dishes-either McRae here...

Earl: 'I'm not doin no fucken dishes.'

Don: 'Me neither.'

Earl: 'We're not here to do gawdamn dishes.'

Don: 'Right. We're writers; let THEM do their own fucken dishes.'

Earl: 'Exactly. Screw them. We're not dishwashers.'

Don: 'Watch out! Here he comes!'

Earl: 'Up his ass.'

Don: 'Up his ass.'"

I saw McRae twice during the following year. On the second visit we met at Moe's World Famous Newport Restaurant, and when we sat down McRae leaned forward across the table.

"Are you drinking, Don?" he asked, his voice awash with concern.

"Lasted eight months," I answered, and he fell back in his chair.

"Don, the last time you were here you were lucid, serious. You had an air of self-confidence about you. You seemed in complete control of yourself. It was *awful*."

We exchanged what news we had heard. Margot and Kevin Anderson had parted, their son going with Margo back to Calgary. Kevin had taken up with a twenty-year-old in Dawson. Big Earl MacKenzie's wife had suffered a stroke. Dave Millar's gold mine had hit hard times, and he was working elsewhere. Jeff Reinebold went 6–26 with his Winnipeg Blue Bombers before being fired in October, '98. Steve Craig busied himself transporting kayaks cross-country, picking them up in the Maritimes and delivering them points west. Last I heard from him he was in Mongolia.

"Bumped into Brad Marsh two months ago," McRae told me. "He said he wanted to arrange a trip by the Senators alumni team to Dawson City sometime in the vague future. Every now and then I think of that trip, especially the snowmobile part, and I can't believe we were part of such an enchanting thing. Yeah, even the God-forsaken sumbitch parts of it warm with memory…those bastids probably still can't believe that you and I hung as tough as junkyard dogs and made it through. I don't know if I'll ever top that for adventure. It all seems now like an incredible dream."

Doc Parsons sent a post card the following January. "As the months go by," he wrote, "most of us are struck by the magnitude of our journey/accomplishment; a magnitude that is more evident the further removed we are from the minutiae of each day of the journey; a magnitude that regretfully we could not graciously and completely embody at the time; a magnitude that flows one's way all too infrequently in a lifetime." He went on to write, "I have 'opted out' for the winter, having not been the first man to come to the realization that certain opportunities come only once in a lifetime. My partner and I have gone to a remote cabin (18' X 18') off the Stewart River about fifty miles from where we spent nite #2 at Scroggie Creek. No electricity, nor running water, phone, radio, watch, amenities, etc. It's as much a soul searching adventure as it is a physical one, more evident over this particular week of -45 degree temps, in the throes of 'duskishness' and cabin fever…" I recently heard that Doc Parsons and his partner Suzanne now have a baby.

"You know, Don," McRae confided, "I miss the whole thing terribly. It's such a letdown being back to normal, it was such an experience, it was so exciting. I feel so…bored. The whole thing was such a pain in the ass, but it was the trip of a lifetime."

We talked about The Movie. Walt Disney Studios had gotten wind of our journey and sent three suits north to confer with the Dawson boys. Three hours late for their meeting in the Eldorado Hotel, Hogan, Duffee, Millar, and Anderson were well oiled by the time they arrived. The Disney people inquired into every aspect of the trip, what we had seen, what we had done, how it was on the trail, the guys answering all their questions until it became apparent that Disney was not interested in doing a movie about the Dawson City Nuggets, but something similar. Anderson stormed out. Disney left, and what appeared in the fall of '99 was an Americanized version of what we had *not* done, entitled *Mystery, Alaska*.

McRae and I talked about how to write this book. I had never written a non-fiction book, and was concerned about the fairness involved with showing a few individuals at what I considered less than their best. McRae has written a couple of books on sports personalities, and enjoys a checkered reputation as a national columnist willing to stir the pot. He has more than his share of enemies, but is adamant in his philosophy: "Hey, the truth is the truth. Everyone's responsible for their own acts. They said they shot all the dogs, they didn't shoot any dogs. They said there was a rope bridge, there wasn't any rope bridge. They said there was a rumor about pulling us off the trail, there wasn't any rumor. They're always leaning on people to see who has a thick skin, well, now we'll see who has the thick skin. *Fuck 'em.*" Margo Anderson had another idea on how to handle the problem.

"I heard what Kulych said to you, and I wanted to slug him," she said to me. "One thing I've learned is that anything someone says to someone else, really means it about himself. When he said you didn't pull your weight, he was saying he felt *he* didn't pull his weight. He didn't even go through the bush! If you really want to get back at them, the worst thing you could do is not mention them at all, for the entire book."

Others were more reserved. I corresponded with Steve Craig on this issue, giving him an example of Dick Van Nostrand dropping his pants on the train. Craig replied, "I don't see any relevance to the story. Dick was in no way connected to the Nuggets. He was a sponsor but was there as a fan. Personally, I can see no reason to relate a thing like that." Van Nostrand himself dismissed out of hand any historical revision, or omission. When I called, concerned after writing about him chasing around a waitress with a ten-inch-long, red dildo sticking out of his pants, I asked if he minded my mentioning it. "Naw," Dick told me, "it's part of the *essence.*"

But it is about neither revenge, nor sugar coating. It's about telling a story with all its warts and scars, revealing a human adventure, a drama, through the power of two dozen conflicting personalities. Historical novelist Kenneth Roberts once wrote that most stories have two sides to them, both equally good. I like to think this story has twenty sides to it, all equally good. This one is simply mine.

THE YUKON TERRITORY
October, 2002

Troy Suzuki released his documentary *From Moccasin Square Gardens* at the Dawson City Film Festival in the spring of 2002. It was played three times, to standing ovations on each occasion. I was told Kevin Anderson and John Flynn both cried. In October I flew north with my two oldest daughters Becky and Sarah to join the team for a "Thank You" tour of the Yukon. Suzuki played the film to First Nation audiences in both Pelly Crossing and Carmacks, in appreciation for their support during our trip. I jumped in the filmmaker's car for the drive from Pelly to Carmacks.

"I'm a builder, I have to build to be emotionally happy," Suzuki tells me. "I am a woodworker, I am a filmmaker. I knew there was no way I could play, but what really screwed me up in Ottawa was I really wanted to play. I was just as nervous as anybody else, and I screwed up the camera work. The boys left it all on the ice in Ottawa, you know that expression. But I couldn't get it out. I found it quite upsetting. I went all the way with the team, I wanted to play in that game. I went the whole way with the guys. I said at the first screening this film was the game for me, this was my contribution. It made the journey complete for me.

"Oh, just a matter of a month before the trip I decided to film it. The idea was chucked around to do a video, maybe two months before. I was playing hockey with all those guys, it was all they were talking about. The choosing process was long and hard, so I knew I wouldn't be playing. I just got this camera, it was one of the first of its kind, so I was just figuring out the camera. I should have spent more time watching the film as I did it, but I didn't look at it till after the trip. All kinds of problems, the lighting was wrong, the sound was wrong, and I came out thinking I had missed it. I wasn't sure I even had a product. I missed so much, there were eighteen guys and everyone had a story. It was four years before I started editing.

"I was looking for the humor, which is always a way into the heart of people, seeing who they really are. I was into the boys, the story about...well, the boys, I guess. Maybe I discovered after I edited, but I always liked these guys. The affection they have for each other, a lot of times hockey teams get pigeon-toed, how would you say, crude, rough people, but they're not necessarily. I think they're all bound more to each other now. It still always comes up, little stories here and there. I think this was the high point for that generation of Dawson hockey, they played together fifteen or twenty years, and it was the center of their life. It was a whole bunch of hockey players that turned thirty-five at the same time, they were a crew of guys who were really tight.

"The team sort of fell apart after. It was never the same, Kevin and Margo broke up. Kevin will be moving away, we'll lose a little heart here. He's great, Kevin's great. He'd be banging his head against the wall, but after… He gave everything to the game, but when it was over, he didn't care if he won or lost. It's a good quality."

I mention that during the trip Duffee, when I asked if Troy Suzuki was related to the famous David Suzuki, had looked at me, shrugged and replied, "I don't know. I never asked him." Troy cast me an incredulous glance, and burst out laughing.

"My father had a huge effect on me, there's no escaping the guy. I tried to run from him in the early years, but no matter what happens I got to admit it's a great thing. I'm just very proud of him. It's like people have preconceived ideas of me because of him. They either think I'm a lot smarter than I am, or a lot stupider. I prefer to be just taken as me. I think the States is the only place he wouldn't be recognized. But in Australia, or particularly Canada, he's treated like a rock star. I saw him give a speech in Toronto last year, and he had an entourage all around him. I couldn't get near him." Troy Suzuki smiles as we barrel down the Klondike Highway toward Carmacks.

"My father loved the film."

The tour brings the team back together, all except Earl McRae who can't make it up from Ottawa, Wes Peterson who's working in Saskatchewan, Poncho Rudniski who's working in the Arctic, and Harvey Downes, who remains in Winnipeg. After showing the film in Pelly and Carmacks, we drove to Whitehorse for a special showing organized by Nancy Houston and the Firth family, for an invited crowd of two hundred former Dawsonites. On Saturday evening we gather for the presentation of Suzuki's film and have time to reminisce before the show. I tell the others of my recent conversation with Harvey Downes.

"I didn't know what to expect," Downes told me over the phone. "Pat Hogan and Kevin Anderson identified themselves as leaders of the group, showed me where my room was and it was a private berth. I'd never been on a train before and I found out not everybody had private rooms…after I found out about the fund raising I felt kinda bad, not guilty, but kinda funny about it. Kevin is the image of the Yukon. The hearty guy who can drink you under the table. I mean, a guy with a name like Poncho Rudniski—who could make that up? It's better than fiction.

"I ended up in the bar car, I guess you'd call it, and I came in and introduced myself and they were all measuring me up I guess, but really I hit it off with most of them. Some of them were quiet. Talked to Poncho quite a bit about his trapping stories, there was a huge chunk of my inner soul that enjoyed that. I was trying to pick everyone's brain, there were a lot of interesting people on the trip, got to know Kevin and Pat 'cuz they were taking care of me. I mean, you could tell some guys could care less if I was there or not, but some guys were more interested in meeting me than others.

"I chummed with Mike Fraser and Kevin, Wes Peterson, a little bit with Steve Craig. One guy I really liked and ended up as my roommate was Bruce Duffee. He is a very funny guy, we had a blast being roomies together. If it wasn't for him I'd have missed my trip home. Got back to the room at eight in the morning and needed to be downstairs to catch the shuttle. After the game people got split up, I ended up in a car with Mike, Jayne, and Kevin, and we went back to that bar on the cobblestone street—I can't remember that bar—the two guys kept the bar open way past closing for us, they put newspapers on the windows. I was so drunk, I walked back with Wes, and I said I gotta change and be ready to go, so I packed and I needed a shower…it was seven A.M., so I got dressed, sat on the edge of my bed and passed out. Bruce woke me up, he woke me up at five to ten, so I had three bags, my hockey stuff, my sticks, my two bags and off I went downstairs and I was just a train wreck, and I saw Kevin and he stuck the *Ottawa Sun* in my face and said, 'Have you seen this?' And I thought why did they put my picture on the front page of the morning newspaper and not someone else? I felt bad. I said 'Kevin, why weren't you on the front?' And he said, 'Don't worry about it, it's not anyone's choice.' Got on the plane—I was really not in good shape, I reeked, I was sitting between these Manitoba judo team guys coming home and I get right between these two guys and they said 'Whoa!' I said look, 'I'll probably snore and sleep the whole way,' and I did. And I had to go straight to work and work all day and take a cab home...

"I traded jackets with Wes Peterson. His leather Dawson City hockey jacket. I wear that jacket all the time. My wife will confirm it. People think my name is Wes. Seriously, I wear it all the time, fall, winter, spring, I wear it all the time. And I get comments all the time from people, where did you get that jacket?

"It's something that's with me every day. I seriously think about it every day. It was an incredible experience. It was not only a great experience that I was there, but it was a learning experience. I learned. When you find out what they did, that my expenses weren't paid by Shell or Exxon, I realized I needed to appreciate it even more. Everybody treated me so well, Kevin and Pat, you...

"For a year people asked me about it all the time. It was hard to come down off of, after we got back. It was a let down. I'm an emotional guy, my wife says I cry at *Little House on the Prairie*, but I get choked up by this stuff. I'm not best friends with these guys, but they accepted me. I was honored to be a part of it, and extremely glad I entered that contest. It's something I'm very proud of. When you see the guys, tell them something from me: Huge thanks for a train-load of the most amazing memories a man could ever be lucky enough to carry with him, from The Southern Nugget...yeah, looking back on it, knowing how it was funded—I'm just proud to be part of it."

I tell them of another phone conversation, with Patricia Dahlquist.

"I remember the actual event itself, performing, and the amount of pride I had being invited to be part of it," our Diamond Tooth

Gertie told me. "Being onstage in the Westin and performing, it was a re-creation, very authentic even though it was a modern hotel, there was an authenticity I appreciate. The next day, walking out onto the ice to sing the national anthem was a thing I'll never forget. I had sung the national anthem on different occasions before, but this was very special to me because it was in Ottawa and for a town I really loved, Dawson City. But with the national anthem, you don't get to sing it very often. I was concerned I'd crack the high notes or forget the words, pregame jitters, but just standing there at center ice it took over, the song itself took on its own entity, its own spirit. A sense of my being the instrument. I did feel nervous. I knew I had many years of singing behind me, that I could trust my training to do it.

"It's a completion when someone puts their whole heart and soul into something and the audience applauds. It completes the circle. It was just such an opportunity, it was one of those things that I said I'm so glad I didn't turn this down, to travel all across the country to per-form in Ottawa. I had done it before, I'd met Trudeau before, but to sit in Parliament... Whoever was speaking at the time, I just remember being acknowledged, and felt so proud."

"You might say my lowest point was I didn't take my son," Roy Johnson tells me. "I was working at Viceroy, I didn't take the trip through the snow to Whitehorse. My highest point was on the ice, you might say. I tried very hard. I tried hard to click with Chester Kelly, but it didn't happen. I request this one point: I tried to get the puck to Freddy Farr, but misjudged. Another turn I didn't look and sent the puck out front, and the puck just jumped over his stick, Budd Docken. Blind passed it. It was a really good pass, but it bounced right over his stick. Budd said, 'I shoulda had that, shoulda had it...'

"If I could go again I would, it's not every day you have six thou-sand people cheering for you. To see the ice at ice level...it was excit-ing, and I just want to go back and try just one more time. Even if I win the lottery, I'll tell the captain, 'Let's go again!' And this time go there to win."

"To be honest with you, I consider the ferry and the train nothing but filler between the skidoos and the game," Bruce Duffee relates. "I can still remember going into a sporting goods store in Ottawa. After our first practice and the Ottawa Senators practiced after us, I watched Brad Marsh shoot, and I went down to Houle's Sporting Goods Store and bought the most expensive shin pads they had there. It never occurred to me at the time that he's not gonna hit me unless he wants to, but if he hits me with one of those…I was amazed at the effect McRae's articles had. I can still remember going into the store, with the sweater on. And this guy said which one are you, and I told him my name, and he said, 'Oh, you're the most hated man in Ottawa.' Sitting here now and someone says, 'You're the most hated man in the Yukon,' I could deal with that. But at the time, very vulnerable. I just felt *awful*…and he said, 'You're the guy who turned Earl McRae around on the skidoo in the wilderness, aren't you!'"

We tell old stories; many laugh when I relate Duffee's feigned ignorance when asked in the bush if Suzuki's father was famous. John Flynn takes particular delight.

"David Suzuki made a documentary with a French Canadian woman who studied moose," he tells me. "She studied their calls during the mating season, their customs and habits. But what happened—to people who hunted moose, this was the greatest way to mimic how to call moose. That documentary was responsible for more moose being killed then anything! Every hunter uses that video—I still listen to it— how the bulls and cows call each other in rutting season. When guys go hunting they want to listen to it, they borrow it. All this from David Suzuki, the environmentalist! I don't think he had that in mind!" Flynn emits his signature cackle.

"Today, every time I play *Orange Blossom Special*," Willie Gordon says, "the boys get all excited and join in a dance to it. Does this make sense? As I look back at the trip, it was quite a fun time, a real eye-opener from all the coverage we got during the trip and it seemed that once we got started, it was almost done so soon. I wouldn't have missed it for the world. I thank the Dawson Nuggets from the bottom of my heart for allowing me to be a part of history, and also thanks to the people of Dawson City for their support, hell the whole of Yukon. Now all that is needed is for the Silver Seven Senators alumni to make a return trip, now that we have an arena to play hockey in!"

Gordon's fiddle is taped up in two places. When I inquire, he shrugs.

"Brawl in The Pit," he says, and smiles that smile.

"The trail was my favorite part of the trip," Pat Hogan reminisces. "From Dawson to Whitehorse. I tell you, the toughest part, the most disorienting, was the train. It rocks and rolls worse than anything. Worse than the boat, worse than a snow machine.

"I know that everyone that saw the film, who hadn't been on the whole trip, said, you know, we heard the stories, but we didn't *know.* We didn't know exactly what you guys went through, what you did going through the bush. And it means so much to see the whole thing. So, bringing Troy along was a great idea. He did a super thing there.

"The problem from day one with the whole event was that the Ottawa Senators were used to having Ottawa Senators alumni events. The Ottawa Senators alumni were playing the Toronto Maple Leaf's alumni. And the draw was, the focus was the Ottawa Senators alumni. Let's face it, these are guys with egos, with determination, or they wouldn't have got to where they got to. But our story was much bigger than their's could ever hope to be. They were supporting actors in the play. They had, if you will, walk on parts. And there was some resentment there. There was some resentment that these goddamn guys are coming across, and they're trash-talking and saying yeah we're gonna kick their ass, and I haven't shaved my beard in twenty years and we're gonna win this game. But you know what? That's the way you play hockey. You don't go to a hockey game to lose.

"They shortened their bench in the third period. They were playing four lines up until the third period, they only played three in the third period because they wanted to run the score up to twenty-three. Or better. But Marsh still couldn't get a goal. They were all feeding him, too. The thing was, he was an all-star defenseman, but he couldn't score worth a shit. And then the last game he ever played for Ottawa, they pumped him the puck to get him a goal. I read an article some place about that, but no way, he couldn't put it in the net, no way. Hands of steel. He was a good guy, though, I have a lot of respect for him. He could understand our position when he applied himself to understanding our position. His heart was certainly in the right place.

"McRae played a major part, building excitement. And making the story known that it was a cross-Canada story, that it was a national story. And it *was* a national story, it took place at one end of the country, one of the most remote ends of the country, and went to the nation's capital. I heard comments when we had the dinner at Moe's. Like, 'I hate that little fucker McRae but I just had to read his articles to see where you guys were.' He does it the way he believes it, and that's OK. People don't like it, but he doesn't care. And it's been successful for him.

"I thought McRae did a great job, he was a tremendous asset to have along. It was absolutely hilarious to have him there. I near killed myself laughing when I saw all the shit he had, he showed up with two huge hockey bags just stuffed. He called me up and said, 'My paper wants me to come and go the whole way, can I come?' Yup, you bet. You're there, buddy. No problem. We'll find a machine for ya, we'll get you down the trail. He said, 'Will I have any trouble?' Naw, piece of cake. 'What'll I need?' Well, you should have this this this and this. He said he walked into a sporting goods store with a checkbook and they went, 'Oooh Boy!'"

McRae, for his part, described his feelings in his final recap of the journey. I found them insightful after having traveled three weeks with the man who strived mightily to appear the four-eyed, lippy little shin-kicker: "And finally, three memories that have captured me most of all," he wrote in the *Ottawa Sun.* "One, the eternal deep, dead silence; utterly profound, haunting, and spiritual; staggering in its dimension; the silence Robert Service talked about and that you can never know unless you go to the Yukon, a place of breathtaking beauty.

"The second, the boat late one night; hearing the distant, melancholy strains of a bagpipe; following the sound to the top deck where stood all alone, playing into the wind, a young carpenter from Ketchikan, Alaska named Ken MacRae. A crowd soon gathered, including fiddler Willie Gordon, and Willie asked the piper if he could play *Amazing Grace* 'for me and in memory of my grandfather because it was his favorite song.' As the piper played, Willie stood off to the side by himself, weeping softly, tears running down his cheeks. 'It's not a sad song for me,' Willie told me later. 'It's a song of hope. I've been there. I've been that poor wretch.'

"The third, walking back to my hotel in Dawson City late one night, the snow-packed streets empty and silent, the windows dark and shuttered, and seeing only the dogs, not stray dogs, but dogs that have homes, trotting alone or in pairs along the streets, in and out of the moon-lit shadows, completely free and unattended. And I remember my childhood, and the small, sleepy village where the dogs roamed freely, and on that night in that magical place, I felt I was in a Sherwood Anderson short story of a time and a town long ago and far away, all so beautiful, so innocent, and I knew then and I knew there that one day the spell of the Yukon would bring me back."

There is something I have to do here tonight. When I had first arrived in Dawson with my daughters, the first familiar face we ran into in the Downtown Hotel's dining room was Dave Millar's. Dave was generous and affable, and even gave us a personal tour of his family's gold operation out on Hunker Creek. From his demeanor and kindness, it was obvious he held no hard feelings toward anything that had occurred between us on the trip. Here in Whitehorse tonight, there is one more guy I need to speak to. When I see Kulych standing alone along a back wall, I approach him and stick out my hand.

"You know, Dale, there's no reason in the world why we shouldn't be friends," I say. Kulych smiles, and grabs my hand.

"No reason at all," he concurs.

Earlier in the week, a group of us had assembled in Bombay Peggy's up in Dawson and ordered a round, Troy Suzuki, Rod Dewell, Steve Craig, Steve's friend Neil West, and myself. We discussed Troy's film, and Troy mentioned the fact that several of the guys cried during its first showing.

"Well," I said, "I loved it, but I didn't cry."

"Oh c'mon, Don," Suzuki said, "you can admit it. You're among men."

"Honestly, I didn't."

The filmmaker looked at me as if to say "I don't really believe you," and we had left it at that. Tonight at the Dawson City showing in Whitehorse, I recall the conversation. I look around at all the guys, and it strikes me that they truly are extraordinary. All with their game jerseys on, all lined up behind the speaker podium as once again Hogan, Flynn, and Anderson give their talks. But it grips me…when I first viewed the film I was alone, away from this all, in Massachusetts. Now, shoulder to shoulder with these guys, it hits me at once, and I am taken with emotion.

We have forged a bond, one of those rare abilities to look one another in the eye, and convey a shared experience. I glance at the rock that is Brian Gudmundson. I see the intense look as Steve Craig is animated, speaking earnestly to someone, as he always does. I see the sheepish grin of Willie Gordon, his wounded fiddle and bow at his sides, waiting to play. I see Doc Parsons, Errol Flynn with a ponytail, laughing as he always is, eyes gleaming. I see Troy Suzuki reserved, thoughtful. As I stand waiting for the film to begin, the emotion overcomes me. These are the guys…I loved the North from afar as a youth, and wanted to move here. I never did. I am surrounded now by those who followed that star, who did what I could not do. I had taken the trail more traveled. But when I glance at my daughters sitting in the front row, their faces beaming among this kaleidoscope of Yukon color, I realize more than ever, aided by that wistful understanding only acquired with age, that the trail I had chosen was the correct one.

Suzuki dims the lights, and starts his film. I stand in back next to a sitting Budd Docken. When the Stanley Cup comes on-screen during the team visit to the Hall of Fame in Toronto, I feel the light tap of a Budweiser bottle against my leg.

The audience loves the film, they howl at every nuance, they catch things viewers in Massachusetts did not, they hang on every word, and when it ends they cheer mightily. Kevin Anderson once again speaks, as the rest of the team lines up behind the podium. When he finishes, he turns and says, "And here is Don Reddick."

Suzuki had asked if I wanted to say a few words this night, and I had declined. Anderson ambushes me now, introducing me out of the blue as I stand behind him. But as I step to the podium—noting the wide grin on his face—I am glad that he has.

"There are so many little stories that will never be told," I tell the crowd. "One of them was in Vancouver when we stepped onto the train platform, and a couple dozen Japanese tourists stood milling around their bags, and Wes Peterson leaned toward me and said, 'Look, Troy's family is here.'" The Dawson alumni laugh, and I continue, "Well, Wes was kidding, of course, but I'm serious when I say that tonight Troy's family *is* here, and we'd like to thank him for this film."

For the first time I publicly extend my heart-felt thanks to Hogan, Flynn, and Anderson, and then Dawson City and the Yukon for including me in their incredible journey. It is also the first time I can say good-bye.

I sent this manuscript up to Bruce Duffee in Dawson City. I had harvested from it arbitrary obscenities and ethnic slurs, leaving only those that expressed emphasis, or provided characterization. I wanted the guys to see it, and tell me if there was anything they strongly disapproved of. McRae had had the same opportunity, and asked only that I delete one incident, relating to an individual he knew personally and had professional contact with. I deleted the story. I received an email from Suzuki, telling me he "burned through it," and enjoyed it immensely. Hogan called and told me that he loved it, and was honored and humbled to be mentioned in the same breath as Joe Boyle. Parsons told Duffee he loved it, and provided the same assessment Duffee had provided me, that he valued it because someday his kids could read it, and see what they had done.

Later, however, during a phone call to Duffee, I was informed that the manuscript had "created something of a firestorm up here in Dawson." There were also teammates who did not like it, including Dale Kulych and Dave Millar. Roy Johnson was also unhappy. He had left me a message that "he wanted to redo his interview," but I never spoke with him again. I was told that Willie Gordon was troubled by voluminous swearing, and that John Flynn had concerns about one particular line. I deleted it. But most disturbing was news that Steve Craig was upset. I asked Duffee if he knew Craig's problems with the manuscript, and he said he did not.

"You know," Duffee told me, "I sent around all those copies with a cover letter saying to contact you if they had any problems, put in your phone number and email address, and no one did. There's a lot that don't like what you wrote, but some I don't think read the whole thing, they just read the parts with them in it. But I think part of it is this. See, here in Dawson City, we're at the top of the world, and we kind of look down on the rest of the world. We think we're better than the rest of the world, and we did this great thing, but when we read something like this, confronted with the truth, with all the arguments, the pettiness, the gaffs and stupidity, well, we realize we're really no different from anybody else."

And so I sit and think about all that's been. The trail, the cold, the train and the journey. I think of the game in Ottawa perhaps least of all. It seems surreal to me now, distant. I think of achieving dreams, of Jeff Reinebold becoming a professional football coach, of Steve Craig roaming the world. Ferrymate Robin Ford is now Robin Dale Ford, accomplished star of the folk music scene. Two friends have seen literary aspirations realized; Adam Killick with his book on the Yukon Quest dog race, *Racing the White Silence*, and hockey scholar Paul Kitchen with his masterful tome on Ottawan hockey, *Win, Tie, or Wrangle*. But most of all I think of the three men primarily responsible. I see Kevin Anderson sitting in some Dawson bar after work, paint splattered on his plaid shirt, a beer in his hand and a gleam in his eye... The Kevin Factor. I see Johnny Flynn, the kid once called a dirty Indian to his face, now considered a pillar of Dawson. And I see the glacier-carved, red-bearded face of Pat Hogan, the man who wouldn't take no for an answer. Three men from Dawson City, Yukon Territory with a dream, and one they would accomplish.

With the passage of time, words to songs long heard sometimes resonate with new meaning. One of my favorite songs is Jerry Jeff Walker's *Song for the Life*, which contains these words, "Somehow I learned how to listen/to the sound of the sun dying down..." There's really no mystery to it all. It's silence we need most, time and distance away from our cell phones and beepers and alarm clocks and palm pilots and emails; quiet time. In our silence, perhaps reminded of time enshrouded within the deep, solitary stillness a lone Yukon winter night provides, bedazzled under the aurora borealis and a Hale-Bopp comet, we may more clearly see what lies just below the surface, our truest concerns too important to ignore, though we all believe we should. We act as though by merely enduring our trials and tribulations, we somehow live a life. Without stealing away in our silent night we might never know how much we can affect someone else, particularly someone we love, by lowering our guard, lowering our sound, and investing in our dreams. In one of his books, Jimmy Buffett advises to begin your adventures as early as you can. I now understand why. I'm proud to know that if someday I find myself with no money, no plastic, I've got a place to go. Don't follow your dreams, lead them.

And so I revel in memories of silence, learning something from my adventures. It is a common sentiment, but too important to be dismissed as sophomoric, or trite—you're reminded of what's truly important. She's doing fine. You know, my daughter; she's doing just fine.

APPENDIX

"I hate quotes. Tell me what you know."

— RALPH WALDO EMERSON, *JOURNAL*, 1849

GAME SUMMARY

Dawson City Nuggets vs. Ottawa Senators Alumni
March 23, 1997
Correl Center, Kanata, Ontario

Ottawa 18, Dawson 0

Goals: (Ottawa)Babin 5, Boschman 3, Hedges 2, Payette 2, Kuntz 1,
Charlebois 1, Hatoum 1, Paterson 1, Skinner 1, O'Donnell 1

Assists: (Ottawa) Boschman 5, Smith 3, O'Donnell 2, St. Marseille 2, Babin 2,
Kitchen 2, Hatoum 1, Paterson 1, Skinner 1, Marsh 1, F. Barrett 1,

Shots on Goal: Ottawa 43, Dawson 22
Penalties: St. Marseille
Attendance: 6,139
Referee: Jeff Johnston

GAME SUMMARY

Dawson City Klondikers vs. Ottawa Senators
January 13, 1905

Ottawa 9, Dawson 2

Goals: (Ottawa) Smith 5, White 2, McGee 1, Westwick 1 (Dawson)
McLennan 1, Kennedy 1

Assists: (Ottawa) White 4, McGee 2, Westwick 1, Smith 1 (Dawson) H. Smith
2, Watt 1

GAME SUMMARY

Dawson City Klondikers vs. Ottawa Senators
January 16, 1905

Ottawa 23, Dawson City 2

Goals: (Ottawa) McGee 14, Westwick 5, Smith 3, White 1 (Dawson) H. Smith 2

Assists: (Ottawa) Smith 9, Westwick 8, White 5, McGee 4, Pulford 3 (Dawson) Kennedy 2, Fairbairn 1

NOTE: Assists were not recorded in 1905. These stats are extrapolated from newspaper accounts of the games in *The Ottawa Citizen*.

1905 Dawson City Klondikers' Team Record

11 Wins, 13 Losses, 0 Ties

Jan. 13 Dawson 2 at Ottawa 9   STANLEY CUP GAMES
Johnstone, Watt, Martin & Young's hometown.

Jan. 16 Dawson 2 at Ottawa 23

Jan. 23 Dawson 2 at Amherst 4

Jan. 24 Dawson 2 at Halifax Wanderers 3

Jan. 25 Dawson 11 at Halifax All-Stars 2

Jan. 26 Dawson 0 at Sydney Victorias 4

Jan. 27 Dawson 3 at Sydney Nationals 7

Jan. 28 Dawson 5 at Cape Breton All-Stars 2

Jan. 29 Dawson 7 at Pictou 3
Dawson & Henderson's hometown.

Jan. 30 Dawson 2 at Amherst 4

Jan. 31 Dawson 7 at Moncton 3

Feb.1 Dawson 4 at St. John 2

Feb. 2 Dawson 5 at St. John 0

Feb. 3 Dawson 2 at Fredericton 0

Feb. 6 Dawson 2 at Trois-Rivieres 7
Forrest's hometown.

Feb. 8 Dawson 1 at Montreal Montagnards 2

Feb. 13 Dawson 5 at Queen's University 15
Eilbeck's hometown, McLennan's alma mater. (Kingston, Ontario)

Feb. 15 Dawson 2 at Brockville 8

Mar. 8 Dawson 8 at Pittsburgh PAC 5

Mar. 10   Dawson 3 at Pittsburgh PAC 4

Mar. 11   Dawson 6 at Pittsburgh PAC 1

Mar. 15.   Dawson 8 at Port Arthur 4

Mar. 20.   Dawson 1 at Winnipeg Vics 8
Smith & Kennedy's hometown.

Mar. 21   Dawson 8 at Brandon 1
Hannay's hometown.

1997 Dawson City Nuggets' Team Record

Mar. 4   Dawson 6 at Pelly Crossing Juniors 11 (road hockey)

Mar. 6   Dawson 11 at Carmacks Juniors 12 (road hockey)

Mar. 9   Dawson x at Whitehorse Old Timers x (road hockey)

Mar. 21   Dawson 4, at Media 2 (hockey, Sandy Hill Arena, Ottawa)

Mar. 23   Dawson 0 at Ottawa Senators Alumni 18
STANLEY CUP REENACTMENT

Mar. 24   Dawson 6 at Kingston All-Stars 6
Queen's game reenactment.

Dawson to Ottawa Reenactment Participants

Dawson City to Ottawa
Pat Hogan, Kevin Anderson, Freddy Farr, Gerard Parsons, Wes Peterson, John Flynn,
Steve Craig, Earl Mackenzie, Dave Millar, Bruce Duffee, Earl McRae, Don Reddick

Dawson City to Carmacks
Rangers Trevor Williams, Bruce Taylor, Agata Franczak

Dawson City to Whitehorse
Larry Smith, Patrick Riopel, Steve Christianson, Brian Gudmundson

Whitehorse to Ottawa
Budd Docken, Dale Kulych, Chester Kelly, Joe Mason, Willie Gordon

Vancouver to Ottawa
Glen Heinbigner, Mike Fraser, Poncho Rudniski, Roy Johnson, Patty Dahlquist

Winnipeg to Ottawa
Harvey Downes

Toronto to Ottawa
Richard Nagano, Bob Sutherland, Chuck Barber, Rod Dewell, Brian Gudmundson

Dawson City Nuggets Roster

2   Bob Sutherland, D, Joliette, Quebec. High School Teacher

3   Brian Gudmundson, D, Arborg, Manitoba. Retired RCMP

4   Pat Hogan, D, Port Hope, Ontario. Building Management

5   Steve Craig, D, Victoria, British Columbia. Hobo

6   Bruce Duffee, D, Maple Creek, Saskatchewan. Heavy
       Equipment Operator

7   Chuck Barber, LW, Dawson City, Yukon. Heavy Duty Mechanic

8   Joe Mason, RW, Dawson City, Yukon. Carpenter

9   Gordon "Budd" Docken, C, London, Ontario. Mining Camp Manager

10   John Flynn, C, Dawson City, Yukon. Gold Miner

11   Glenn Heinbigner, LW, Hague, Saskatchewan. Building Maintenance

13   Dale Kulych, C, Edmonton, Alberta. Marketing Representative

14   Kevin Anderson, C, Port Alberni, British Columbia. Painter

15   Gerard "Doc" Parsons, LW, Gander, Newfoundland. Doctor

16   Mike Fraser, C, Arivda, Quebec. Carpenter

19   Chester Kelly, RW, Aklavik, Northwest Territories. Engineering
       Inspector

20   Harvey "Lorne Hannay" Downes, D, Winnipeg, Manitoba.
       Security Analyst

27   Roy Johnson, RW, Dawson City, Yukon. Heavy Equipment Operator

31   Steven "Poncho" Rudniski, G, Dawson City, Yukon. Miner,
       Heavy Equipment Operator

33   Richard Nagano, G, Dawson City, Yukon. Driver Trainer

69   Freddy Farr, RW, Dawson City, Yukon. Surveyor

     Wes Peterson, Coach, Wadena, Saskatchewan. Carpenter

     Dave Millar, Assistant Coach, Dawson City, Yukon. Gold Miner

     Earl "Joe Boyle" MacKenzie, Team Manager, Wolfville,
       Nova Scotia. Entrepreneur

     Patricia "Diamond Tooth Gertie" Dahlquist, Kaslo, British
       Columbia. Actress

     Rod Dewell, Trainer, Toronto, Ontario. Carpenter

     Ronnie McPhee, Honorary Teammate, New Glasgow, Nova
       Scotia. Fisherman

     Willie Gordon, Team Fiddler, Acklavick, Northwest Territories.
       Musician

     Earl "Wrong Way" McRae, Team Columnist, Ottawa, Ontario. Writer

     Troy Suzuki, Team Filmmaker, Vancouver, British Columbia.
       Filmmaker

     Don "Dangerous Don" Reddick, Team Novelist, Norwood,
       Massachusetts. Word Dink

Ottawa Senators Alumni Roster

1   Gerry Armstrong, G, Ottawa, Ontario.

2   Bill Kitchen, D, Schomberg, Ontario.

3   Fred Barrett, D, Ottawa, Ontario.

4   Mitch Babin, LW, Kapuskasing, Ontario.

5   Randy Pierce, RW, Arnprior, Ontario.

6   John Barrett, D, Ottawa, Ontario.

7   Roland Hedges, D, Ottawa, Ontario.

8   Murray Kuntz, LW, Ottawa, Ontario.

9   Eddie Hatoum, D, Beirut, Lebanon.

10   Larry Skinner, C, Vancouver, British Columbia.

14   Brad Marsh, D, London, Ontario.

15   Frank St. Marseilles, C, Levack, Ontario.

16   Laurie Boschman, RW, Major, Saskatchewan.

17   Bob Charlebois, RW, Cornwall, Ontario.

18   Fred O'Donnell, RW, Kingston, Ontario.

19   Jean Payette, LW, Quebec, Quebec.

20   Rick Smith, D, Kingston, Ontario.

30   Mark Paterson, D, Ottawa, Ontario.

Noel Price, D, Brockville, Ontario.

Moe Robinson, D, Winchester, Ontario.

Claude Julien, D, Blind River, Ontario.

Kevin Kemp, D, Ottawa, Ontario.

Pete LaFramboise, C, Ottawa, Ontario.

Gord McTavish, C, Guelph, Ontario.

Bryan McSheffrey, Coach, Ottawa, Ontario.

Doug Smith, Coach, Ottawa, Ontario.

Mike Foley, Equipment Manager, Ottawa, Ontario.

Gold Contributors

Allan Fry, Bert Liske, Joe Fellers, Greg Hakonson, Keiran Daunt, Art Sailor,
Ian Fraser, Stuart Schmidt, Dave Millar, Duncan Spriggs, Paul Henderson,
Jim Christy, Don Sandberg, Barry Graham, Marty Knutson, Lyle and
George Gatenby, Daryl Morgan, Jimmy Lynch, Joel White, Peter Erickson,
Ivan Burian, Lenore Calnan, Chris Krieger, Peter and John Gould, Pete Erickson,
Norman A. Ross, Viceroy Resource Corporation, Nugget Hill Placers,
and Whitehorse Old Timers Hockey League.

Harvey Downes' entry for Winnipeg's
"Be Lorne Hannay" contest.

ODE TO A HACKER

My first year on blades
I was just five years old
Now thirty-one years later
I'm still in the fold.

I still have the passion
A burning desire
To strap on the gear
I'll never retire.

The legs now move slower
The shot not as hard
But I can still get one by
If goalies drop their guard.

Now there's no winner's trophy
What we play for all year
Is the respect of your teammates
And more importantly, COLD BEER!!

Hockey I know is the greatest
Sport you can play
If my wife would just let me
I'd play every day.

But for now I get by
On two games a week
Not bad for a hacker
Whose equipment just reeks!

The flash of LaFleur
Or the Golden Jet's blast
I once thought I had them
They're now a thing of the past.

Rogie and Sawchuck
The Espositos and Shore
Bower, Beliveau, and Gordie
And the great Bobby Orr.

Glenn Hall and Mikita
Dionne and Ellis

All stars of the past
Of whose talent I'm jealous.

Now there's Mario and 'Mess'
And my man Stevie Y
Chelios and Coffey
And the 'Great One' on high.

Now Dutchie, the 'Postman'
Iron Mike, Lep, and Rocki
Ricky, the 'Beer Guy'
Vic, Shark, and Ozzie.

Manson and Taylor
Les, Maz, and 'the Hack'
Makin' up for with hustle
For the talent we lack.

Not names you've heard of
Just hackers on a mission
AMBASSADORS to the game
Carrying on a tradition.

Now a long time ago,
By dogsled and train
A team traveled cross-country
For the sake of a game.

In the 'Peg they picked up
One extra player
Now they need one again
Some hack present dayer.

To fill out the squad
They need one more on the roster
Forget Bure or Fedorov
They need a Ciccarelli impostor.

To be picked as that player
Would be like a dream
To help us remember
It's about the game and the team.

Because I just love to play
And this may sound cocky
But the greatest game on this planet
Is the game we call HOCKEY!!!!